OECD Studies on SMEs and Entrepreneurship

D1825130

Mexico:
Key Issues and Policies

This work is published on the responsibility of the Secretary-General of the OECD. The opinions expressed and arguments employed herein do not necessarily reflect the official views of the Organisation or of the governments of its member countries.

This document and any map included herein are without prejudice to the status of or sovereignty over any territory, to the delimitation of international frontiers and boundaries and to the name of any territory, city or area.

Please cite this publication as:
OECD (2013), *Mexico: Key Issues and Policies*, OECD Studies on SMEs and Entrepreneurship, OECD Publishing.
http://dx.doi.org/10.1787/9789264187030-en

ISBN 978-92-64-18692-7 (print)
ISBN 978-92-64-18703-0 (PDF)

Series: OECD Studies on SMEs and Entrepreneurship
ISSN 2078-0982 (print)
ISSN 2078-0990 (online)

Foreword

S*mall and medium-sized enterprises (SMEs) and entrepreneurs are fundamental drivers of innovation, economic growth and job creation. As a result, they also play an important role in fostering social development and cohesion. Because SMEs account for a large share of employment in Mexico, policies to foster entrepreneurship could be front and centre in the reform agenda of the new Mexican Government.*

This "Review of SMEs and Entrepreneurship Issues and Policies in Mexico at National and Local Level" shows that the framework conditions for SMEs and entrepreneurship have improved in recent years. Reforms such as regulatory simplification, the expansion of the national loan guarantee programme and the integration of the micro-enterprise sector into the public business support system played a key role in this respect. Nonetheless, the share of SMEs in Mexico's total value added remains lower than in other OECD countries, suggesting that there is much potential for relying on SMEs as a powerful driver of growth.

Our review takes stock of the progress made in recent years and identifies areas for further strengthening, as well as guidance for future policy adjustments. In particular, administrative burdens on start-ups remain high, and SMEs still face restricted access to credit and limited new opportunities in innovative sectors. More needs to be done to reduce informality, improve access of SMEs to financing and generate greater numbers of medium-sized companies able to innovate and internationalise. There is also scope for simplifying rules and operations of the SMEs Fund, which is one of the main sources of financing for SMEs and entrepreneurship, and for strengthening professional capacities in intermediary organisations providing business support services on behalf of the government.

This review is part of the series of OECD Studies on SMEs and Entrepreneurship at national and local levels. The series provides a tool for assessing and improving the design and implementation of SMEs and entrepreneurship policy and for sharing policy experiences among OECD member and partner countries. The reviews provide a benchmark for SMEs and entrepreneurship performance and assess the impacts of the institutional and economic framework. Furthermore, they offer recommendations to improve the design and implementation of existing policies and programmes. They are based on a standard methodology, which includes a diagnostic questionnaire completed by the national authorities, study missions and fieldwork, and a peer review by Delegates in the OECD Working Party on SMEs and Entrepreneurship (WPSMEE).

This report aims at providing valuable insights not only for policymakers in Mexico, but also for other OECD member and partner countries, especially in Latin America. The OECD will continue to work hand in hand with Mexico to support reforms across a range of policy areas, including SMEs and entrepreneurship. I am confident that Mexico's efforts to implement the necessary structural changes will bear fruit, resulting in better policies for better lives for all of its citizens!

Angel Gurría

Secretary-General
Organisation for Economic Co-operation and Development

Table of contents

Acknowledgements

The review was undertaken by the OECD Centre for Entrepreneurship, SMEs and Local Development (CFE) at the request of the Mexican Ministry of Economy and the Association of State Economic Development Secretaries (AMSDE). It is part of the Programmes of Work of the OECD's Working Party on SMEs and Entrepreneurship (WPSMEE) and the Local Economic and Employment Development Committee (LEED).

The preparation of the report has been guided by an OECD Steering Group comprising government delegates from Australia, Canada and Italy and representatives of the Andean Development Corporation (CAF) and the United Nations Conference on Trade and Development (UNCTAD). The information within the report is based on responses to a Fact-Finding Questionnaire sent to the Mexican authorities in August 2011 and information gathered during study missions to the states of Morelos and Querétaro in October 2011 and to Mexico City in November 2011.

The report was prepared by Mr Marco Marchese (OECD), Dr Jonathan Potter (OECD), Professor David Smallbone (Kingston University, United Kingdom), Ms Lois Stevenson (consultant, Canada) and Professor David Storey (University of Sussex, UK). Professor Maryann Feldman and Professor Tom Kemeny (both of the University of North Carolina, US), Professor Helen Lawton-Smith (Birkbeck College, University of London, United Kingdom) and Professor Andy Pike (University of Newcastle-upon-Tyne, United Kingdom) contributed to Chapter 5. Mr Benjamin Dean (OECD) provided the research assistance.

The project was led by Dr Jonathan Potter under the direction of Miriam Koreen, Deputy Director of the OECD Centre for Entrepreneurship, SMEs and Local Development.

List of abbreviations

CANACINTRA	*Cámara Nacional de la Industria de transformación* (National Chamber of Industry Transformation)
COMPITE	*Comité Nacional de Productividad e Innovación Tecnológica* (National Committee of Productivity and Technological Innovation)
CONACYT	*Consejo Nacional de Ciencia y Tecnología* (National Council of Science and Technology)
CRM	Customer Relationship Management
EDP	Entrepreneurial Development Plan 2001-06
ESP	Economy Sectoral Programme 2007-12
EU	European Union
FDI	Foreign direct investment
FIT	*Fondo de Innovación Tecnológica* (Technological Innovation Fund)
FOCIR	*Fondo de Capitalización e Inversión del Sector Rural* (The Rural Sector Capital Investment Fund)
FUMEC	*Fundación México-Estados Unidos para la Ciencia* (The United States-Mexico Foundation for Science)
GDP	Gross Domestic Product
GEM	Global Entrepreneurship Monitor
ILO	International Labour Organisation
INEGI	*Instituto Nacional de Estadística y Geografía* (National Institute of Statistics and Geography)
IO	Intermediary organisation
IPR	Intellectual property right
MEC	*Centros* México Emprende (Mexico Enterprise Centre)
SME	Micro, small and medium enterprise
MXN	Mexican Peso
NAFIN	*Nacional Financiera* (National development bank)
NBFI	Non-bank financial institution
NDP	National Development Plan
NTBF	New technology based firm
OECD	Organisation of Economic Co-operation and Development
PNF	*Programa nacional de franquiciamiento* (National Programme of Franchises)
PyME	Pequeña y mediana empresa (Small and medium-sized enterprise)
R&D	Research and Development
RFC	*Registro Federal de Contribuyentes* (Federal Register of Taxpayers)
SDP	Suppliers Development Programme
SEDECO	*Secretaría de Desarrollo Económico* (Ministry of Economic Development)
SOFOLES	*Sociedad Financieras de Objeto Ilimitado* (Limited Purpose Financial Entity)
SIEM	*Sistema de Información Empresarial Mexicano* (Mexican Business Information System)
SME	Small and medium-sized enterprise
UK	United Kingdom
US	United States of America
USD	United States dollar
VAT	Value-added tax

BASIC STATISTICS OF MEXICO

2010 unless otherwise indicated

THE LAND

Area (sq. km)	1 964 375	**Inhabitants in major metropolitan areas** (millions)	
Agricultural area (sq. km) (1990)	394 000	Mexico City	20.1
		Guadalajara	4.4
		Monterrey	4.1

THE PEOPLE

Population (thousands)		**Distribution of employment**[1] (% total employment, 2009)	
	108 396		
Inhabitants per sq. km	58	Agriculture	13.3
Annual population growth (1990-2010)	1.5	Industry	23.9
Unemployment rate (% labour force)	5.4	Services	62.1
Employment rate (%)	60.3		

ECONOMY

GDP (USD billions)	882.9	**Structure of production** (% of total, 2009, 2003 prices)	
GDP per capita (USD, current prices and PPPs)	15 204	Agriculture	3.7
Real GDP growth (%)	5.5	Industry	29.8
Gross fixed capital formation (% of GDP)	20	*of which:* Manufacturing	16.6
Consumer price index annual change (%)	4.2	Services	64.5

GOVERNMENT AND PUBLIC FINANCES

Federal Presidential Constitutional Republic

President	Felipe Calderón		**Composition of Parliament**	

Public sector indicators[2] (per cent of GDP, 2009)			**Senate**	**Chamber of Deputies**
Public sector expenditure	26.0	**PRI**	50	240
Public sector revenue	23.7	**PAN**	33	142
Oil-related revenue	7.4	**PRD**	24	68
Gross public debt (December)	37.1	**Other**	21	50
		Total	128	500

FOREIGN TRADE

Exports of merchandise (per cent of GDP)	29.2	**Imports of merchandise** (per cent of GDP)	29.5
Main exports (per cent of total, 2009)		**Main imports** (per cent of total, 2009)	
Manufactures	82.4	Intermediate goods	76.2
Petroleum products	14.0	Capital goods	10.0
Agriculture	2.9	Consumer goods	13.7

THE CURRENCY

Monetary unit: Peso	**Currency units per USD**, average of daily figures	
	2010	12.07
	2011	12.63

1. People economically active according to results of the *Quarterly National Employment Survey*.
2. Central government and public enterprises.
Source: INEGI, OECD, *OECD Economic Surveys: Mexico 2011* and OECD, *OECD Factbook Statistics 2012*.

OECD Studies on SMEs and Entrepreneurship: Mexico
© OECD 2013

Executive summary

*SME and entrepreneurship policies have been
established and embedded in the policy
framework*

Twelve years ago, the Mexican government started a concerted policy effort to support small and medium-sized enterprises (SMEs – firms with up to 250 employees) and stimulate new firm creation in order to accelerate economic growth, create jobs and reduce poverty. During 2001-06 this involved the creation of an Under Ministry of Small and Medium Enterprises in the Ministry of Economy to promote and co-ordinate policies, the establishment of a central budget in the SME Fund, and the creation of SME programmes focused on access to finance and innovation.

Since then, the effort has been strengthened. There are increased resources to the SME Fund. Programme support has been extended to include nascent entrepreneurship and micro-enterprises. New intermediary organisations are involved in delivering SME Fund programmes. And business service structures for policy delivery and outreach to the clients have been enhanced, such as a doubling of the number of business incubators and the introduction of Mexico Emprende Centres, acting as one-stop shops.

The policy effort is bearing its fruits. Mexico has one of the highest business birth rates among OECD countries and in the Latin American region and its business stock is growing rapidly. Favourable macroeconomic conditions have been installed, burdens on starting a business have been reduced substantially, investments in human capital and technology transfer have increased, and financial markets have been deepened.

The present report takes stock of developments over 2007-12. It assesses the achievements made and offers advice to SME and entrepreneurship policy makers and other stakeholders on how to respond to current challenges.

*There are high enterprise birth rates but a
predominance of micro and informal enterprises*

SMEs account for 99.8% of enterprises and 72.3% of employment in Mexico. This is a significantly greater share than in most other OECD member countries. These firms are a vital part of the Mexican economy.

As well as the sheer size of the SME sector in Mexico, one of its distinctive features is its high share of very small enterprises. Micro-enterprises (employing less than 10 people) account for 96.1% of all businesses in Mexico, one of the highest rates in OECD member countries. They therefore also represent the majority of Mexican SMEs.

13

However, micro firms have low productivity. Together they contribute only 18% of Mexican output compared with 40% of employment. Moreover, their productivity levels actually reduced during 2003-08. Low micro firm productivity is partly tied up with the large numbers of Mexican enterprises operating outside of the formal sector. These informal firms lack access to credit and seek to stay under the horizon rather than grow. Greater efforts are needed to help these firms to modernise, formalise and increase their productivity and contribution to value added.

The flip side of the dominance of micro firms is a gap relative to other countries in middle-sized SMEs, those in the range of 50-250 employees. These firms tend to have much greater productivity and better innovation and internationalisation performance than SMEs in general. They are therefore an important target for policy seeking to improve the structural characteristics of the Mexican SME economy.

Entrepreneurial intentions are positive in Mexico, however, and the business birth rate is one of the highest in the OECD area, with a growing stock of SMEs.

Macro conditions and regulations have improved but gaps in finance, innovation, skills and administrative simplification remain

Framework conditions for SMEs and entrepreneurship have improved dramatically in recent years. This has been underpinned by stable macroeconomic conditions and by multilateral and bilateral trade agreements which have stimulated exports and foreign direct investment inflows. Regulatory reforms have also simplified starting and running a business. For instance, between 2003 and 2010, the days needed to open a business fell from 58 to 6. Efforts have been made to close tax loopholes, with the adoption of the alternative minimum tax on business income being a good practice.

However, bank supply of credit to SMEs is relatively low. It is partly associated with lack of product market competition in the banking sector, and while the national loan guarantee system is helping to address the problem in the medium term, it services only 70 000 to 80 000 enterprises per year, compared with more than 4 million enterprises in Mexico, which can be considered relatively low given the strong existing barriers to access to finance in Mexico at this time. There are also weaknesses in Mexico's investments in innovation, such as on R&D and patenting. Thus in 2009, government expenditure on R&D stood at 0.25% of GDP in Mexico and business expenditure on R&D stood at 0.18%, significantly below OECD median values of 0.72 and 1.12% respectively. The education system still does not produce enough people with entrepreneurial or business management skills, despite government efforts in these areas. And despite improvements, regulatory burdens still act as a disincentive to the participation of firms in the formal sector. Further public actions are needed to strengthen the business environment in these areas.

A sound strategic framework is now in place,
but there is scope for strengthening intermediary
organisations and streamlining SME Fund
regulations

The Economy Sectoral Programme 2007-12 took over from the Entrepreneurial Development Plan of 2001-06 and expanded the former SME programmes into new areas. This new policy framework is appropriate to the challenge and based on a sound diagnosis of the areas warranting government intervention.

Many of the government actions are bound together through the SME Fund, while co-ordination with complementary bodies and programmes such as CONACYT and the Innovation Fund is managed by the Under Ministry for SMEs. The portfolio of SME Fund expenditures is organised in model fashion, responding in an integrated and holistic manner to the needs of nascent entrepreneurs, micro-enterprises, established SMEs and gazelles, as well as exploiting larger "tractor' enterprises for the upgrading of SMEs in their supply chains.

Outreach to the very large population of Mexican SMEs is facilitated by the use of a network of intermediary organisations such as universities, chambers of commerce and business associations. These organisations deliver business services and support to firms and entrepreneurs in their networks on behalf of government. At the same time, however, the penetration of programmes into the population of SMEs and entrepreneurs needs to be increased further.

One of the constraints is that the operational procedures of the SME Fund are burdensome for intermediaries and potential intermediaries in terms of reporting requirements, compliance procedures, annual rather than multi-annual budgeting and payment delays. This complexity reduces the degree of leverage of federal government financial resources and the government's ability to reach out to the full potential client group.

In addition, there is scope to increase the quality and capacity of intermediary organisations through the strengthening of competitive selection procedures and capacity building measures, including training for management and front line staff and the development of learning networks amongst business service delivery organisations.

Comprehensive and good practice programmes
should be extended in priority areas

The Mexican government offers a comprehensive set of support measures for entrepreneurs and enterprises as they develop, and by investing strongly in financing and training and consultancy, policy is on the right course.

Furthermore, support has evolved effectively over time in order to meet new priorities and respond to changing economic conditions. This is illustrated, for example, in the shift of access to finance programmes from the initial SME subsidies toward building of credit and equity markets, and in the extension of the scope of policy to cover new entrepreneurs, micro-enterprises and gazelles as well as mainstream SMEs.

Several of Mexico's programmes are international good practice, offering models for policy development elsewhere. They include the business accelerators programme, the national guarantee programme, the supplier development programme, the modernisation and integration programmes and the Federal Commission for Regulatory Improvement.

However, support for the development of risk capital markets is still at its beginnings, and the available support for seed capital is not promoted sufficiently to potential beneficiary enterprises and incubators. And while there is a growing network of incubators, only a small proportion concentrates on innovative and knowledge-intensive start-ups.

Given the scale of the needs, efforts must be made to increase the proportions of micro-enterprises benefiting from mentoring and consultancy support and support for access to finance. The Modernisation and Integration Programmes and the National Loan Guarantee Programme are making a real difference in this area and need to be maintained, with potential refinements based on evaluation results. However, the number of beneficiaries is small relative to the massive number of micro firms in Mexico, both formal and informal. For example, the government's target for 2011 was to reach 10 000 micro-enterprises with training and consultancy support, but this represents a tiny proportion of the more than 4.9 million enterprises in the business population. The loan guarantee scheme is only able to reach around 70 000 micro-enterprises per year, despite its high leverage of private finance.

Moreover, innovative SMEs and start-ups require greater attention. They received only 6.6% of the total SME Fund budget for SME productive projects in the period 2009-11. Similarly, only 4% of business incubators are currently targeting high technology start-ups, while the Technological Innovation Fund is oversubscribed.

More attention is also needed to the promotion of women's entrepreneurship and ensuring equal access to public programmes.

National-local coherence should be pursued

SME and entrepreneurship policy in Mexico has an important local dimension, given the size of the country, the decentralisation of many powers and budgets to States, and the strong diversity in conditions for business activity across Mexico's various regions and localities. This is recognised through arrangements for the co-funding by federal and state governments of SME Fund-supported programmes, co-selection of SME Fund-supported projects, and the opportunity for states and municipalities to run intermediary organisations for policy delivery in their areas. These arrangements help to secure the tailoring of policy to local needs and coherence between national and local policy actions.

There is nonetheless some scope to pursue this co-ordination further. In particular, simplification of the SME Fund operating procedures will facilitate the co-funding of SME Fund programmes by state and other local level partners. Furthermore, new structures can be introduced for the exchange of information on policy needs and good practice responses between the federal and state levels and among the local partners in different states.

Evaluation activity should be expanded to focus policy on achieving high impacts

One of the requirements for further strengthening of SME and entrepreneurship policy in Mexico, and securing its maximum contribution to economic growth, job creation and poverty reduction, is to focus on, and scale up, those programmes that make the most difference to SME and entrepreneurship development and those intermediaries that deliver support with the greatest effectiveness and efficiency. Robust programme evaluation is required to inform this effort. It needs to be undertaken across the full portfolio of SME and entrepreneurship policies in order to allow a comparison of the costs and benefits of the different interventions and intermediaries.

Many of the conditions for sound evaluation are already in place. In particular there are good data on programme expenditures and inputs. There is also the possibility to pull together further existing information across government that will be extremely useful for impact evaluation by using a single serial number for each enterprise that has interactions with government, and ensuring that this same code is used by and shared by all government departments. This will enable the tracking of the support used by enterprises and of trends in their performance and provide for comparisons of outcomes, such as growth and survival rates, for "treated" and "non-treated" enterprises.

Currently, however, there are few evaluations available that reliably establish programme impacts and it is difficult to compare the cost-benefit ratios of different programmes and intermediary organisations from existing evidence. Furthermore, there are currently only limited capacities for evaluation across government programme managers, although there is some important external evaluation expertise.

The way forward

This report documents the great strides that have been taken by the Mexican government to strengthen SMEs and entrepreneurship in recent years and offers best practice lessons to other countries in many areas. It is now crucial to secure these gains and maintain the good practice structures and programmes that have been put in place.

At the same time, new efforts should be undertaken to reflect the changing environment and changing priorities. The key steps that need to be taken now concern addressing remaining weaknesses in the business environment and framework conditions for SME and entrepreneurship development, supporting further those enterprise segments with the greatest potential to contribute to growth and job creation, and bringing all programme activities and services up to the level of the best.

With this in mind, the directions recommended for future policy development in Mexico include:

● developing micro-enterprises and reducing informality, including through increasing the numbers of micro-enterprises benefiting from mentoring and consultancy support and further reducing regulatory burdens on business;

● developing access to entrepreneurial financing such as through additional decentralised credit guarantee mechanisms, improved credit bureau data, promotion of community-based banks, facilitating competition in the banking sector, and creation of new fiscal mechanisms aimed at channelling investment by private savers into equity funds that invest in innovative and high-growth SMEs;

● stimulating innovative SMEs and start-ups by expanding existing programmes such as the business accelerators, the supplier development programme and high technology business incubators so that they can help more of these high-potential beneficiary firms, and introducing new initiatives such as vouchers for innovation purchasing;

● adjusting the management of the SME Fund's intermediary organisation system to reinforce the competitive element of the processes through which intermediaries are selected, specifying clear performance criteria for funding, offering capacity building training and good practice exchange for the management and front-line staff of intermediaries, and streamlining the SME Fund operational procedures to reduce the administrative burden on intermediary organisations in terms of applications and payments and facilitate the development of longer-term projects;

● reinforcing impact evaluation, and using it to scale up those programme initiatives and intermediary organisations with the greatest impacts, including better tracking of beneficiaries through programme monitoring activities, the creation of a single cross-government database using common enterprise serial numbers to record enterprise interactions with government and enterprise performance subsequent to support, installing a government organisation for SME and entrepreneurship policy evaluation, and drafting a self-standing cross-government policy statement of objectives and targets for SME and entrepreneurship policy.

This report assesses the policy framework in Mexico today and identifies lessons for future SME and entrepreneurship policy development. Its objective is to:

● provide an overview of SME and entrepreneurship activities and how they perform against international benchmarks;

● outline the strengths and weaknesses of the business environment and framework conditions;

● assess the current SME and entrepreneurship policy framework and measures, taking stock of the progress made and identifying new challenges;

● show the relationships between federal and state governments in SME and entrepreneurship policy design and implementation;

● review the policy evaluation system;

● provide recommendations on opportunities for policy development in the next presidential period.

Introduction

Overview

In 2000, the Mexican government acknowledged the key role that small and medium-sized enterprises (SMEs) and entrepreneurship play in guaranteeing the future prosperity of Mexico by making "more and better jobs, more and better enterprises and more and better entrepreneurs" the foundation of a new SME and entrepreneurship policy agenda. This agenda was carried through by the actions of the Entrepreneurial Development Plan (EDP) 2001-06, co-ordinated by a newly created Under Ministry of SMEs within the Ministry of Economy. The achievements of that period were assessed in an OECD review of SME policy in Mexico published in 2007 [OECD (2007), *SMEs in Mexico: Issues and Policies*, OECD Publishing, *http://dx.doi.org/10.1787/9789264031791-en*].

Following the OECD recommendations and an internal review, the Under Ministry of SMEs embarked in 2007 on a new policy agenda under the SME pillar of the Economy Sectoral Programme (ESP) 2007-12. This new agenda marked a departure with the past. In addition to the traditional activities to strengthen the competitiveness of existing Mexican SMEs, new measures were introduced for SME productivity growth and internationalisation and to stimulate a pipeline of new, competent future entrepreneurs and upgrade micro-enterprises.

This introduction puts the review in context by documenting the main steps taken by the Mexican government in introducing an SME and entrepreneurship policy to Mexico over the last 12 years.

Early days: The Entrepreneurial Development Plan (EDP) 2001-06

The Mexican government's emphasis on the SME sector (firms with up to 250 employees) began in earnest in 2001, when it developed and launched a new national policy framework, the Entrepreneurial Development Plan (EDP) for the period 2001-06. This introduced a coherent set of actions to support SME competitiveness, replacing a few scattered programmes that existed previously within the broad ranging framework of industrial policy and foreign trade.

At the same time, the government created the Under Ministry for Small and Medium Enterprises in the Ministry of Economy to oversee the planning, design and implementation of the SME policy and programmes. Consensus building and collaboration among the main stakeholders were fostered with mechanisms to improve participatory processes and vertical and horizontal policy co-ordination. Administrative powers were decentralised, opening up space for state and local governments as well as to other intermediaries to tailor the design and implementation of SME policy initiatives. The legal framework for these steps was the Law for Development of the Competitiveness of Micro, Small and Medium Enterprises, published in December 2002.

The policy efforts focused on the removal of general impediments to entrepreneurial activity rather than selective sector intervention, as had been the case in the past. A number of important measures were introduced. They included the National Supplier Development Programme, the National Guarantee System, the National Financial Extension Programme, the Programme for Training and Strengthening SME Capabilities, the PYMExporta Centre Network and the Impulsoras Programme for Exportable Offer, the National System of Business Incubators, measures for the procurement of public goods and services from SMEs.

Assessing the EDP: The 2007 OECD Review

The OECD review of these policies highlighted many positive developments. For instance, the number of SMEs benefitting from SME support programmes increased from 13 000 to 254 000. Improved access to finance was shown by lower risk premiums (the average spread between SME loan charges to short-term interest rates narrowed by 7-8 basis points) and lower transaction costs. Administrative lead times for firm creation decreased substantially, and firm survival rates improved. The report commended the Mexican authorities for the policies introduced and for having regrouped SME programmes around four major action routes (innovation and firm creation, access to finance, production networks and access to foreign markets).

The report also identified a number of areas for improvement. The main recommendations involved the introduction of measures to:

● strengthen policy co-ordination among ministries and state governments;

● enhance the capacity of states and local authorities to implement federal policy initiatives;

● provide financial resources, advice and basic training to micro-enterprises;

● build networks of micro suppliers around large enterprises;

● widen the range of federal SME programmes to address the needs of all categories of SMEs;

● acknowledge regional differences in economic environments;

● strengthen policy evaluation.

To assist with the implementation of these recommendations, and in light of the scale of the SME sector's structural problems, the report recommended that additional resources be allocated to the SME Fund.

Evolution: The Economy Sectoral Programme 2007-12

With the OECD review's recommendations in mind, the Ministry of Economy embarked on the Economy Sectoral Programme (ESP) 2007-12. This placed greater emphasis on promoting entrepreneurship on growing higher potential enterprises and on upgrading micro-enterprises.

To configure the activities, the Under Ministry for SMEs developed a 5-by-5 framework covering:

● Five target segments: entrepreneurs (women and men in the process of creating, developing or strengthening an enterprise); micro-enterprises; SMEs; gazelles (newly established SMEs with potential for above average job generation) and tractor enterprises (large enterprises at the centre of supply chains involving SMEs).

● Five main service offerings: financing, training and consultancy, management, marketing and innovation.

The previous thirteen programmes of the EDP were regrouped, replaced or discontinued. The result was the following five core programmes:

● New Entrepreneurs National Programme;

● National Programme for Micro-Enterprises;

● National SMEs Programme;

● National Programme for Gazelle Enterprises;

● National Programme for Tractor Enterprises.

In this reformulation, funding for certain pre-existing programmes, such as the Centres for Productive Articulation and Innovation Laboratories, was discontinued; funding for other programmes, such as the Impulsora Exportable Offer and PYMExporta Centres was reallocated to ProMexico;* new programmes were created, and the network of business development centres was replaced with a new system of standardised Mexico Emprende Centres.

The overall effect of the policy changes was to enable a rapid scaling up of a number of previous programmes, following a number of the recommendations of the *2007 OECD Review*. Among the most notable developments were:

● the introduction of the National Programme for Micro-Enterprises, including its Integral Modernisation Programme;

● the enlargement and strengthening of the National SME Guarantees Programme, with about MXN 8.9 billion of public resources allocated and channelled through financial intermediaries during 2007-12 compared to MXN 1.2 billion during 2001-06, and almost 320 000 SMEs supported (compared to 157 877 in the previous period);

● an expanded network of Mexico Emprende Centres taking over from the former business development centres, with 200 centres in operation in 2011 compared to 155 in 2006;

● an expanded network of business incubators, numbering 500 at the end of 2011 compared with 254 in 2006.

The policy was also flexible enough to turn to the problems of the global financial and economic crisis that began in 2008. The associated downturn in the United States had strong adverse effects on the Mexican economy, with GDP contracting 6 and 5.5% in 2009 and 2010, respectively. This was the most serious decline in economic growth in Latin America, and reflected the relative openness of the Mexican economy and its strong economic ties with the US. The available policy measures such as financial guarantees played a key role in helping SMEs weather the crisis.

Table 1 shows the progress that has been made in implementing the OECD recommendations from its 2007 review. However, there are new challenges, some persistent weaknesses in framework conditions, and gaps to be filled in policy support. This report examines the state of play today and recommends how to respond.

---

* Following the creation of ProMexico as the national agency for exports and investment promotion under the Ministry of Economy at the end of 2007, the actions and strategies implemented by the Under Ministry for SMEs regarding the development of exportable offer, were gradually transferred to ProMexico. Most of the PYMExporta Centres were rationalised or closed.

Table 1. **Progress in implementation of the 2007 OECD review's recommendations**

2007 Recommendations	Actions taken since 2007	Current assessment
Improve policy co-ordination		
Conduct a methodological review to enhance policy co-ordination among all SME stakeholders.	The Ministry of Economy carried out an extensive review of the SME policy framework and introduced a new programme structure.	The adjustments to the policy framework reduced overlap, improved co-ordination and enhanced visibility and access to SME support.
Review programmes for technological development and regional and sector development with a view to harmonisation.	The new policy framework integrates the technological development and regional and sector development actions within the actions for target enterprise segments. Mexico Emprende Centres were established to achieve greater harmonisation among programmes.	Important synergies have been achieved. Communication and networking among intermediary organisations could be developed for the sharing of good practice.
Use the natural sequence of "service stations" or "support units" to co-ordinate and integrate policy.	The new policy framework offers support to entrepreneurs and enterprises as they progress from start-ups, to micro-enterprises, to small and medium enterprises, to gazelles to tractor firms.	The framework provides effective policy co-ordination and integration.
Conduct an inter-institution review across federal government, states and local authorities to identify where reorganisation of programmes could increase efficiency.	Concurrent sector programmes have been prepared by different Federal ministries incorporating SME development measures. The Ministry of Public Education, the National Council for Science and Technology, the Ministry of Agriculture, and the Ministry of Tourism have laid out budgetary commitments in support of the SME sector.	Better inter-institution co-ordination could be achieved through development of a high-level SME and entrepreneurship policy statement that encompasses the SME development actions of each of these ministries and councils and through the reactivation of the National Council on the Competitiveness of SMEs.
Better communicate the SME Policy Framework		
Issue a succinct central policy statement on SME policy, explaining in simple terms the essence of each policy action route.	A broad vision has been set for SME policies involving "more and better jobs, more and better enterprises and more and better entrepreneurs". However, a new strategic statement cannot be made before revision of the National Development Plan after 2012.	A cross-government policy statement should be issued early in the next presidential term.
Conduct regular surveys of SMEs' views on different policy options.	Opinions of SMEs are sought in the process of programme evaluations.	Further consultation on SME views on policy options should be undertaken. This could be facilitated by creation of an SME Advisory Council to the Ministry of Economy formed by SME owners and entrepreneurs.
Simplify the language used by business support organisations with clients and introduce "policy disseminators" to make services clear to potential customers.	The Ministry of Economy has introduced a web-based platform to allow project applicants to submit proposals online and track the progress of project approval. A clear set of SME Fund operating rules and procedures and guidelines for project applicants are on the website. A new system of Mexico Emprende Centres has been introduced to provide a one-stop entry point for potential customers.	Communication about SME policy measures delivered through the SME Fund is transparent and easy to understand. The new system of Mexico Emprende Centres helps policy dissemination. Further training should be offered to Mexico Emprende Centre staff to communicate available services to potential clients and deliver good quality services.
Enhance the capacity of states and local authorities to absorb federal policy impulses and to take policy initiatives		
Expand programmes for capacity building in states and local governments to increase their ability to deliver policy to SMEs and entrepreneurs.		Federal government provides no formal capacity building support for state and local government policy makers. Training in policy design, delivery and evaluation should be provided for economic development professionals. Sharing of good practice among intermediary organisations should be encouraged, particularly among the newly-launched Mexico Emprende Centres and members of the national incubation system.
Strengthen states' capacity to issue effective guidelines for the use of SME Fund resources by service deliverers and intermediary organisations.		States do not issue guidelines about the use of the SME Fund. To increase take up of SME Fund resources in under-represented states, clear information should be provided by all states to potential service deliverers about the objectives and procedures of the Fund and how to draw down funding efficiently.

Table 1. **Progress in implementation of the 2007 OECD review's recommendations** (*cont.*)

2007 Recommendations	Actions taken since 2007	Current assessment
Support states and local authorities in their efforts to draw up tailor-made programmes of institutional-capacity building for less privileged regions.	Flexibility has been increased to allow specific local projects from under-represented and poorer regions to draw on the SME Fund. However, there has been no specific institutional capacity building for these regions.	States have substantial flexibility to tailor SME Fund programmes to local development priorities because local intermediaries can be used to design and deliver projects and certain applications can be shortlisted at state level. However, SME Fund expenditure is overly concentrated in and around the Capital region. Institutional capacity building for use of the SME Fund in non-Capital regions would help to rebalance expenditure.
Build further synergies between federal, state and local programmes.	The operational procedures of the SME Fund have been designed to encourage synergies among programmes at federal and state levels, and often involve equal federal and state level co-funding of projects. Local governments do not have many responsibilities in the area of economic development support.	Current SME Fund operating arrangements permit synergies among government levels, but simplification of SME Fund rules and procedures would help state and local actors to increase their utilisation of the Fund increase its adaptation to emerging local policy needs. It would also be useful to increase the involvement of the state level Federal Delegate Offices and other state level stakeholders in policy development discussions at federal level.

Create an efficient evaluation culture at all levels of government, support units and intermediate organisations

Develop comprehensive and systematic evaluation procedures that estimate and communicate policy impacts.	Each ministry has evaluation procedures in place concerning its support instruments for SMEs, and there is a range specific evaluation bodies at federal level, including the Superior Auditing Body of the Federation, the Internal Control Organ, the National Centre for Evaluation, the INEGI and the SHCP. Each assesses the programmes under their responsibility. All states and municipal governments have their own mechanisms for monitoring and control.	Evaluation procedures are currently fragmented across government with important variations in quality and coverage. Many current evaluations focus on measuring activities and outputs rather than impacts, and policy impact estimates that are offered are not always based on robust methodologies. Evaluation would be improved by the creation of a politically influential organisation within federal government using robust methods to evaluate policies and programmes and using the results to formulate future policy.
Undertake a formal gap analysis to determine SME policy needs.		Undertaking formal research on the challenges faced by SMEs and how they can be addressed by policy would be helpful, but is no longer of the highest priority.
Make best-practice evaluation procedures an integral part of each policy programme.	There has been an increase in programme evaluation activities. There are considerably more data available on the clients of public programmes.	Much of the data required for evaluation studies is now available. However, the evaluations undertaken to date – with perhaps one notable exception – have not used the most robust approaches available for establishing impact.
Establish an independent evaluation agency.	There are several government organisations that undertake evaluation but no single independent evaluation agency for SME and entrepreneurship policies.	The establishment of an independent evaluation agency would promote the use of best practice evaluation procedures and enable more comprehensive and systemic evaluation across government including comparison of results across programmes.

Increase micro firms' take-up of programmes

Create and extend institutional networks making use of mobile business development centres.	Mobile business development centres have not been introduced, but the proportion of microenterprises benefitting from support policies has increased thanks to the new Mexico Emprende Centres.	There has been an appropriate response to the problem of increasing access of micro entrepreneurs to policy support.
Enlarge the presence of micro credit institutions making use of mobile micro banks.	The microcredit organisation infrastructure has been strengthened although mobile micro banks have not been a key feature of the improved support.	There is good public support for microcredit. The priority for the future should be on encouraging increased private sector delivery of microcredit, including through increasing competition in the banking sector.

Table 1. **Progress in implementation of the 2007 OECD review's recommendations** (*cont.*)

2007 Recommendations	Actions taken since 2007	Current assessment
Develop new tailor-made financial products to micro firms.	The National Programme of Micro-enterprises (2007-12) was introduced to provide tailored support for micro-enterprises. It offers access to training and consulting services in the first stage and access to funding for equipment to meet the modernisation needs of their micro-enterprises in the second stage (for graduates of the training and consultancy phase).	The Ministry of Economy has worked effectively in co-operation with non-bank financial institutions in particular to develop and offer new loan products for microenterprises.
Encourage micro firms to join associations, to help in the design and implementation of tailor-made policies.	The development of microenterprise programmes has emerged from dialogue with microenterprise associations, which has allowed the strengthening of these business associations.	Microenterprises are still not well represented in business associations. Actions should be taken to encourage their greater participation, and to consult with the microenterprise sector to ensure their needs are understood by policy makers.
Increase resources for SME policy		
Increase financial resources available to the SME Fund.	Total resources allocated to the SME Fund have increased to MXN 17.6 billion (USD 1.4 billion) for 2007-12. Spending for entrepreneurial training and infrastructure averages MXN 3.5 billion (USD 277 million) per year, compared to an average of MXN 2 billion (USD 158 million) per year in 2004-06. MXN 8.9 billion (USD 705 million) are allocated to the National SME Guarantee through the SME Fund.	SME Fund resources have increased. An amendment to the 2002 Law for Competitiveness of SMEs in 2011 ensures that the budget allocated to the SME Fund cannot be less than in the immediately preceding year.
Use incremental resources generated in the federal budget by economic growth to extend SME programmes and create an effective evaluation culture.	Incremental resources for the SME Fund were allocated in 2007-08. This included resources for SME programmes and for evaluation.	The additional resources have permitted improvements in the collection of evaluation data and increased programme support. Further efforts are needed to embed a culture of evaluation and scale up the most effective and efficient policies.
Other recommendations		
Improve data collection on SMEs to help policy analysis.	The collection of information on SMEs is carried out by programme, but an analysis through time of the evolution of these companies is not carried out.	A database covering all enterprise interactions with government should be developed. All enterprises should have a single code to be used in all circumstances so as to minimise the bureaucratic burdens on enterprise and enable government to be more responsive to the needs of SMEs.
Lighten the administrative burden on businesses.	The government launched a major regulatory reform and simplification effort in 2009. Many administrative and regulatory procedures affecting SMEs were reviewed and actions taken. The government also implemented an online system for registering a business and dealing with all start-up requirements.	These actions have significantly eased business start up and operation but further administrative simplification is required.
Facilitate regulatory compliance by SMEs.		There is scope to increase transparency in regulations.
Review inheritance tax policies to ease procedures for change in SME ownership.		Measures to provide fiscal incentives for investment in innovative SMEs are desirable, as well as actions to facilitate financing of the transmission of enterprises to new generations of owners.
Improve and broaden entrepreneurial education in schools and universities.	The Ministry of Economy has promoted entrepreneurship in universities and, in co-ordination with the Ministry of Education, established a Board for Financing Entrepreneurship Initiatives that provides funding for entrepreneurship skills programmes and extra-curricular activities in higher education.	Entrepreneurship education and start-up support initiatives should be expanded to schools and technical colleges.

Reference

OECD (2007), *SMEs in Mexico: Issues and Policies*, OECD Publishing, doi: *http://dx.doi.org/10.1787/ 9789264031791-en.*

Chapter 1

SME and entrepreneurship performance in Mexico

This chapter examines the current state and recent evolution of entrepreneurship and SME performance in Mexico. It presents key structural indicators such as the SME share in enterprises, employment and GDP, the sector and size distribution of SME activity, business start-up rates, entrepreneurial intentions, numbers of growth firms and the size of the informal economy. It also analyses performance indicators including productivity, exports, investment and innovation.

1.1. The size and structure of the SME sector

1.1.1. The SME definition in Mexico is as follows

Table 1.1. **Definition of SMEs in Mexico**

Size	Sector	Range of number of workers	Range of amount of annual sales (MXN million)	Combined ceiling[1]
Micro	All	To 10	Up to 4	4.6
Small	Trade	From 11 to 30	4.01 to 100	93
	Industry and services	From 11 to 50	4.01 to 100	95
Medium	Trade	From 31 to 100	100.01 to 250	235
	Services	From 51 to 100		
	Industry	From 51 to 250	100.01 to 250	250

1. Combined = ceiling (employees) x 10% + (annual sales) x 90%. The size category of the company is determined from the score obtained from the following formula: Points of the company = (number of employees) x 10% + (annual sales amount) x 90%. This must equal or be lower than the combined ceiling for its class.
Source: www.compite.org.mx/DOFNuevaEstratificacionDeLasPyMEs.htm.

The Mexican authorities estimated the SME population in Mexico to be 4.1 million in 2010, accounting for an estimated 52% of GDP and 78.5% of total employment. It is difficult to produce accurate descriptions of the size distribution of enterprises because of variations between different databases. However, according to the Economic Census in 2008, the number of economic units in the 3 major sectors (commerce, non-financial services and manufacturing) totalled 3 643 982 firms of which only 5 944 were large firms (i.e. 0.2%). Therefore, in 2008 a total of 3 638 038 firms are classified as micro, small or medium enterprises (SMEs), representing 99.8% of all enterprises.

Tables 1.2 and 1.3 compare data for enterprises Mexico with a mix of countries in terms of levels of economic development, thereby providing benchmarks against which to identify distinctive features of the size structure of enterprises in Mexico.

Table 1.2. **Size distribution of enterprises in Mexico and various countries, 2007**
As a percentage of total enterprises

	Micro	Small	Medium	Large
Brazil	66.4	26.6	5.7	1.3
United States	76.9	19.9	2.0	1.1
United Kingdom	87.9	10.1	1.6	0.4
Spain	92.6	6.5	0.8	0.1
France	93.0	5.9	0.9	0.2
Mexico	**94.5**	**4.4**	**0.9**	**0.2**
Portugal	94.5	4.7	0.7	0.1
Greece	96.7	2.9	0.4	0.1

Source: OECD Structural and Demographic Business Statistics.

Table 1.3. **Employment distribution of enterprises in Mexico and various countries, 2007**

As a percentage of total enterprises

	Micro	Small	Medium	Large
Brazil	7.3	19.7	21.7	51.3
United States	11.1	23.0	13.2	52.7
United Kingdom	21.5	17.4	15.2	45.9
France	24.3	20.4	15.8	39.5
Spain	38.3	24.5	14.8	22.4
Mexico	**39.5**	**16.2**	**16.7**	**27.6**
Portugal	41.8	23.0	16.4	18.9
Greece	58.2	17.5	10.7	13.6

Source: OECD Structural and Demographic Business Statistics.

As well as accounting for the vast majority of all enterprises, SMEs provide almost three quarters of total employment in Mexico, compared with about one-half in the US, at one extreme, and 86% in Greece at the other extreme. As in most countries, the share of the business stock accounted for by SMEs in Mexico is higher than their share of total employment.

The exceptionally high proportion of microenterprises in Mexico is confirmed by Figure 1.1. Of the 35 countries shown, Mexico has the third highest proportion of its business stock accounted for by micro-enterprises. The corollary is that Mexico appears to suffer from a dearth of medium-sized enterprises.

Figure 1.1. **Enterprises by size class, 2008 or latest available year**

Percentage, by size of firm

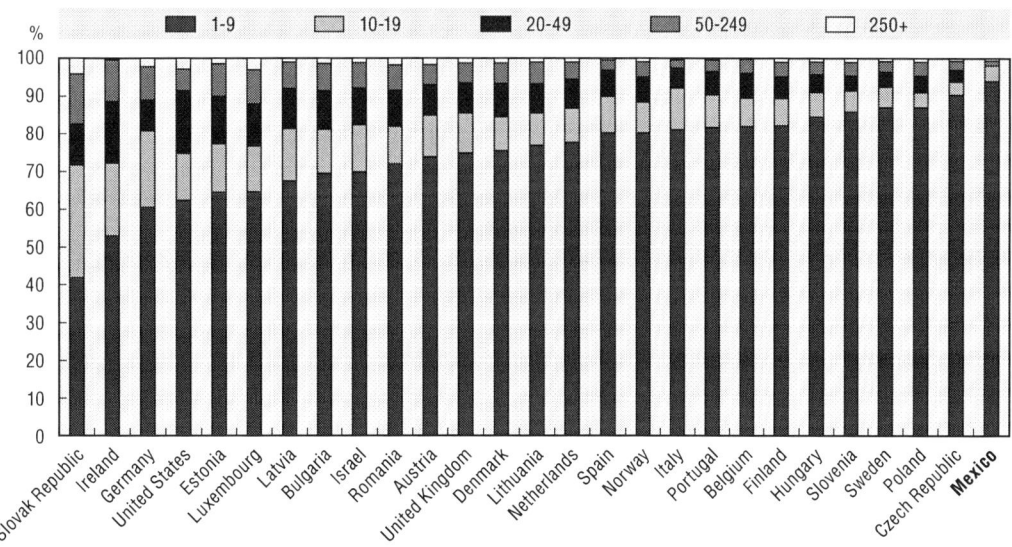

Notes: The unit of measure is enterprises for all counties, except Japan and Korea where establishments is the unit. For Ireland, only enterprises with three or more persons employed are covered, while the data for Japan and Korea do not include establishments with fewer than four and five persons employed, respectively. For the United States, employment in enterprises refers to the number of employees and not the number of persons employed. Data cover the market economy, excluding financial intermediation; for Brazil, Ireland, Israel, Japan, Korea, Luxembourg and the Slovak Republic they cover manufacturing sectors only. The statistical data for Israel are supplied by and under the responsibility of the relevant Israeli authorities. The use of such data by the OECD is without prejudice to the status of the Golan Heights, East Jerusalem and Israeli settlements in the West Bank under the terms of international law.
Source: OECD, Entrepreneurship at a Glance, 2012.

The size structure of enterprises can be affected by the sector composition of national economies. However, the predominance of microenterprises in Mexico relative to other countries is shown even more starkly when taking manufacturing alone. Mexico's micro-enterprise share in manufacturing, at 94% of the total, is the highest among the 27 benchmarked countries shown in Figure 1.2.

Figure 1.2. **Manufacturing enterprises by size class, 2008 or latest available year**

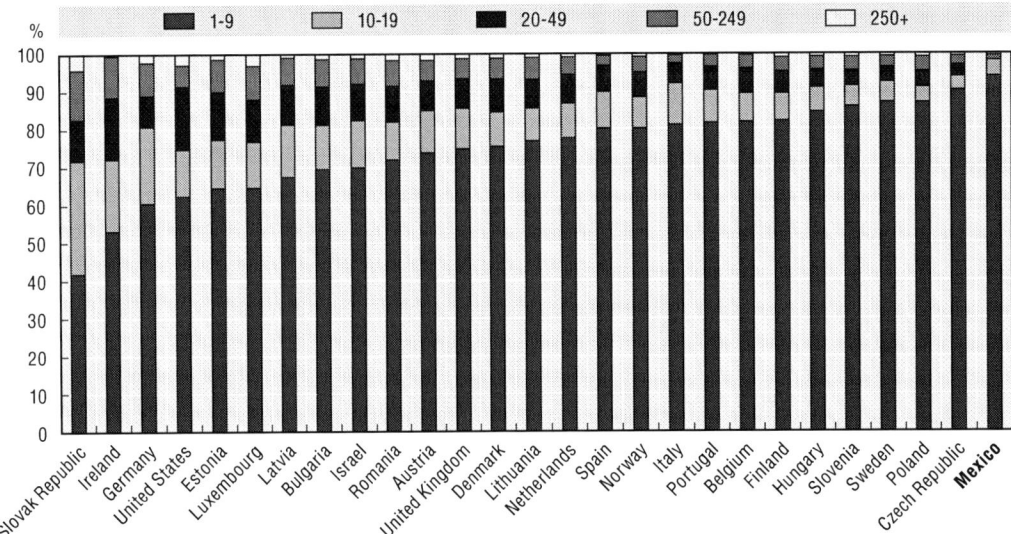

Notes: Data for Israel uses the ISIC Rev. 3 classification. The statistical data for Israel are supplied by and under the responsibility of the relevant Israeli authorities. The use of such data by the OECD is without prejudice to the status of the Golan Heights, East Jerusalem and Israeli settlements in the West Bank under the terms of international law. The size classes 10_19 and 20_49 are aggregated for Mexico; the exact list of size classes for Mexico is the following: 0_10, 11_50, 51_250, 251+. Size classes for US are 1_9, 10_19, 20_99, 100_499 and 500+.
Source: OECD Structural and Demographic Business Statistics Database.

Figure 1.3 shows the percentage of total employment in each of the enterprise size classes. It further emphasises the exceptional nature of Mexico's enterprise size distribution internationally in which micro-enterprises are more prevalent than in most of the other countries. Employment creation has been an important target of government policy in recent years and micro-enterprises are contributing to that objective. However, given the greater export propensity and productivity levels of medium-sized firms compared with micro and small firms, the weighting of the size distribution to micro firms in Mexico constrains export and productivity performance.

The aggregate picture masks variation in the contribution of SMEs between sectors. Micro-enterprises are most dominant in commerce, where they make up 97.5% of firms, compared with 94.5% of firms in non-financial services and 92.5% in manufacturing. However, SMEs above the micro firm threshold are rare in each of the sectors, representing 2.45% of enterprises in commerce, 4.63% in non-financial services and 5.12% in manufacturing. There is a significant gap in medium-sized SMEs in each of the three broad sectors of the economy, but this is particularly marked in manufacturing.

One of the distinctive features of the Mexican economy is that SMEs make a considerably lower contribution to value-added than in benchmark countries. As shown in Figure 1.4, SMEs as a whole account for only 53.6% of value added in Mexico, far behind the corresponding figure for most other OECD economies.

Figure 1.3. **Employment by enterprise size class, 2008 or latest available year**

Percentage

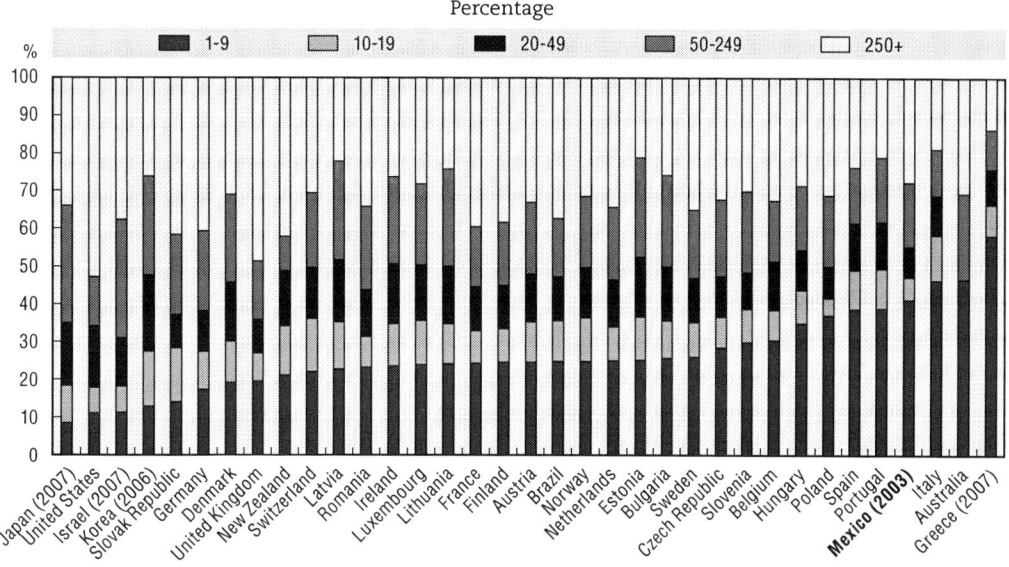

Notes: The unit of measure is enterprises for all counties, except Japan and Korea where establishments is the unit. For Ireland, only enterprises with three or more persons employed are covered, while the data for Japan and Korea do not include establishments with fewer than four and five persons employed, respectively. For the United States, employment in enterprises refers to the number of employees and not the number of persons employed. Data cover the market economy, excluding financial intermediation; for Brazil, Ireland, Israel, Japan, Korea, Luxembourg and the Slovak Republic they cover manufacturing sectors only. The statistical data for Israel are supplied by and under the responsibility of the relevant Israeli authorities. The use of such data by the OECD is without prejudice to the status of the Golan Heights, East Jerusalem and Israeli settlements in the West Bank under the terms of international law.
Source: OECD (2012), *Entrepreneurship at a Glance 2012.*

Figure 1.4. **Value added by enterprise size class, 2008 or latest available year**

Percentage

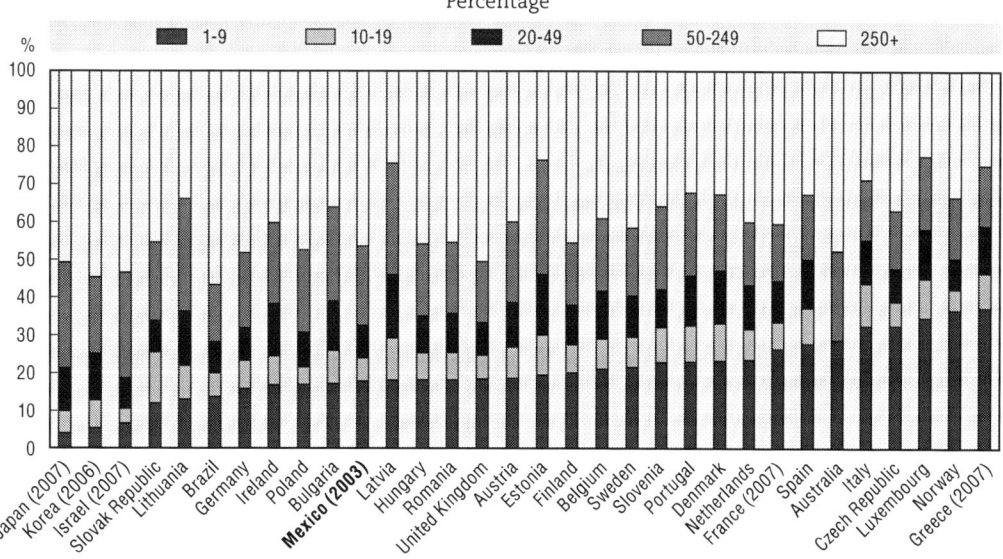

Notes: The unit of measure is enterprises for all counties, except Japan and Korea where establishments is the unit. For Ireland, only enterprises with three or more persons employed are covered, while the data for Japan and Korea do not include establishments with fewer than four and five persons employed, respectively. For the United States, employment in enterprises refers to the number of employees and not the number of persons employed. Data cover the market economy, excluding financial intermediation; for Brazil, Ireland, Israel, Japan, Korea, Luxembourg and the Slovak Republic they cover manufacturing sectors only. The statistical data for Israel are supplied by and under the responsibility of the relevant Israeli authorities. The use of such data by the OECD is without prejudice to the status of the Golan Heights, East Jerusalem and Israeli settlements in the West Bank under the terms of international law.
Source: OECD (2012), *Entrepreneurship at a Glance 2012.*

Given that SMEs contribute approximately three-quarters of employment in Mexico, this signals an SME productivity deficit. In large measure this reflects the relative weighting of the Mexican SME sector towards micro-enterprises, but it also reflects relatively low productivity within the micro-enterprise sector compared with other countries.

1.2. The informal economy

Informal economic activity is difficult to measure accurately because of the lack of recording in official statistical sources and the blurred distinction between formal and informal businesses. There are different degrees of informality. Within the informal sector there are firms that are not registered and not compliant with business and tax laws and regulations. Alongside these firms are those which are registered, but evade some of their taxes by declaring only some of their workforce. Then there is a third set of fully formal businesses that are legally registered and totally compliant with tax and business rules and labour regulations.

Taking the broader definition of informality including firms that evade some taxes, a 2008 survey by INEGI found 6.44 million businesses that were unable to provide any proof of purchase for commercial transactions. They accounted for 80.1% of the businesses surveyed. Many of these firms, however, are not operating entirely in the informal economy. Other estimates suggest that the contribution of the informal sector to GDP may lie in the range of 12 to 30% of GDP (Brambila, 2008; INEGI, 2000; World Bank, 2004). It is difficult to compare the level of informality across countries, but one estimate suggests that Mexico's informal sector may be large by international standards (see Figure 1.5).

A more direct estimate by the ILO based on the share of urban population without coverage for health and/or pension also suggests that Mexico's informal sector may be large by international standards, but not the largest in the Latin American context (see Figure 1.6).

Whilst the informal activity provides jobs and may contribute to reducing social and economic exclusion in the short term, it is a drag on economic growth and job generation in the longer term. This reflects lack of access to credit, training and legal protection in the informal sector, which reduces the ability of informal firms to invest and introduce best practice operating models (Brandt 2011), together with a tendency to remain small in order to hide activities. Furthermore, the informal sector is not contributing to tax collection and hence to the development of public services and infrastructures. Firms that are not registered and not compliant with business laws and regulations also represent unfair competition to legal businesses.

In this context, policy intervention designed to promote formality and discourage informality is warranted in Mexico. Detailed research on the nature of informal activity in Mexico and the motives of participants running businesses informally would help in the design of government initiatives in this area, together with evaluation evidence on the impacts of the initiatives already taken.

Figure 1.5. **Informality across countries, 2007**[1]

Schneider definition

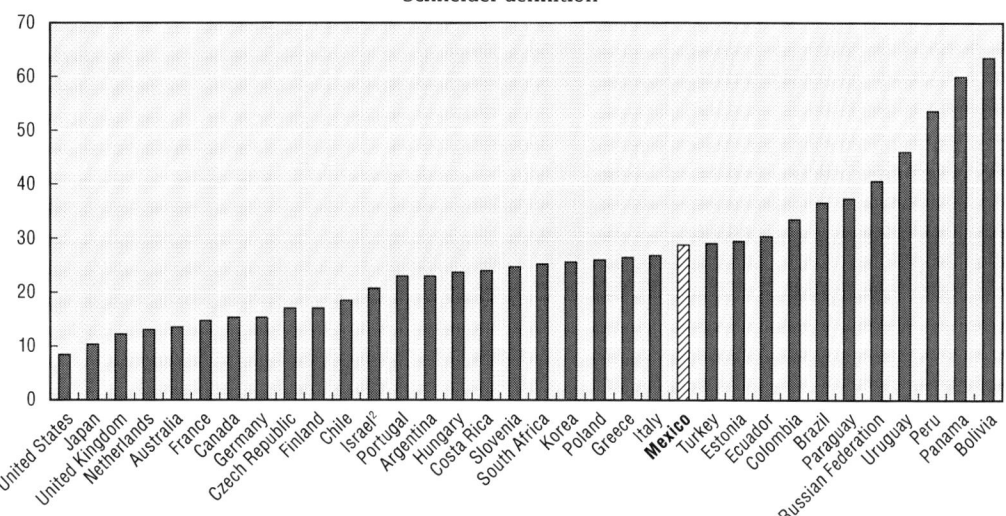

1. The Schneider definition of the shadow economy uses a multiple indicator multiple cause model to estimate the shadow economy econometrically with a structural equation with one latent variable. It is an attempt to estimate all market-based legal production of goods and services that are deliberately concealed from public authorities to avoid payment of income taxes, social security contributions, respect of legal labour market standards and administrative procedures. While the method relies on strong assumptions and results thus have to be interpreted with caution, this is the only indicator of the informal economy that allows a comparison across a wide range of countries.
2. The statistical data for Israel are supplied by and under the responsibility of the relevant Israeli authorities. The use of such data by the OECD is without prejudice to the status of the Golan Heights, East Jerusalem and Israeli settlements in the West Bank under the terms of international law.
Source: OECD Economic Surveys: Mexico 2011, based on ILO (2009), Labour Overview – Latin America and the Caribbean; F. Schneider, A. Buehn and C. Montenegro (2010), "New Estimates for the Shadow Economies all over the World", International Economic Journal, 24:4; ILO, Key Indicators in the Labour Market.

Figure 1.6. **Informality across Latin American countries**

ILO definition[1]

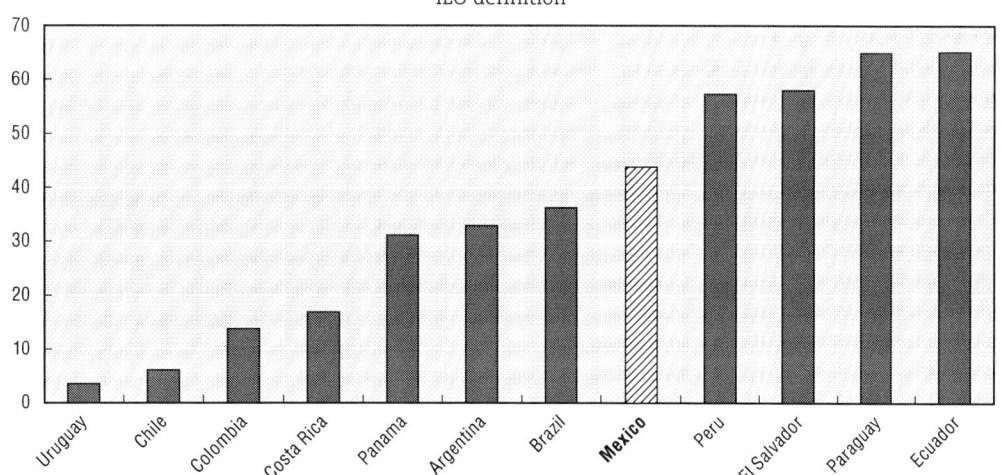

1. ILO definition: Urban population without coverage for health and/or pension in 2008. For Mexico, this measure is corrected by subtracting those self-employed workers who are registered with tax or local authorities or with a business association.
Source: ILO (2009), Labour Overview – Latin America and the Caribbean.

1.3. Entrepreneurship

1.3.1. Attitudes towards entrepreneurship

Table 1.4 compares the entrepreneurial attitudes and perceptions of adults in Mexico with those in other OECD economies. Mexicans have an above-average propensity to perceive good opportunities for starting a business in the next six months. They are also very confident about having the knowledge and skills to start a business and less likely to be held back from starting a business by fear of failure. They are more likely to expect to start a business in the next three years than the average for OECD economies.

Attitudes in society towards entrepreneurship are in line with other OECD member countries in terms of seeing entrepreneurship as a good career choice and considering that entrepreneurship features frequently in the media. However, slightly lower proportions of Mexicans than other OECD residents see successful entrepreneurs as having high status. This suggests that there is an issue to address concerning the status given to entrepreneurs in society.

Table 1.4. **Entrepreneurial attitudes and perceptions in OECD economies, 2011**

As a percentage of population aged 18-64

	Perceived opportunities	Perceived capabilities	Fear of failure[1]	Entrepreneurial intentions[2]	Entrepreneurship as a good career choice	High status to successful entrepreneurs	Media attention for entrepreneurship
Australia	48	47	43	12	54	68	70
Belgium	43	44	41	11	64	55	47
Chile	57	62	27	46	73	69	65
Czech Republic	24	40	35	14	..	49	..
Denmark	47	35	41	7	..	..	..
Finland	61	38	32	7	46	83	67
France	35	38	37	18	66	68	47
Germany	35	37	42	6	55	78	50
Greece	11	50	38	11	61	69	33
Hungary	14	40	35	20	54	78	34
Ireland	26	46	33	6	46	82	56
Japan	6	14	42	4	26	55	57
Korea	11	27	45	16	61	67	62
Mexico	**43**	**61**	**27**	**24**	**57**	**58**	**48**
Netherlands	48	42	35	9	83	67	62
Norway	67	33	41	9	53	80	60
Poland	33	52	43	23	73	64	58
Portugal	17	47	40	12	..	..	..
Slovenia	19	51	31	9	54	70	45
Spain	14	51	39	8	65	67	45
Sweden	72	40	35	10	52	71	62
Switzerland	47	42	31	10	..	..	..
Turkey	32	42	22	9	..	..	..
United Kingdom	33	42	36	9	52	81	47
United States	56	31	11	..	..	..	..
Average (unweighted)	35	43	36	16	58	69	53

1. Denominator is 18-64 age group perceiving good opportunities to start a business.
2. Respondent expects to start a business within 3 years, as a proportion of 16-64 year olds currently not involved in entrepreneurial activity.

Source: Global Entrepreneurship Monitor.

1.3.2. Self-employment

Self-employment includes business owners who employ themselves alone and those who employ others but are registered as sole proprietors or partners. These people tend to have low growth ambitions. The most recent data on self-employment in Mexico are sample estimates from the National Micro business survey (ENAMIN). In 2008, out of 8 108 755 micro businesses, 1 044 460 (12.9%) were regarded as employers whereas 7 064 295 (87.1%) were regarded as self-employed. The number of self-employed people had increased by 10.9% from 2002-08.

Figure 1.7 shows self-employment as a percentage of total employment in selected OECD and Latin American countries. The scale of self-employment in Mexico is second only to that in Ecuador. A high level of self-employment, combined with the predominance of micro-enterprises, is distinctive feature of entrepreneurship in Mexico. It suggests that policy needs to prioritise support for entrepreneurs with the ambition and capability to grow a business in order to increase the proportion of larger businesses.

Figure 1.7. **Self-employment in OECD and selected non-OECD countries, 2008**

As a percentage of total employment

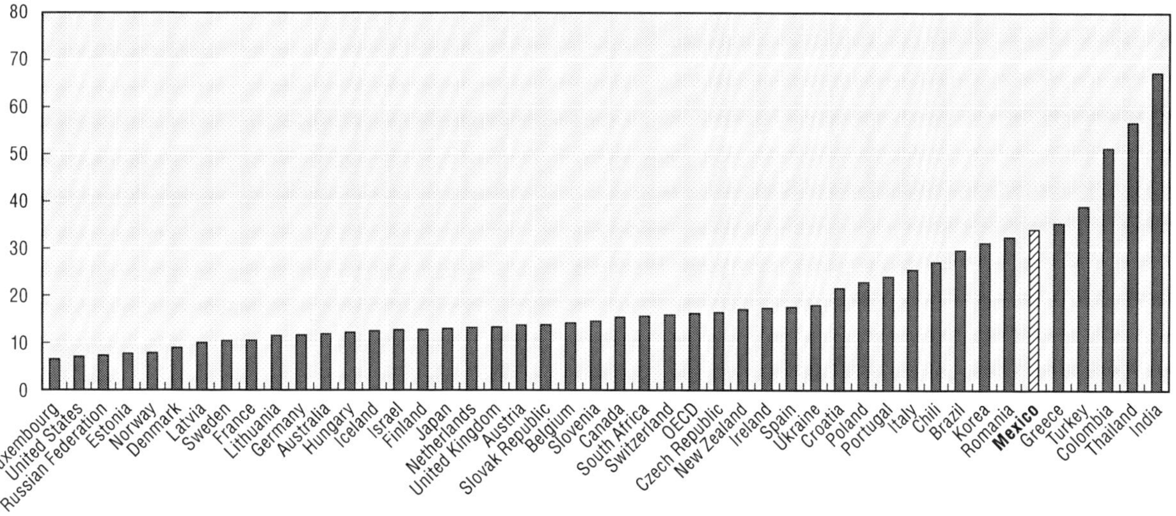

Source: World Bank, World Development Indicators Database.

1.3.3. Gender differences in entrepreneurship

The Global Entrepreneurship Monitor provides data on people involved in early-stage entrepreneurial activity, either as nascent entrepreneurs who have taken their first steps to starting a firm or as owners of a young business up to 42 months old. In 2001, there were 2.4 Mexican men engaged in early-stage entrepreneurship for every Mexican woman. However, by 2010, this ratio was almost 1:1.

Figure 1.8 shows that Mexico has become one of the countries with the highest female entrepreneurship rates in the OECD area. This increase suggests a dramatic improvement in entrepreneurship rates in Mexico as a whole, given that rates for one-half of the population have risen. Furthermore, the high female entrepreneurship rate does not appear to be more strongly weighted to necessity entrepreneurship than the average for efficiency-driven economies.

Figure 1.8. **Women entrepreneurship, 2005 and 2010**

As a percentage of all entrepreneurs

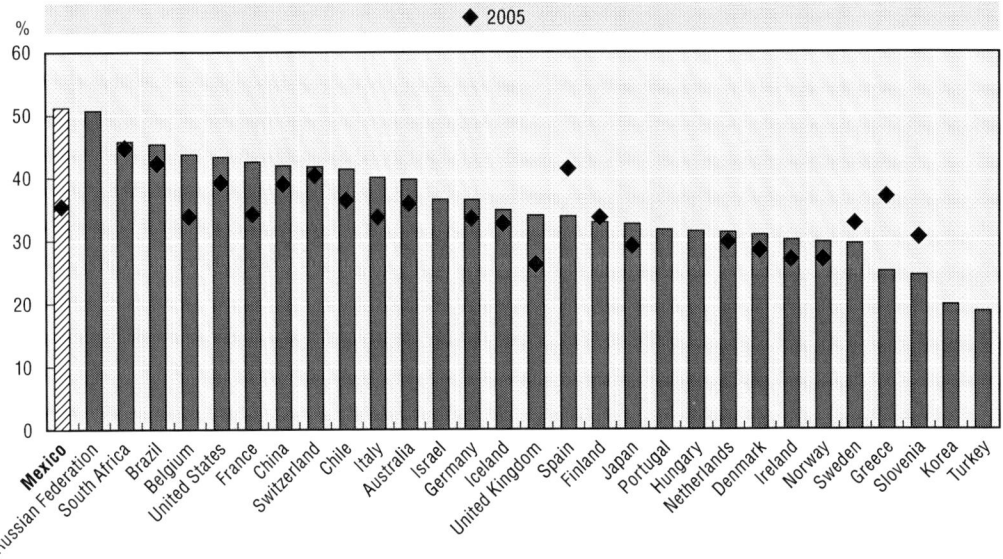

Source: Global Entrepreneurship Monitor.

1.3.4. Enterprise births and deaths

Business creation is an important aspect of business dynamism. New firms are often more innovative than incumbents because they have to establish a market position through new products, processes or services. Various studies have shown how greater start-up rates are associated with more rapid economic growth (Audretsch and Keilback, 2005; Erken *et al.*, 2008). Furthermore, the creation of employer enterprises is associated with greater employment and growth impacts than self-employment (OECD, 2012).

Figure 1.9 makes an international comparison of employer enterprise birth rates, calculated from the total number of active enterprises with at least one employee. Mexico is the top ranked country in both manufacturing and services. This signals the progress that has been made by the government in lowering entry barriers to start-ups and facilitating the development of a positive entrepreneurial culture and other entrepreneurship framework conditions.

Figures 1.10 and 1.11 show that a disproportionate share of business creation takes place in employer enterprises hiring between 1 and 4 employees. This is a trend common to all countries and true for both manufacturing and services. They also show that Mexico outperforms the comparator countries with regard to firm creations in the larger size brackets. This is a further very positive feature of the Mexican SME economy, and might signal that Mexico is beginning to move away from an overwhelming predominance of micro-enterprises.

Figures 1.12 and 1.13 compare the birth rates of enterprises in Mexico with their death rates in an international context. This reveals the change in small business stock. An excess of business births over deaths leads to a growth in the stock and contributes to job creation. Business births are running at much higher rates than business deaths in Mexico. At 0.3%, Mexico's manufacturing enterprise death rate in 2006 was the lowest of any country shown and well below the birth rate of 6.1% in 2007. Similarly, at 7.9%, the business

Figure 1.9. **Employer enterprise birth rate by sector, 2008**

Percentage

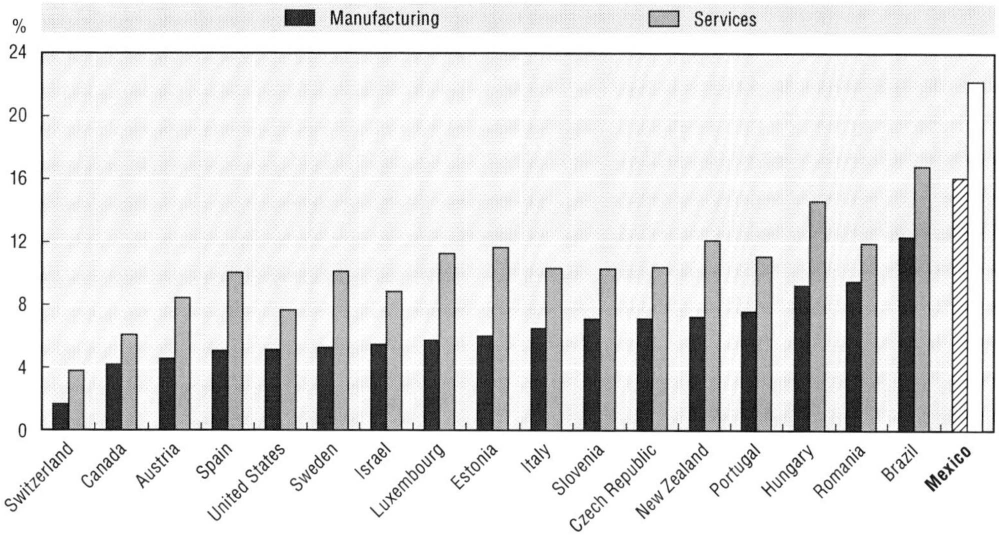

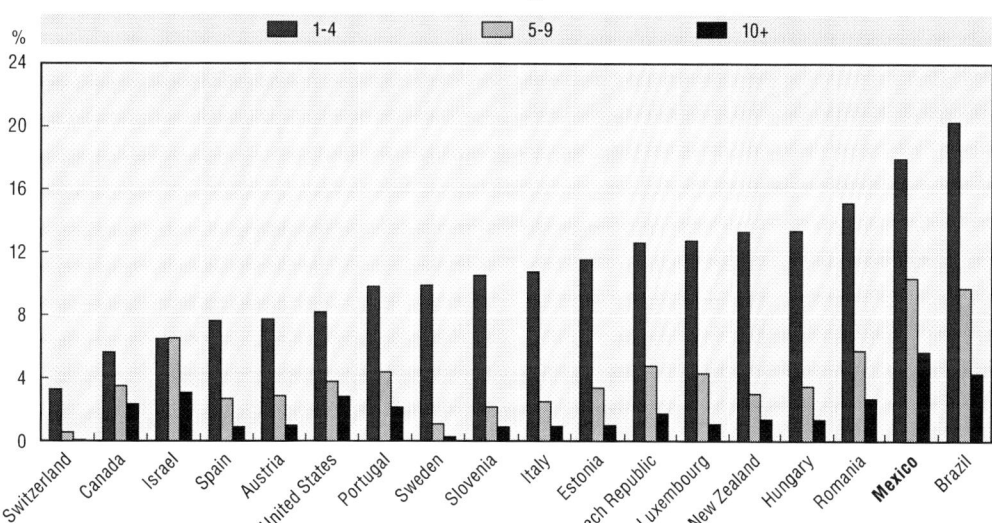

Source: OECD (2012), *Entrepreneurship at a Glance.*

Figure 1.10. **Employer enterprise birth rate by size class, manufacturing, 2008**

Percentage

Source: OECD (2012), *Entrepreneurship at a Glance.*

birth rate in services in Mexico was well above the death rate of 1.8%. This was the lowest death rate of service enterprises of any country shown.

The data indicate a growth in the SME stock. This is confirmed by a complementary analysis of Economic Census data, which shows that between 2003 and 2008 the enterprise birth rate across all sectors was 8.15% compared with a death rate of 4.45%, leading to an increase of 3.7% in the enterprise stock.

While growth in enterprise numbers is important to job creation when there are unused resources in the economy, low enterprise death rates in the long run would indicate a relatively low churn in the enterprise stock and potential problems in releasing

Figure 1.11. **Employer enterprise birth rate by size class, services, 2008**

Percentage

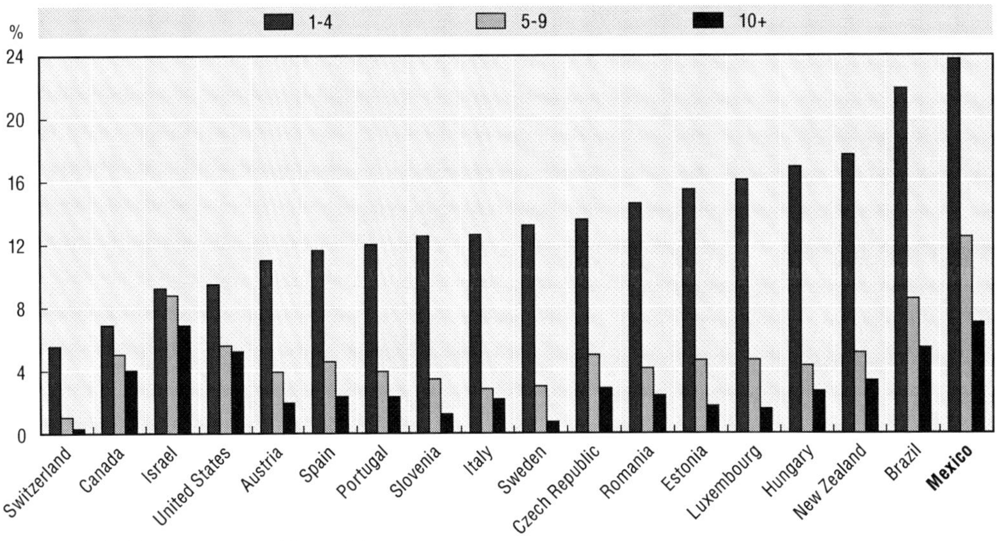

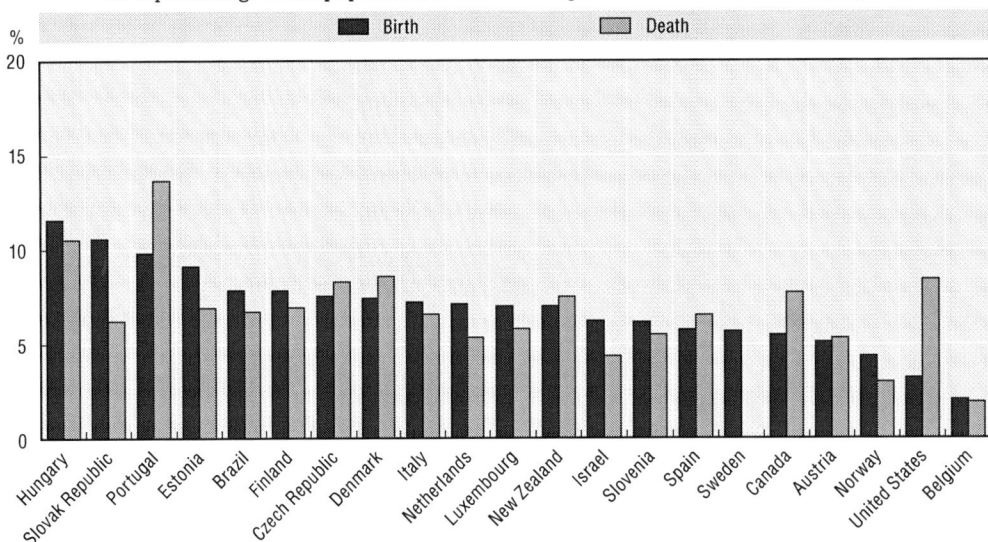

Source: OECD (2012), Entrepreneurship at a Glance.

Figure 1.12. **Employer enterprise birth rate (2007) and death rate (2006) in the manufacturing sector**

As a percentage of the population of active enterprises with at least one employee

Note: The statistical data for Israel are supplied by and under the responsibility of the relevant Israeli authorities. The use of such data by the OECD is without prejudice to the status of the Golan Heights, East Jerusalem and Israeli settlements in the West Bank under the terms of international law.
Source: OECD (2011), Entrepreneurship at a Glance.

resources from low productivity to higher productivity uses. In this context, a review of barriers to exit in the Mexican economy may be justified.

1.3.5. High growth firms

There is substantial evidence that a minority of rapidly-growing SMEs typically generate a majority of jobs. They also tend to be associated with better export performance. For example, Smallbone et al. (1995) showed that 23% of established

Figure 1.13. **Employer enterprise birth rate (2007) and death rate (2006)**
in the services sector

As a percentage of the population of active enterprises with at least one employee

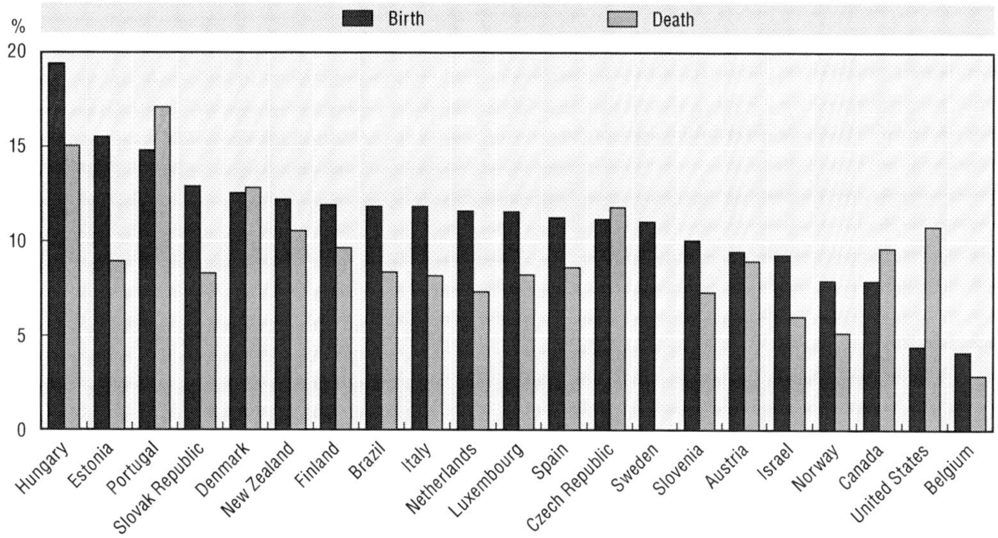

Note: The statistical data for Israel are supplied by and under the responsibility of the relevant Israeli authorities. The use of such data by the OECD is without prejudice to the status of the Golan Heights, East Jerusalem and Israeli settlements in the West Bank under the terms of international law.
Source: OECD (2011), *Entrepreneurship at a Glance.*

manufacturing SMEs (i.e. those achieving high growth) generated 71% of new jobs over a ten-year period, and Anyadike-Danes, Bonner, Hart and Mason (2009) showed that the 6% of UK businesses with the highest growth rates generated half of the new jobs created between 2002 and 2008. This makes high-growth firms an important target of policy. A recent study in Brazil, Chile and Mexico (Loosens, 2009) identifies some of the distinctive characteristics of the entrepreneurs leading high growth SMEs in the region. The ventures are typically founded by entrepreneurial teams; the entrepreneurs are typically educated to postgraduate level with qualifications in the technical field; most had considerable experience in the field; many had sought external support for the management of the business, often turning to external consultants and/or business incubators. Many of the ventures were also suppliers to inward investors, which had encouraged them in product, process and organisational innovation.

Managing intellectual property was an issue for the firms. Very few had generated patents and licenses. Instead most sought to protect their intellectual capital through confidentiality clauses or nurturing the loyalty of their personnel. Financing was a further issue. The companies were heavily reliant on their own capital resources, which may be due to a risk-averse stance of commercial banks towards entrepreneurial ventures.

These observations suggest how policies may identify high-growth potential firms and the types of actions that may assist their development, including in the areas of incubation, consultancy, intellectual capital management and access to financing.

1.4. SME performance

1.4.1. Growth of the SME sector

Figure 1.14 shows that annual growth rates for the output and value added of the SME sector were significantly above the increase in employment during the period 2003-08,

Figure 1.14. **Annual growth rate for employment, output, and value added in Mexico, 2003-08**

As a percentage, by size of firm

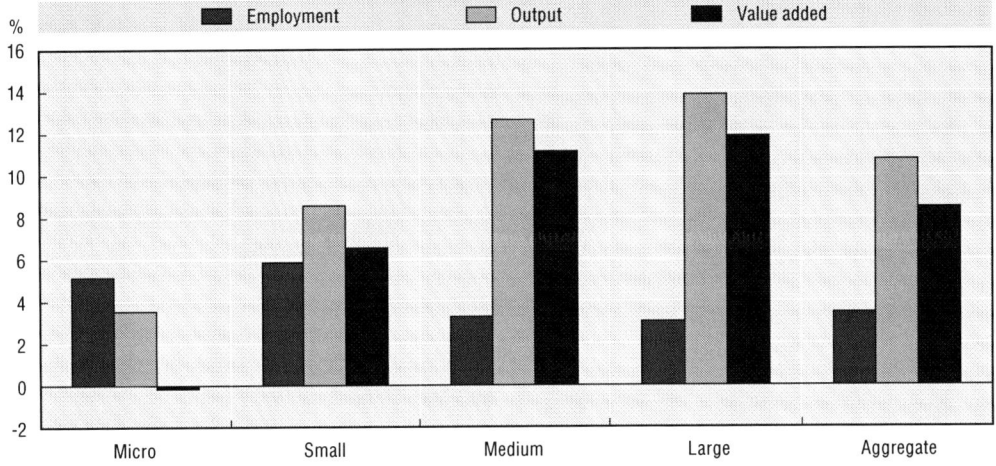

Source: Elaboration based on Economic Census for 2003 and 2000, undertaken by INEGI.

suggesting an upward trend in productivity. However, the high rates of increase in output are mainly a feature of medium-sized and large enterprises. The trend is much less healthy for micro-enterprises, for which value added actually declined. On the other hand, small firms and micro-enterprises make a relatively strong contribution to employment growth.

The growth patterns of SMEs vary by sector. During 2003-08, employment grew fastest in non-financial services, whereas output and value added grew fastest in manufacturing (Table 1.5).

Table 1.5. **Annual growth rate for employment, output, and value added in Mexico by sector, 2003-08**

As a percentage, by size of firm

Sector	Firm size	Employment	Output	Value added
Commerce	Micro	5.19	2.57	-0.83
	Small	2.90	4.56	2.06
	Medium	5.16	9.35	6.52
	Large	-4.02	3.48	-0.70
	Total	4.19	5.22	1.61
Non-financial services	Micro	7.77	10.78	9.99
	Small	7.27	8.59	8.49
	Medium	3.56	8.40	7.83
	Large	6.63	10.36	6.10
	Total	6.79	9.79	7.29
Manufacturing	Micro	7.24	4.41	3.12
	Small	1.59	5.13	4.59
	Medium	-0.30	11.11	10.86
	Large	1.08	13.33	10.21
	Total	2.11	12.28	9.80

Source: Economic Census for 2003 and 2000, undertaken by INEGI.

Table 1.6 shows the productivity and profitability trends for firms of different sizes and sectors for 2008-11. Large firms were the most productive and profitable, followed by medium, small and micro enterprises. Productivity and profitability were highest in manufacturing and significantly lower in non-financial services and commerce. Furthermore, whereas large and medium-sized firms raised their productivity by between 30 and 35% over the period, the productivity trend among micro-enterprises was negative. Trends in profitability largely followed those of productivity. This is highlighted again in Table 1.7.

Table 1.6. **Productivity and profitability of firms in Mexico, 2008 and 2011**

In MXN thousands, by sector and firm size

		2008 productivity[1]	2011 productivity[1]	2008 profitability[2]	2011 profitability[2]
Commerce	Micro	77	72	110	97
	Small	302	317	3 752	3 638
	Medium	396	445	22 672	23 820
	Large	402	504	81 112	87 525
	Aggregate	175	180	338	322
Non-financial services	Micro	129	140	162	180
	Small	224	232	2 240	2 284
	Medium	330	378	15 345	17 154
	Large	482	534	207 027	216 079
	Aggregate	251	273	653	676
Manufacturing industries	Micro	106	98	104	95
	Small	425	472	2 844	3 022
	Medium	1 006	1 393	36 457	50 179
	Large	1 624	2 290	345 123	446 283
	Aggregate	1 046	1 391	3 390	3 783
All sectors	Micro	109	104	137	123
	Small	322	347	3 110	3 129
	Medium	597	775	26 637	33 158
	Large	1 324	1 785	457 838	606 268
	Aggregate	547	693	1 356	1 737

1. Thousands of MXN of annual product per employee.
2. Thousands of MXN of value added per firm annually.
Source: Economic Census undertaken by INEGI.

Table 1.7. **Changes in productivity and profitability, 2008-11**

As a percentage, by firm size

Enterprise size class	Productivity change 2008-11	Profitability change 2008-11
Micro-enterprise	-4.6	-10.2
Small	7.8	0.6
Medium	29.8	24.5
Large	34.8	32.4
All	26.7	25

Source: Own compilation based on data supplied by the Ministry of economy drawn from the economic Census for 2003, 2008.

1.4.2. SME internationalisation

Important internationalisation opportunities for Mexican SMEs have been opened up by the multilateral and bilateral international trade agreements signed by the Mexican government in recent years, including membership of the North American Free Trade

Agreement (NAFTA), which means that Mexico can act as a production platform for the US and Canada. However, whilst Mexico generates substantial exports, they are dominated by a few hundred large enterprises, while the SME sector makes a small contribution.

Mexican SMEs face distinctive challenges when engaging in export activity. In seeking to supply Canada and the United States, a priority is to upgrade in terms of design, quality, marketing and innovation and to use up-to-date production equipment to reduce price. In particular, Mexican SMEs tend to be relatively high cost producers compared with foreign SMEs and larger Mexican enterprises (Rostro, 2010).

Aside from direct exports, there is strong potential for internationalisation of Mexican SMEs through accessing global value chains as suppliers to international companies, particularly within the context of a manufacturing base for the NAFTA region. The so-called maquila industry was established in Mexico in the mid-1960s, with the Programme of Bordering Industrialisation, which aimed to attract foreign investment with tax and other incentives in a 10-mile strip along the northern border of Mexico. This provides important opportunities for SMEs to enter supply chains through linkages with foreign direct investment operations.

1.4.3. Innovation in SMEs

Mexico has one of the lowest levels of business expenditure on R&D as a percentage of GDP among the OECD member countries. In 2005, it stood at only 0.23% of GDP (OECD, 2009). This low expenditure in large part reflects the low level of research and development undertaken by Mexican SMEs. In 2005, SMEs with at least 50 employees accounted for 60% of business expenditure on research and development compared with 96% of the business stock. By contrast, large firms accounted for 40% of business expenditure on research and development from only 4% of the remaining business stock. Whilst not all innovation is derived from R&D, these figures suggest that in order to increase the innovation rate in the economy as a whole, it is necessary to increase innovation among SMEs.

1.5. Regional and local variations

Mexico is a country of contrasts. Within the OECD area it is the second most unequal country with regard to the regional distribution of income, as shown in Figure 1.15.

The income disparities across Mexico's regions are illustrated in Figure 1.16. GDP per capita is five times higher in the Federal District than in Chiapas, the poorest state of the country, while elsewhere in the country the higher incomes are particularly concentrated in the northern states bordering the United States and in the south of the Gulf of Mexico (Campeche and Tabasco). The former states have benefited since 1994 from the free trade agreements with the US and Canada in attracting foreign direct investment (FDI) in low-tech manufacturing, whereas the latter concentrates tourism investment in Mexico. States on the south Pacific coast (e.g. Chiapas, Oaxaca, and Guerrero) are the most stricken by poverty.

While there are remarkable income disparities across Mexican states, a moderate process of convergence has been occurring. During the period 2003-08, the GDP per capita of the bottom quartile of Mexican states grew by 21%, whereas that of the top quartile grew by 11%. Of the seven fastest growing states over this period, two were in the bottom quartile (Nayarit and Zacatecas), three in the second-lowest quartile (Hidalgo, Veracruz and San Luis Potosi), and only two in the top quartile (Campeche and Tabasco) of GDP per capita. This convergence process is illustrated by the moderately negative relationship between recent GDP growth rates and current GDP per capita (Figure 1.17).

Figure 1.15. **Gini coefficient of income inequality across OECD countries, latest year available**

(0 = lowest inequality – 1 = highest inequality)

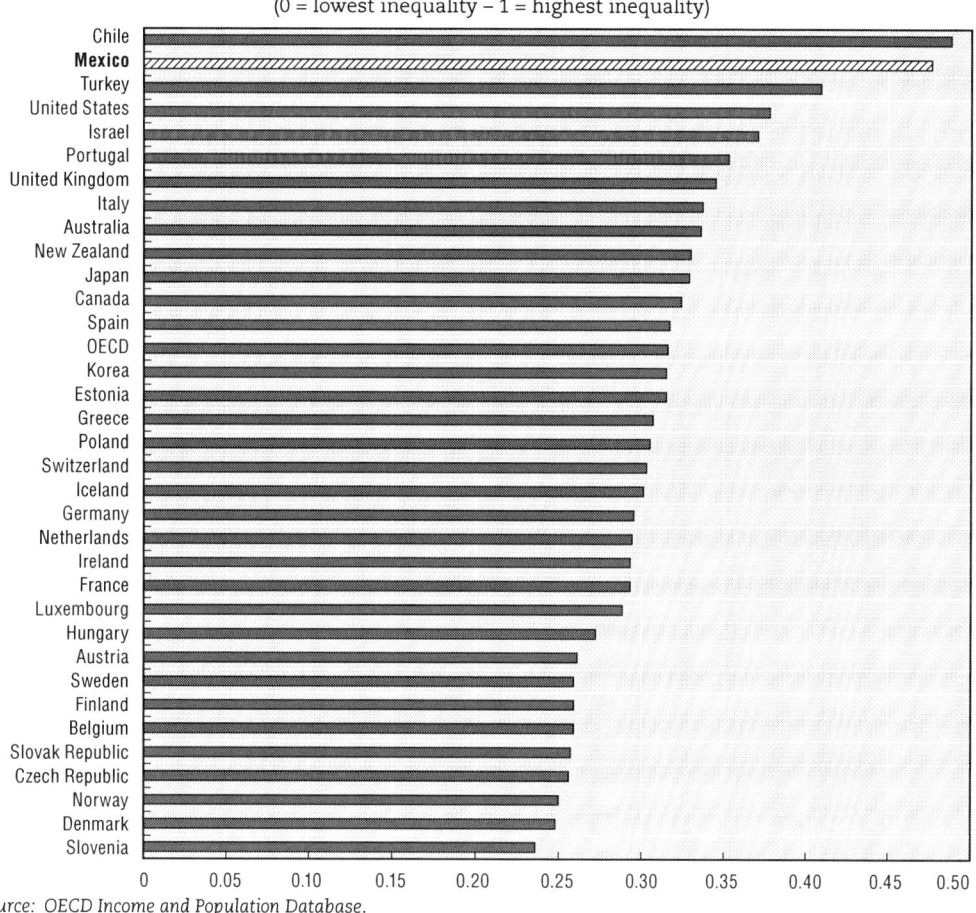

Source: *OECD Income and Population Database.*

There are also important spatial disparities in SME and entrepreneurship activity in Mexico. The pattern is one in which regions with the lowest incomes have the highest business densities, as shown in Figure 1.18. Thus the density of businesses (which is dominated by SMEs) is highest in Oaxaca (62.2 firms per 1 000 population) and lowest in Baja California (31.0 firms per 1 000 population). More generally, SME activity rates are relatively high in the poor states of the south Pacific coast (Oaxaca, Guerrero and Michoacán) and relatively low at the border with the United States. This appears to reflect a domination of FDI and large establishments in the north, including *maquilladoras*, and a lack of alternative job opportunities and high rates of necessity entrepreneurship in the poorer states.

This is confirmed by data on spatial variations in SME performance in terms of productivity, profitability and output. The patterns that emerge match the core-periphery divide noted above, with performance tending to be better in the central and southern states and lower in the north (Figure 1.19).

The spatial challenge for Mexico is, therefore, to promote not only self-employment but also opportunity-driven and higher productivity entrepreneurship in the poorer regions, and to nurture the diversification of the higher income regional economies beyond the mere attraction of FDI towards building complementary SME sectors.

Figure 1.16. **GDP per capita in Mexico by state, 2008**
MXN pesos, constant prices 2000

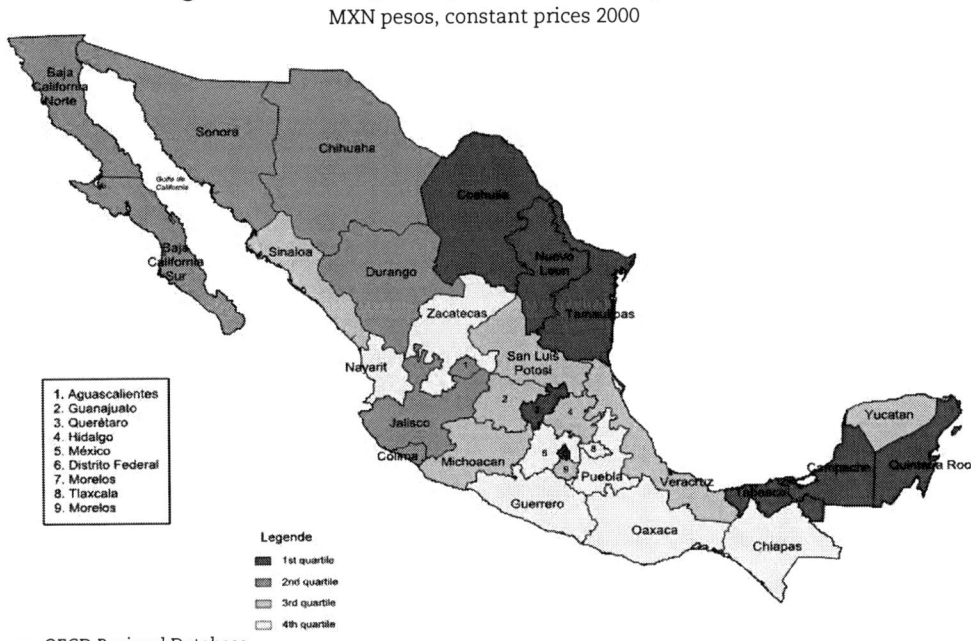

Source: OECD Regional Database.

Figure 1.17. **The relation between GDP growth rate (2003-08) and GDP per capita (2008)**
Various

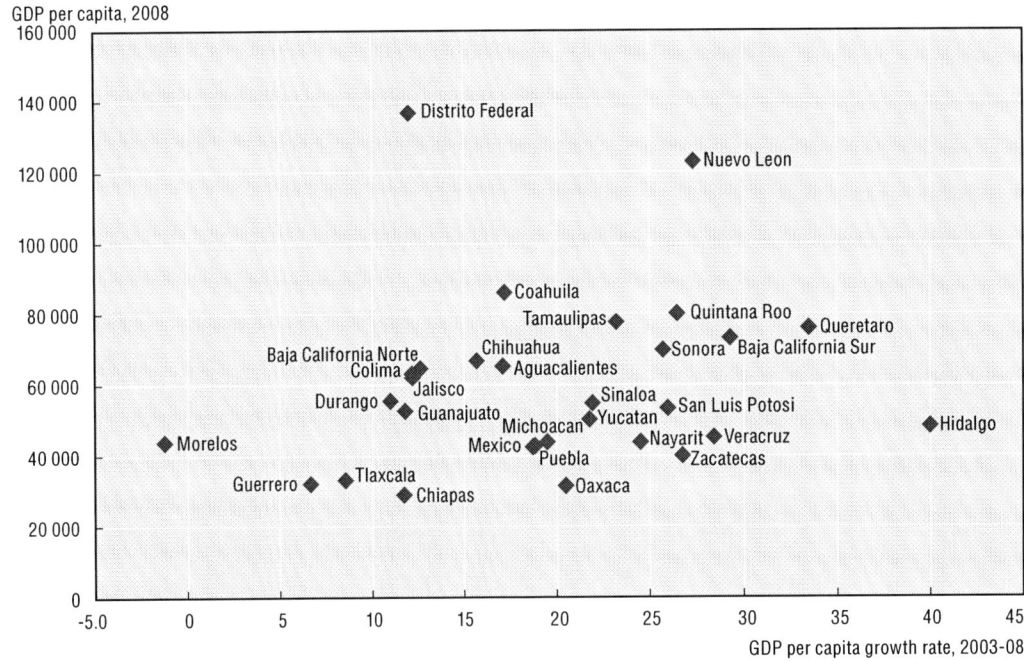

Note: The states of Tabasco and Campeche are excluded since they have much higher values than the average and represent statistical outliers.
Source: OECD Regional Database.

Figure 1.18. **Business density in Mexico by state, 2008**

Number of firms per thousand population

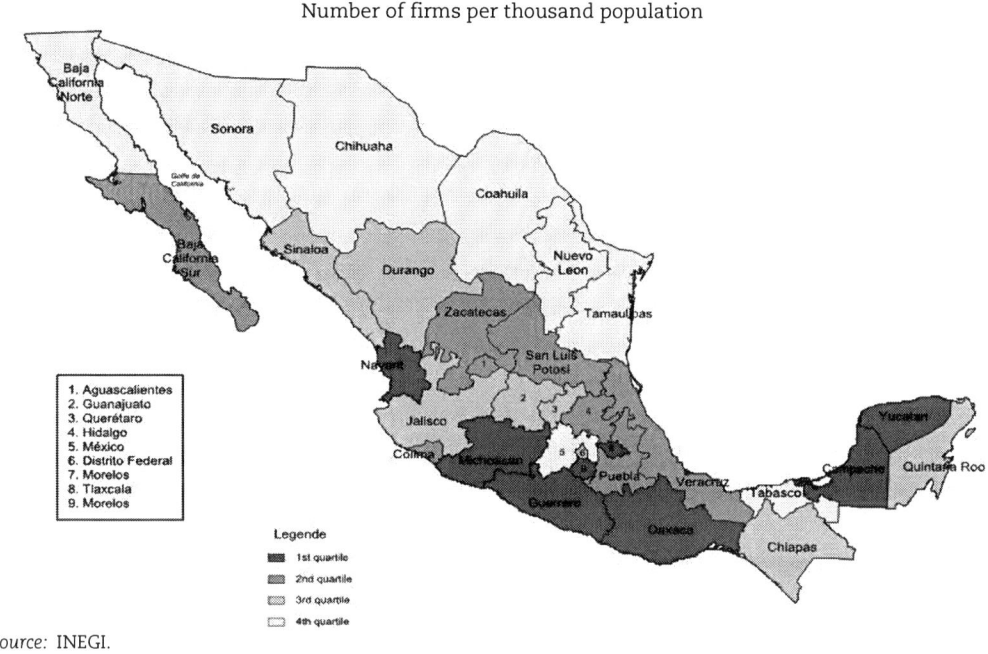

Source: INEGI.

Figure 1.19. **Most and least productive states, 2008**

SME labour productivity, MXN thousands

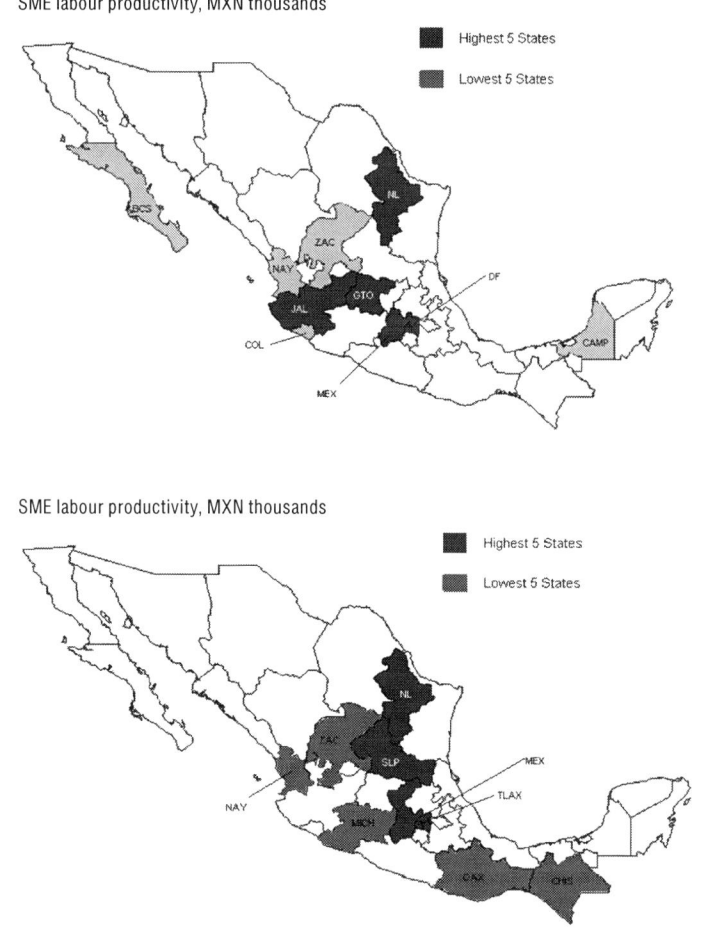

SME labour productivity, MXN thousands

Figure 1.19. **Most and least productive states, 2008** *(cont.)*

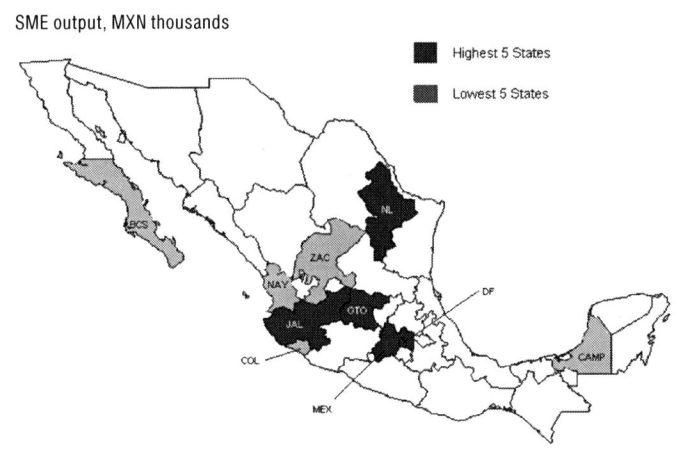

SME output, MXN thousands

■ Highest 5 States

■ Lowest 5 States

Notes: Due to insufficient data at the state level, Mining and Electricity, Water, and Gas Supply were excluded.
Source: INEGI.

1.6. Conclusions

The SME and entrepreneurship sector in Mexico has a number of important strengths. The SME sector is a large one in terms of the numbers of firms and their contribution to employment. There are positive attitudes in society towards entrepreneurship. There has been significant growth in self-employment activity. The female entrepreneurship rate matches that of men. The business birth rate is one of the highest in the OECD area. There has been substantial growth in the stock of SMEs and in value added and output. There is an upward trend in productivity among SMEs above the micro firm size threshold.

Alongside these strengths, there are the following key challenges:

- increasing productivity and profitability in micro-enterprises and reducing the scale and scope of the informal economy;
- rebalancing the SME economy towards larger SME size bands by nurturing more gazelles and high-growth SMEs and facilitating an evolution of smaller firms towards the mid-size range;
- improving the innovation performance of SMEs;
- arresting the perpetuation of regional economic imbalances by increasing business births and stocks and SME productivity, profitability and output performance in the periphery.

Box 1.1. Specific recommendations on SME and entrepreneurship performance

Strengthen micro-enterprises and support a shift from the informal to the formal sector

- Provide advice and basic training to micro-enterprises on how to increase productivity and profitability.
- Develop an active strategy to reduce the informality in the economy, recognising the multifaceted nature of informal activity. Provide advice and basic training for firms operating informally and interested in making the transition to the formal economy. Offer help in accessing finance and in negotiation with tax authorities.

Box 1.1. **Specific recommendations on SME and entrepreneurship performance** *(cont.)*

● Commission research to identify the main segments within the informal sector; assess the scope and methods most appropriate to reduce the level of informality in the economy.

Encourage the growth of SMEs towards larger size bands

● Nurture more high-growth start-ups and SMEs.

● Favour growth of firms across size bands.

Increase support to innovative SMEs

● Support innovative SMEs through expanded advice, leadership training and access to appropriate financial packages.

Address spatial disparities in SME and entrepreneurship activity

● Ensure that programme support is sensitive to regional differences in the environment for small business development.

● Make additional policy efforts in regions with low business stocks and birth rates to break out of self-reinforcing disparities.

References

Anyadike-Danes, M., K. Bonner, M. Hart and C. Mason (2009), "Measuring Business Growth: High-Growth Firms and their Contribution to Employment in the UK", *National Endowment for Science, Technology and the Arts*, London.

Audretsch, D. and M. Keilbach (2005), "Entrepreneurship Capital and Regional Growth", *The Annals of Regional Sciences*, Vol. 39, pp. 457-69.

Brambila, M. (2008), *Modelling the Informal Economy in Mexico. A Structural Equation Approach*, Unpublished (*http://mpra.ub.uni-muenchen.de/8504*).

Brandt, N. (2011), "Informality in Mexico", *OECD Economics Department Working Papers*, No. 896, OECD Publishing, *http://dx.doi.org/10.1787/5kg3nzlp1vmq-en*.

Erken, H., P. Donselaar and R. Thurik (2008), "Total Factor Productivity and the Role of Entrepreneurship", *Jena Economic Research Papers*, 2008-19.

ILO (2009), *Labour Overview – Latin American and The Carribean*, ILO, Geneva.

INEGI (2000), *Censo General de Poblacion y Vivienda*, INEGI, Mexico City.

Loosens, R. (2009), *High Growth SMEs, Innovation, Entrepreneurship and Intellectual Assets: A Study of High Growth SMEs in Brazil, Chile and Mexico*, Inter-American Development Bank.

OECD (2009), *OECD Reviews of Innovation Policy: Mexico 2009*, OECD Publishing, *http://dx.doi.org/10.1787/9789264075993-en*.

OECD (2012), *Entrepreneurship at a Glance 2012*, OECD Publishing, *http://dx.doi.org/10.1787/entrepreneur_aag-2012-en*.

Rostro, F. (2010), "General Diagnosis of Mexican SMEs from the Perspective of Marketing Practices Efficiency", *Concyteg*, Mexico City.

Schneider, F., A. Buehn and C. Montenegro (2010), "New Estimates for the Shadow Economies all Over the World", *International Economic Journal*, 24,4, 443-461.

Smallbone, D., R. Leigh and D. North (1995), "The Characteristics and Strategies of High Growth SMEs", *International Journal of Entrepreneurial Behaviour & Research*, 1, 3, 44-62.

World Bank (2004), *Doing Business in 2004, Understanding Regulation*, World Bank, Washington, DC.

ANNEX 1.A1

Firm size classes for Figures 1.1 and 1.2

Country	Micro	Small	Medium	Large
Australia	1-9	10-49	50-199	200+
Austria	1-9	10-49	50-249	250+
Belgium	1-9	10-49	50-249	250+
Brazil	1-9	10-49	50-249	250+
Czech Republic	1-9	10-49	50-249	250+
Denmark	1-9	10-49	50-249	250+
Estonia	1-9	10-49	50-249	250+
Finland	1-9	10-49	50-249	250+
France	1-9	10-49	50-249	250+
Germany	1-9	10-49	50-249	250+
Greece	1-9	10-49	50-249	250+
Hungary	1-9	10-49	50-249	250+
Iceland	1-9	10-49	50-249	250+
Ireland	3-9	10-49	50-249	250+
Israel	1-9	10-49	50-249	250+
Italy	1-9	10-49	50-249	250+
Japan	4-9	10-49	50-249	250+
Korea	1-9	10-49	50-199	200+
Latvia	1-9	10-49	50-249	250+
Lithuania	1-9	10-49	50-249	250+
Luxembourg	1-9	10-49	50-249	250+
Mexico	**1-9**	**10-49**	**50-249**	**250+**
Netherlands	1-9	10-49	50-249	250+
New Zealand	1-9	10-49	50-99	100+
Norway	1-9	10-49	50-249	250+
Poland	1-9	10-49	50-249	250+
Portugal	1-9	10-49	50-249	250+
Slovak Republic	1-9	10-49	50-249	250+
Slovenia	1-9	10-49	50-249	250+
Spain	1-9	10-49	50-249	250+
Sweden	1-9	10-49	50-249	250+
United Kingdom	1-9	10-49	50-249	250+
United States	1-19	20-99	100-499	500+

Chapter 2

Business environment and framework conditions in Mexico

This chapter examines the framework conditions and business climate for SMEs and entrepreneurship. It covers ease of doing business, macro-economic conditions, human resources, access to financing, tax and social security, product market conditions, business law and regulation, foreign direct investment and the innovation system. Strengths and challenges are identified and policy recommendations are offered.

2.1. Macroeconomic conditions

Macroeconomic conditions have an important influence on SME and entrepreneurship development, for example through the market and investment opportunities afforded by GDP growth, through the levels and stability of exchange rates and their influence on the ability to supply domestic and international markets, and the impact of interest rates on the ability to obtain finance and undertake profitable projects.

In recent years, Mexico has secured favourable macroeconomic conditions compared with OECD countries in general. This has been underpinned by prudent public finances and central bank monetary policy and effective regulation and supervision of the financial system. Further features of the benign macro environment are the opportunities opened up for SME exporting and global value chain participation by Mexico's engagement in new trade agreements, including NAFTA. Competition has also been favoured by liberalisation, deregulation and international trade flows, including lifting of price controls and reductions in financial market restrictions.

The progress has not been without its challenges, given the global macroeconomic context. Thus despite its very strong export orientation (Mexico accounted for 57% of total manufacturing exports of Latin American countries in 2009 according to United Nations Comtrade data), Mexico is recovering better from the global economic and financial crisis than many other OECD countries. Mexico's strong exposure to international markets led it to suffer an export-induced shock and deep recession with an annual GDP contraction of 6.1% in 2009 (see Figure 2.1). But since then its economy has achieved a strong recovery with real GDP growth rates of 5.5% in 2010 and 4.5% in 2011.

Figure 2.1. **Shock to exports and GDP slowdown in Latin American countries, 2009**
As a percentage

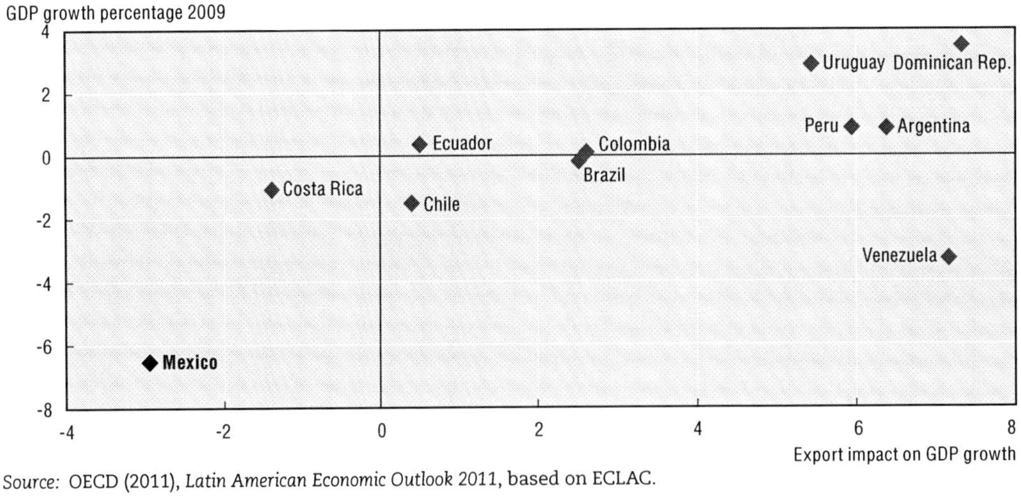

Source: OECD (2011), *Latin American Economic Outlook 2011*, based on ECLAC.

Mexico's labour market is also recovering well from the crisis. Unemployment rates have not reached the high levels recorded in the OECD area as a whole, and stood at only 5.2% in 2011, one of the lowest rates in the OECD area (Figure 2.2).

Figure 2.2. **Harmonised unemployment rates in OECD countries, 2011**
As a percentage of the civilian labour force

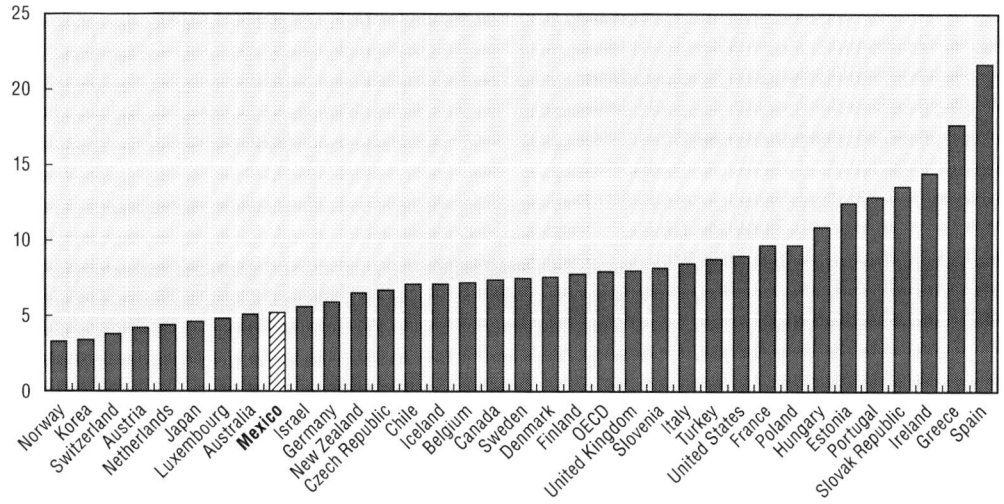

Notes: The OECD average is computed by taking a simple average of country-level point estimates. For each economy, only the latest available year of survey data is used in this computation.
Source: OECD (2012), *OECD Main Economic Indicators*, June.

Public debt has been kept under control at levels well below those of many other OECD countries. Ministry of Finance data show that Mexico's gross total public debt in December 2011 was only 33.8% of GDP, compared with 35.5% for example in Korea, 74.1% in Spain, 97.6% in the United States, 98.6% in France and 112.6% in Ireland. This has helped Mexico to achieve historically low inflation rates and low interest rates (Figures 2.3 and 2.4).

Figure 2.3. **Consumer price indices, 1998-2011**

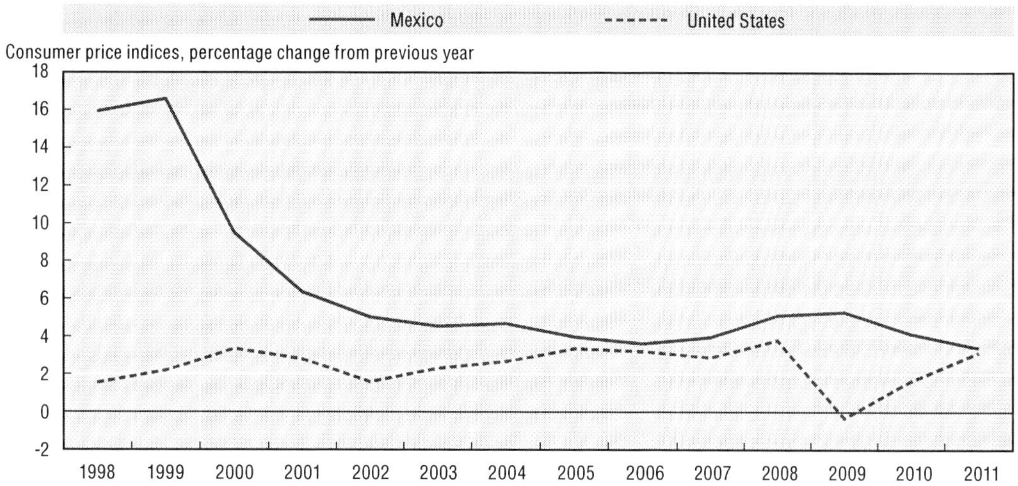

| Mexico | - - - - - United States |

Consumer price indices, percentage change from previous year

Source: OECD Economic Outlook 91 Database.

Figure 2.4. **Short-term interest rates, 1998-2011**

Per cent, per annum

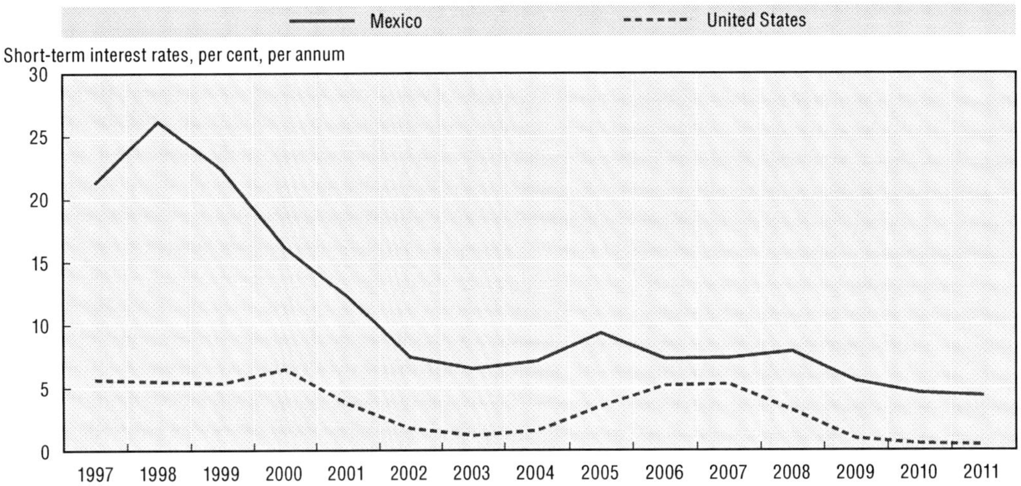

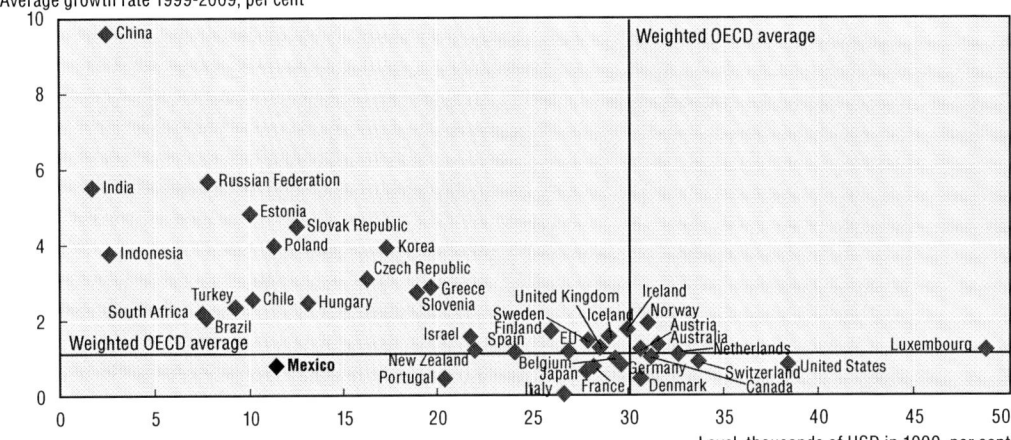

Note: Three-month money market rates where available, or rates on similar financial instruments. For further information, see *OECD Economic Outlook* "Sources and Methods".
Source: OECD Economic Outlook 91 Database.

Figure 2.5 nonetheless indicates that Mexico has a medium-term growth problem in comparison with the OECD average, underlining the need to raise SME productivity growth.

Figure 2.5. **GDP per capita levels and growth rates**

Various

Notes: GDP per capita is given in constant PPPs. In the case of Luxembourg, the population is augmented by the number of cross-border workers in order to take into account their contribution to GDP. For Norway, data refer to GDP for mainland Norway, which excludes petroleum production and shipping. While total GDP overestimates the sustainable income potential, mainland GDP slightly underestimates it since returns on the financial assets held by the petroleum fund abroad are not included.
Source: OECD, National Accounts Database and OECD Economic Outlook, No. 88; Statistics and Projections Database.

2.2. Ease of doing business

Mexico has made significant progress in improving its business environment in recent years, as witnessed by improved rankings on three major international indices with respect to the most relevant pillars for SMEs and entrepreneurship. The relevant rankings and recent changes are shown in Table 2.1. Mexico's performance is generally above average for the countries assessed and is generally rising.

Table 2.1. **Mexico's rankings on international competitiveness indexes**

	World Bank Doing Business		World Economic Forum		Institute for Management Development	
	Ease of doing business	Starting a business	Global index	Business sophistication	Overall index	Business efficiency
Number of countries	183	183	142	142	59	59
Mexico's position 2012	53	75	58	56	37	42
Mexico's position 2009	56	115	60	62	46	46
Improvement	+3	+40	+2	+6	+9	+4
Methodology	Analysis of regulations	Analysis of regulations	Analysis of data, business surveys	Analysis of data, business surveys	Analysis of data, business surveys	Analysis of data, business surveys
Content of index	Starting a business, dealing with construction permits, registering property, getting credit, protecting investors, paying taxes, trading across borders, enforcing contracts, resolving insolvency and, new this year, getting electricity.	Minimum capital requirements (% of income per capita); procedures (number), time (days) and costs (% of income per capita).	Institutions, infrastructure, macroeconomic environment, health and primary education, higher education and training, goods market efficiency, labour market efficiency, financial market development, technological readiness, market size, business sophistication, innovation.	Local supplier quality, state of cluster development, nature of competitive advantage, value chain breadth, control of international distribution, production process sophistication, extent of marketing, willingness to delegate authority.	Economic performance, government efficiency, business efficiency, infrastructure.	Productivity and efficiency, labour market, finance, management practices, attitudes and values.

Source: World Bank, World Economic Forum and Institute for Management Development.

The World Bank's Enterprise Survey provides further information on the factors influencing the performance of businesses in Mexico and the main obstacles perceived by their managers. Figure 2.6 presents the top 10 constraints identified by businesses (large firms and SMEs taken together) benchmarked against the average for Latin America. The most commonly reported constraints relate to the practices of the informal sector (which are typically viewed as unfair competition by formal businesses), tax rates, and access to finance.

Figure 2.6. **Obstacles to all businesses in Mexico, 2010**

As a percentage of firms identifying the main problems as an obstacle

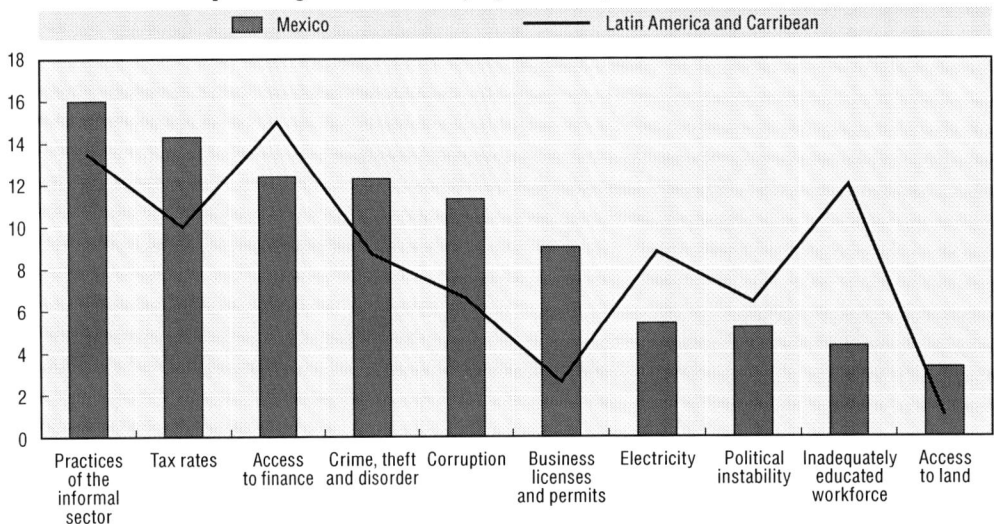

Notes: Regional averages of indicators are computed by taking a simple average of country-level point estimates. For each economy, only the latest available year of survey data is used in this computation.
Source: World Bank Enterprise Survey, 2010.

Figure 2.7 shows that the constraints encountered vary to some extent between firms of different sizes. The practices of the informal sector were viewed as a barrier by firms of all sizes. The particular concerns of medium-sized firms were crime, theft and disorder and tax rates, while the particular concerns of smaller firms were tax rates and access to finance. It should nonetheless be noted that there are special tax regimes for small businesses, and it is possible that the impediment being signalled by managers is linked to the complexity of the tax rules, which force SMEs to acquire specialised accounting services, rather than the nominal tax rates available.

This information signals not just the progress that has been made, but also where obstacles to business could be further alleviated. In this respect, the World Bank study indicates that there is no single predominant and major barrier, but rather a broad set of issues each picked up by a minority of firms. It is likely that the absence of any single major constraint is partly because framework conditions have already attracted considerable attention from Mexico's policymakers.

2.3. Human resources

Mexico has made considerable progress in human capital development in recent years, with the share of public education spending in GDP rising to 4.8%, close to the OECD average of 5.2% (OECD, 2010a). Nevertheless, the amount spent per student is low by international standards, reflecting the relative youth of Mexico's population. Improving

Figure 2.7. **Obstacles to businesses in Mexico by firm size, 2010**

As a percentage of firms identifying the main problems as an obstacle

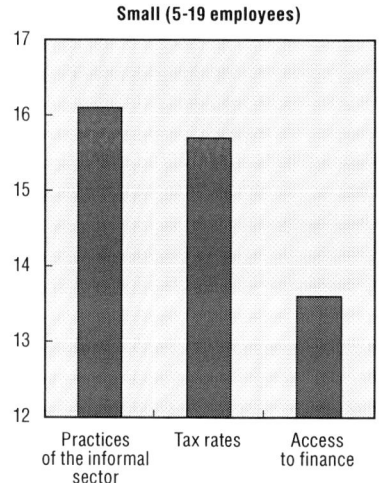

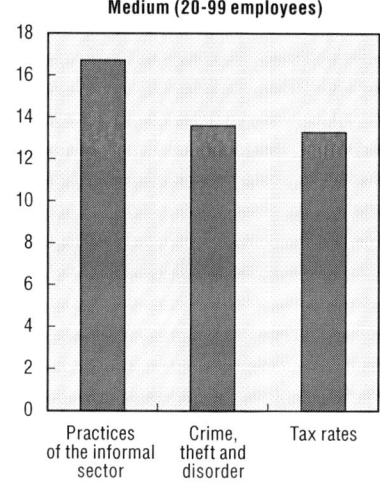

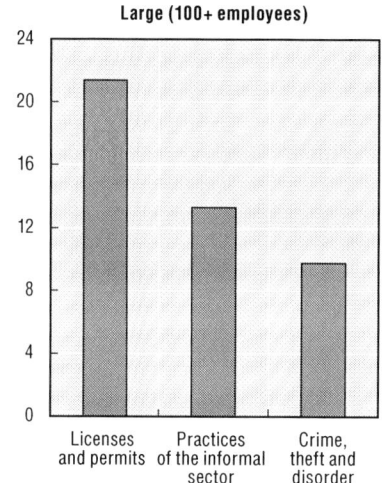

Source: World Bank (2010), *Enterprise Survey.*

general education levels is one of the keys to improving SME productivity and competitiveness through improved workforce skills and should remain a high priority of the government, including investment in secondary and vocational education in particular.

In addition to barriers in general education levels, SME and entrepreneurship development in Mexico is affected by a lack of leadership qualities and entrepreneurial orientation in the young population. This affects the capacities of the population to create successful firms and operate and growth successfully. It implies the need for more business management training (e.g. accounting, finance, marketing, human resource management, as well as specific trade skills), including for micro-enterprises. It also implies greater attention to entrepreneurship education aimed at improving the ability to be innovative and creative, to take risks and manage them, and to have can-do attitude and the drive to make ideas happen. Enterprise education has been a priority for the Mexican government, but it is still only partially applied across formal education institutions and is stronger in universities than vocational colleges and schools. Training and support measures to entrepreneurship teachers are also required.

2.4. Access to finance

SMEs typically face more severe problems in accessing debt and equity financing than large corporations. Furthermore, the challenge can be expected to be particularly great in an economy such as Mexico where the predominant type of business is the micro-enterprise, and informality affects large numbers of micro and small firms.

Having said this, only 12% of firms identified access to finance as the main obstacle they faced in the World Bank's enterprise survey. In part, this appears to reflect the substantial progress Mexico has made during the last decade in reducing the interest rates that SMEs face in the market. The remaining difficulties appear to be connected to limited credit amounts accessed by SMEs from the banking sector rather than their cost.

Figure 2.8 shows that domestic credit to the private sector is low as a percentage of GDP compared to OECD member country and Latin American and Caribbean (LAC)

Figure 2.8. **Domestic credit to the private sector**

As a percentage of GDP

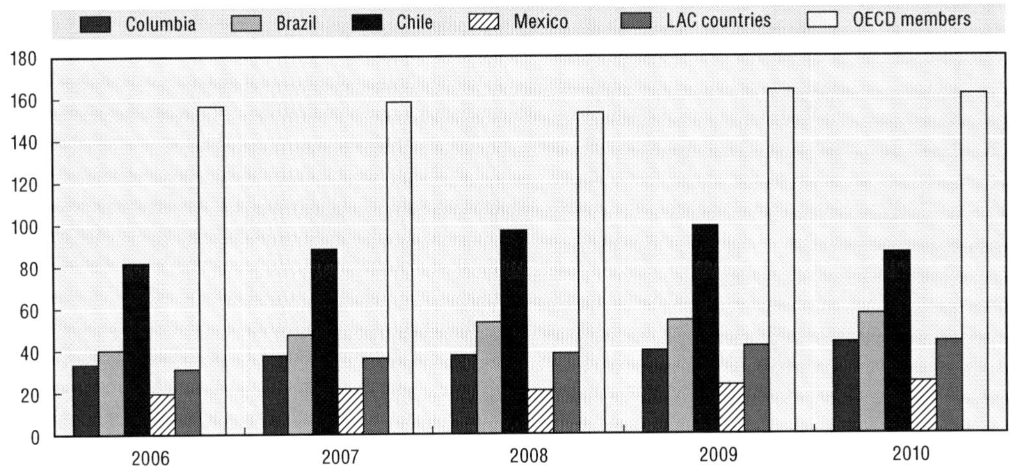

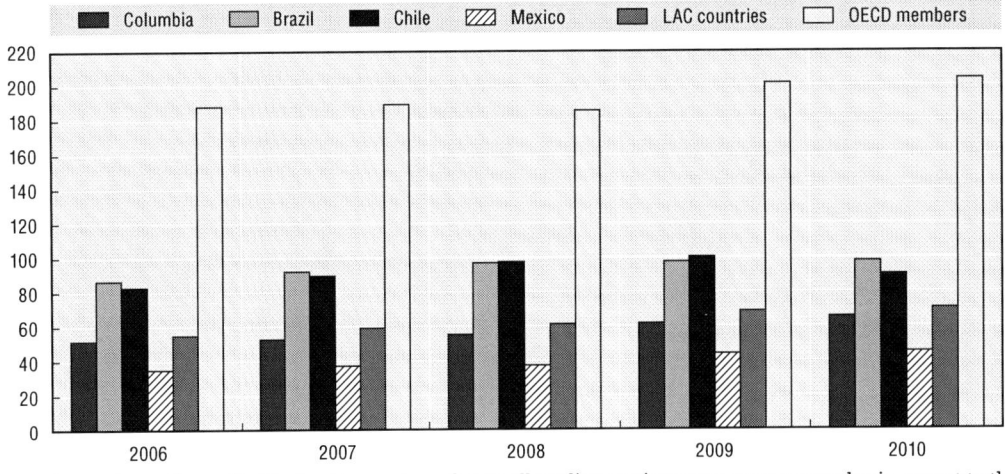

Note: Domestic credit to the private sector refers to financial resources provided to the private sector, such as through loans, purchases of non-equity securities, and trade credits and other accounts receivable, that establish a claim for repayment (definition from World Bank, 2011).
Source: World Bank, *World Development Indicators Database.*

country benchmarks. Figure 2.9 shows that the same is true of domestic credit provided by the banking system.

Figure 2.9. **Domestic credit provided by the banking system**

As a percentage of GDP

Note: Domestic credit provided by banking sector refers to all credit to various sectors on a gross basis, except to the central government, which is net. The banking sector includes monetary authorities, deposit money banks, and other banking institutions for which data are available (definition from World Bank, 2011).
Source: World Bank, *World Development Indicators Database.*

Low levels of bank credit are also related to the prevalent financial culture of SMEs in Mexico, which have traditionally not looked to banks for credit. Figure 2.10 shows that the proportion of firms using banks for credits and deposit accounts is lower in Mexico than in the rest of Latin America or in upper-middle income countries.

Constrained bank credit is compensated to some degree by financing from other sources. As shown in Figure 2.11, internal finance is the most common source of enterprise

Figure 2.10. **Proportion of firms with access to finance, 2010**

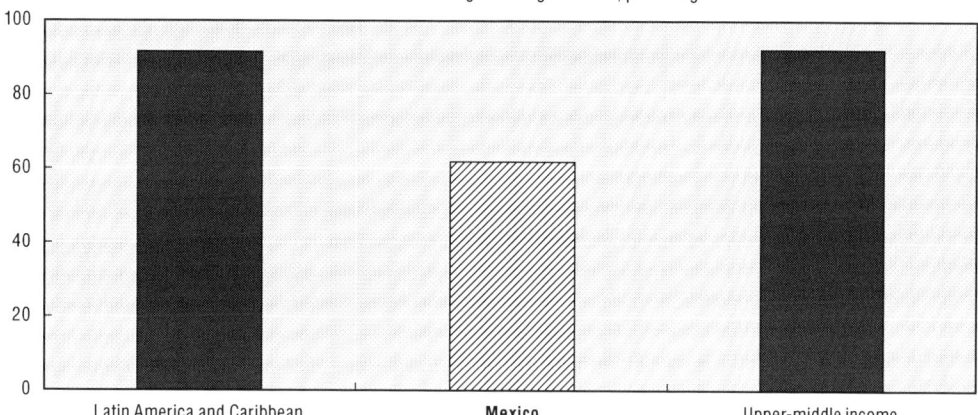

Access to a bank loan/line of credit, percentage

Access to a checking or savings account, percentage

Note: Regional and world averages of indicators are computed by taking a simple average of country-level point estimates. For each economy, only the latest available year of survey data is used in this computation.
Source: World Bank, *Enterprise Survey*, 2010.

Figure 2.11. **Enterprises' sources of finance for investment, 2010**

As a percentage

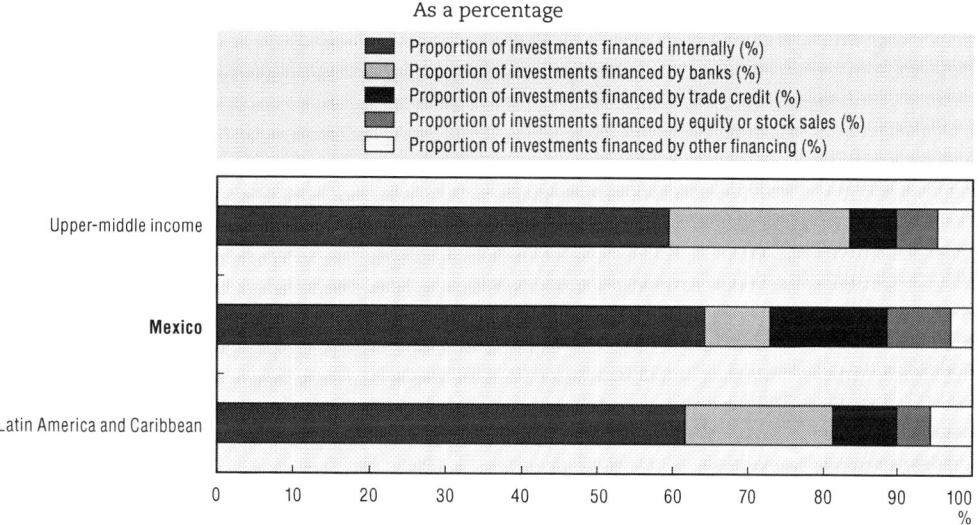

■ Proportion of investments financed internally (%)
■ Proportion of investments financed by banks (%)
■ Proportion of investments financed by trade credit (%)
■ Proportion of investments financed by equity or stock sales (%)
□ Proportion of investments financed by other financing (%)

Note: Regional and world averages of indicators are computed by taking a simple average of country-level point estimates. For each economy, only the latest available year of survey data is used in this computation.
Source: World Bank *Enterprise Survey*, 2010.

finance for investment in Mexico. This is little different from other Latin American countries or upper middle income countries. Where Mexico is distinct, however, is in the much greater reliance of its SMEs on trade credit. Bank of Mexico data show that in 2009, for every 10 pesos of financing to small enterprises, 6.3 pesos came from their suppliers whereas only 1.7 pesos came from commercial banks and 1.6 pesos from development banks.

Notwithstanding the ability of some SMEs to mitigate the lack of bank credit through internal finance and trade credit, there is a clear debt finance gap for Mexican SMEs that needs to be addressed by policy.

One of the obstacles appears to be high operating costs in large banks, which makes micro credits and small loans very expensive to offer. These high costs appear to be related to limited competition in the banking market. Stimulating greater competition, and particularly the entry of new small banking institutions, could help bring down these costs and increase finance supply to SMEs and entrepreneurs.

Another obstacle is the high levels of collateral demanded by commercial banks to secure loans. Figure 2.12 shows that the collateral required in Mexico is typically greater than twice the loan value. This is high by the standards of OECD member countries although it is similar to levels in the Latin American region and upper middle income countries in general, and acts as a constraint to small firms in obtaining lending. In addition, some types of collateral involved in enterprise lending (e.g. machinery and equipment, inventories) are difficult to value in comparison with real estate, and this has reduced the amount of collateral that businesses have at their disposal.

Figure 2.12. **Value of collateral needed for a loan, 2010**

As a percentage of the loan amount

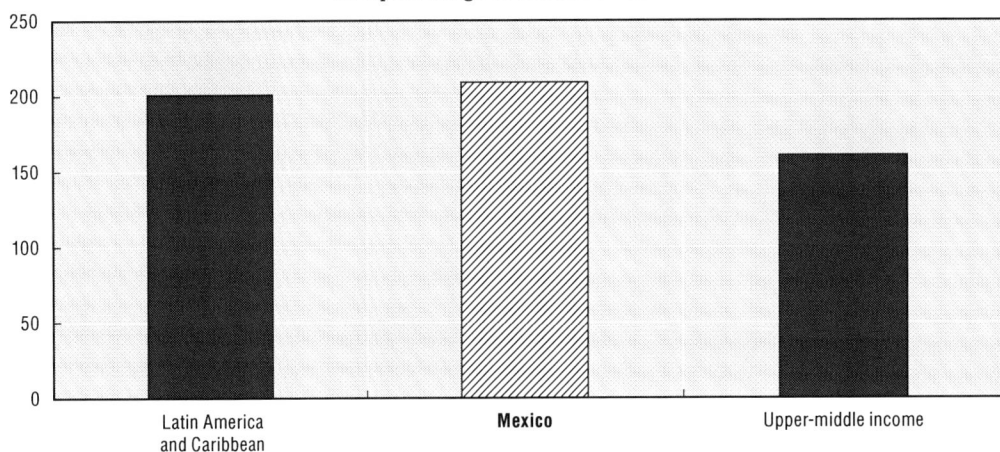

Note. Regional and world averages of indicators are computed by taking a simple average of country-level point estimates. For each economy, only the latest available year of survey data is used in this computation.
Source: World Bank *Enterprise Survey*, 2010

A further problem affecting debt financing is that credit bureaus in Mexico face particular difficulties in tracking the credit history of companies given the large size of the informal sector.

Among the government's most important achievements in responding to these problems has been the creation of the national credit guarantee programme operated by the NAFIN development bank and funded through the Ministry of Economy's SME Fund. This programme is described in Chapter 4.

Alongside the national credit guarantee programme, another important action taken by the Mexican government to improve access to credit has been the August 2009 amendment to the Commercial Code providing for a Unified Registry of Movable Property Collateral. This has expanded the types of collateral allowable from real estate and other immovable assets to enable the use of movable assets such as machinery and equipment as collateral in loan contracts. The World Bank estimates that with the new registry, lenders have multiplied the number of loans to businesses by 4, for an estimated value of more than USD 50 billion in additional financing to firms and that borrowers have saved USD 1.1 billion in registration fees associated to registration of collateral.

As a result of these measures, bank credit requirements have been softened (e.g. banks will now accept simple bank statements instead of audited statements), and the interest rate for the broad range of loans between MXN 250 000 and MXN 4 million is now competitive in the market (10% in 2010, 2% lower than the rate applied by most public programmes in the same range of loan size). Figure 2.13 confirms the progress that Mexico has made with regard to the ease of access to loans. It is still found towards the bottom of the ranking when compared with among OECD countries, but progress is encouraging.

Figure 2.13. **Ease of access to loans, 2007-08 and 2009-10**

Scale from 1 to 7 from hardest to easiest, weighted averages

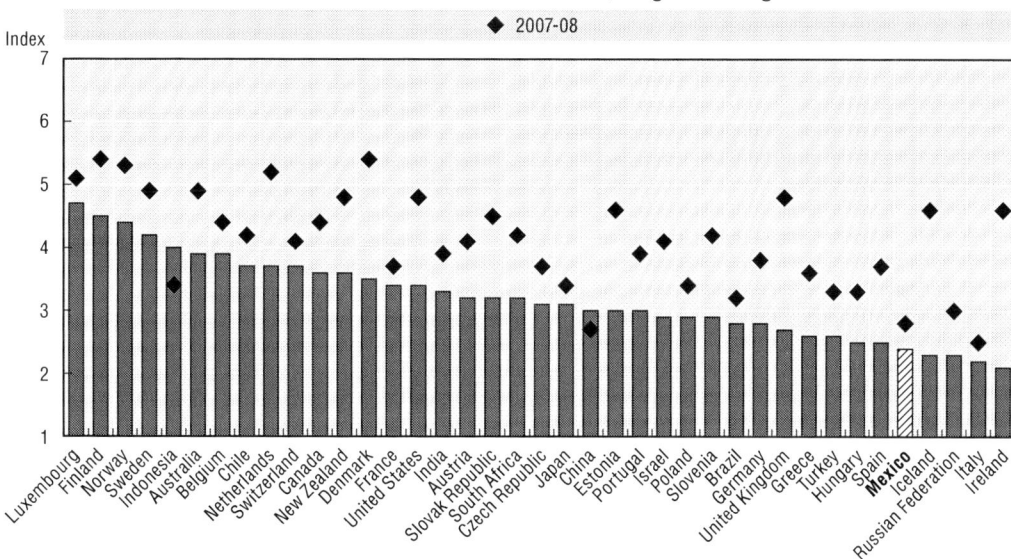

Note: The statistical data for Israel are supplied by and under the responsibility of the relevant Israeli authorities. The use of such data by the OECD is without prejudice to the status of the Golan Heights, East Jerusalem and Israeli settlements in the West Bank under the terms of international law.
Source: OECD (2011c), *STI Scoreboard 2011*, based on World Economic Forum (2010) and World Economic Forum (2008).

Whereas most attention has been on debt finance, the nature of investment projects in innovative SMEs is well suited to equity investment and mixed debt and equity instruments. This is a branch of finance with well documented market failures internationally (OECD, 2006). This is also the case in Mexico, where the venture capital market remains small. There are nevertheless signs that Mexico's venture capital industry is beginning to take off under the impulse of government initiatives. For example, Mexican pension funds have recently been allowed to invest in private equity and a Fund of Funds has recently been established. Further stimulus to equity investment could be provided through the introduction of new fiscal incentives for investment by private savers in innovative SMEs.

2.5. Tax, social security and employment protection

Tax, social security and employment protection all affect incentives for business creation, operation and growth, and can act as a brake on formal sector entrepreneurship. The issues involved concern both rates of levies on enterprises, which determine the underlying cost of complying with regulation, and the complexity of understanding and conforming to the system.

Figure 2.14 presents the rates of corporate taxation for a wide group of countries. At 30%, Mexico's corporate tax rate is one of the highest within the OECD but still lower than that of major economies such as the United States, Japan, Germany and France. High corporate taxation rates can reduce business start-up and growth rates, although they are also important for the provision of public infrastructures and services that strengthen the economy. Careful assessment is needed of whether the rates are set at the appropriate level for national economic objectives.

Figure 2.14. **Taxation on corporate income, 2010**

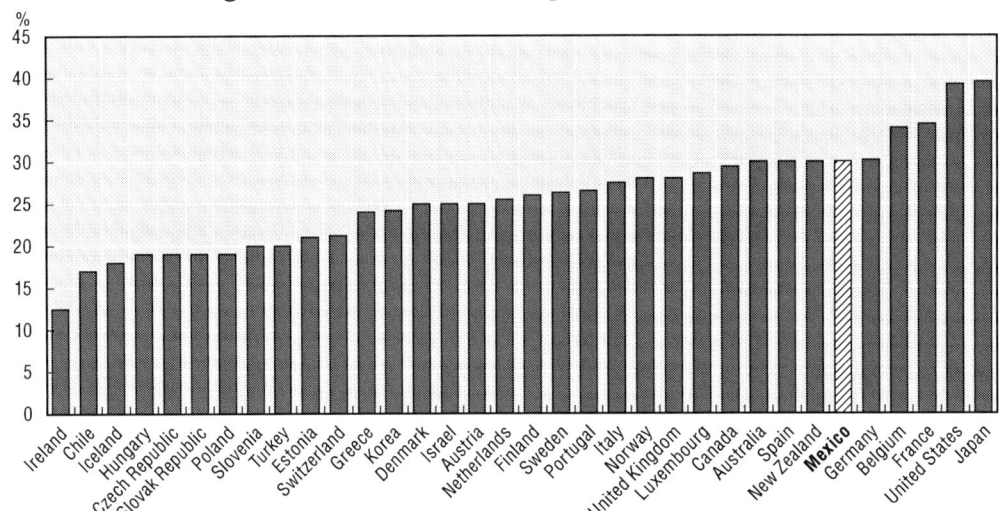

Notes: Corporate income tax shows the basic combined central and sub-central (statutory) corporate income tax rate given by the adjusted central government rate plus the sub-central rate. For differences between countries, please refer to Annex 2.A1. The statistical data for Israel are supplied by and under the responsibility of the relevant Israeli authorities. The use of such data by the OECD is without prejudice to the status of the Golan Heights, East Jerusalem and Israeli settlements in the West Bank under the terms of international law.
Source: OECD (2011), *Taxing Wages 2009-2010*, OECD, Paris.

Aside from the rates of taxation, entrepreneurs signal complexity of the tax system as a barrier together with lack of information on taking advantage of fiscal benefits. Many SMEs have been forced to hire a tax advisor to assist them in these processes. However, significant progress has been made by the government in recent years regarding simplification of the tax system, including a substantial decrease in the number of taxes levied on businesses.

High non-wage labour costs in the form of labour taxes and social security payments can also hamper business activity and act as a disincentive for firms to operate in the formal sector. Whilst labour taxes in Mexico may be moderate, regressive social charges represent a high burden on the lowest paid (OECD, 2011a).

In addition, as shown in Figure 2.15, employment protection legislation in Mexico is relatively stringent, while there are relatively few restrictions on the use of temporary employees. This encourages firms to subcontract or outsource to access lower cost unregistered labour. One way of closing the loophole would be to ensure that only registered labour is used by subcontractors or by those involved in supplying outsourcing companies (OECD, 2011a).

Figure 2.15. **Employment protection legislation (EPL) for regular workers, 2008**

Scale from 0 (least restrictions) to 6 (most restrictions)

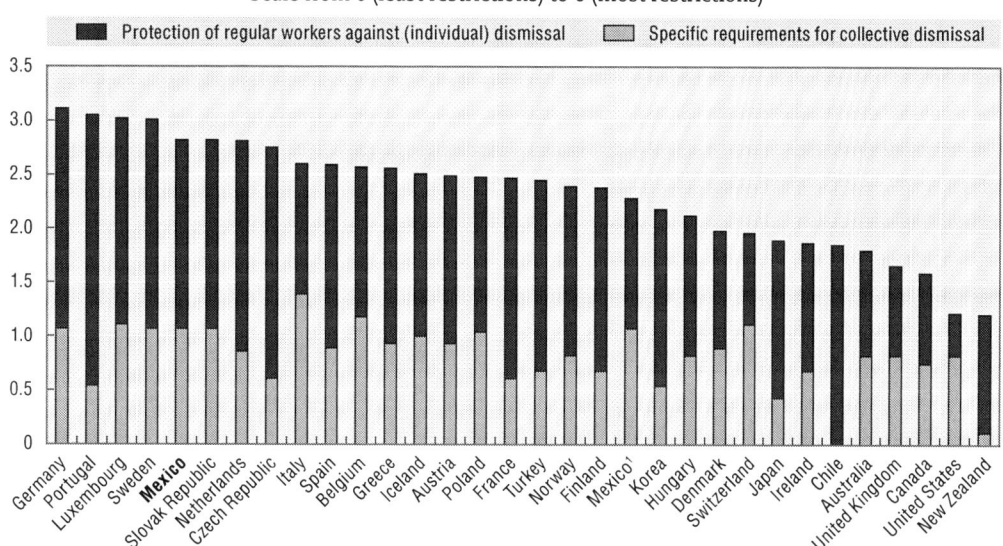

1. Estimate takes into account a recent, proposed reform that would limit the accumulation of due wages during labour trials to 6 months, limit the costs of dismissal and the uncertainty surrounding it, introduce short-term trial and training contracts, ranging from one to six months and make it easier to contract employees for intermittent tasks, such as seasonal work and work that does not have to be performed the full week, month or year.

Source: OECD Indicators on Employment Protection Database.

A reduction in the cost of employing labour formally, if combined with tighter policing of regulatory non-compliance, is likely to have some effect on encouraging movement from the informal to the formal economy. For example, a recently introduced employment subsidy will help to address this problem by reducing costs for firms that hire workers that are registered with social security agencies for the first time.

2.6. Product market conditions

Product market competition is weak in many sectors, with state owned monopolies dominating in electricity and oil production. This closes down opportunities for new firm entry and SME growth. Research undertaken jointly by the Mexican competition authority and the OECD suggests that the average Mexican household spends almost one third of its budget on goods produced in monopolistic or oligopolistic conditions (OECD, 2011a). On the other hand, Mexico is not significantly worse in terms of product market regulation than many comparable countries (Figure 2.16) and authorities in Mexico continue to recognise the need for further competition law reforms which they are actively pursuing with technical assistance from OECD.

Figure 2.16. **Product market regulation in selected OECD and non-OECD countries, 2008**

Scale from 0 to 6 from least to most restrictive

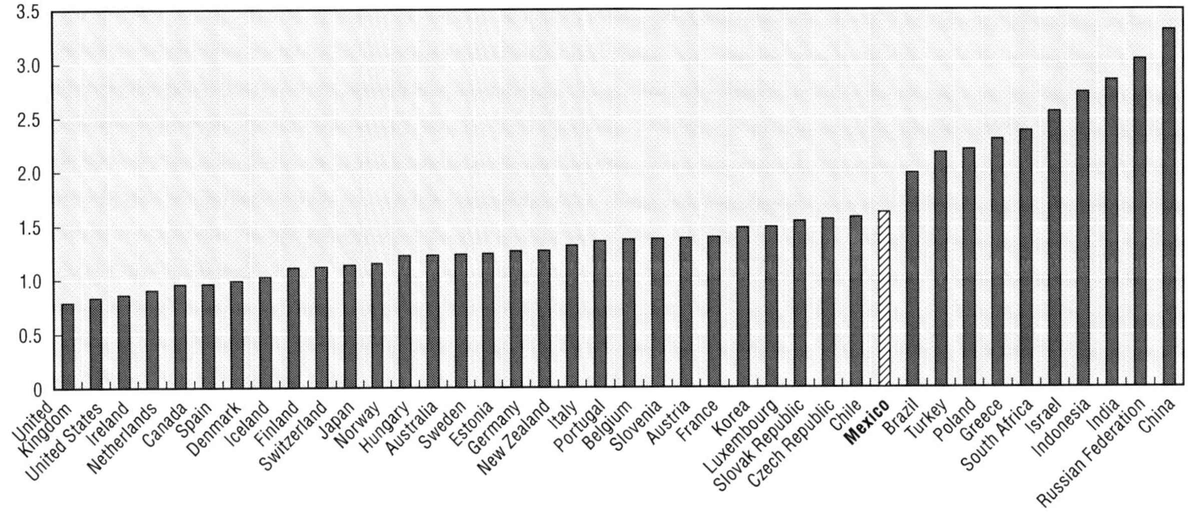

Source: OECD Product Market Regulation Database.

2.7. Business law and regulation

As stated in the OECD Bologna Charter on SME Policies of 2000, policy can promote SME competitiveness by providing "a regulatory environment which does not impose undue burdens on SMEs and is conducive to entrepreneurship, innovation and growth". Unnecessary regulations and inefficiency and inconsistency in the way regulations are applied can be particularly burdensome at start-up and daunting for individuals considering starting a business.

Figure 2.17 shows that the average number of days needed to complete the procedures necessary to start a business was lower in Mexico in 2010 than the OECD average. It also shows the rapid improvement in Mexico compared with other countries needed since 2003.

The improvement reflects early recognition by the Mexican government of the need for business regulatory reform and actions such as the introduction of the Rapid Business Opening System (SARE programme) in 2002, which introduced municipal one-stop shops for business registration. Bruhn (2008) estimated that the implementation of the rapid opening system for enterprises boosted the number of new firms by 5% with an increase of 2.8% in the number of new jobs created. The establishment of a new single point of entry for new business registration through the portal, *www.tuempresa.gob.mx* in 2009, has resulted in further improvements. OECD research suggests that this internet entry site has helped bring down the costs for entrepreneurs to comply with start-up formalities from 16% of per capita GDP to 5.5%, although it is not yet the most widely used mechanism to start up a business (OECD, 2011a). These improvements have been coupled with the development of new options for online payment to government. In late 2011, Congress also passed a bill to eliminate the minimum capital requirement for a limited liability company, although this only applies at the Federal level, not at the State level.

Attention is now turning to the state level, since there are state and local procedures and regulations and compliance procedures as well as federal ones. This leads to significant burdens as well as differences in regulatory environment across the states. Figure 2.18, for example, shows how the number of days required to start a business varies across Mexico by state. The World Bank has assisted the federal government by conducting

Figure 2.17. **Time needed to start a business, 2003 and 2010**

Days

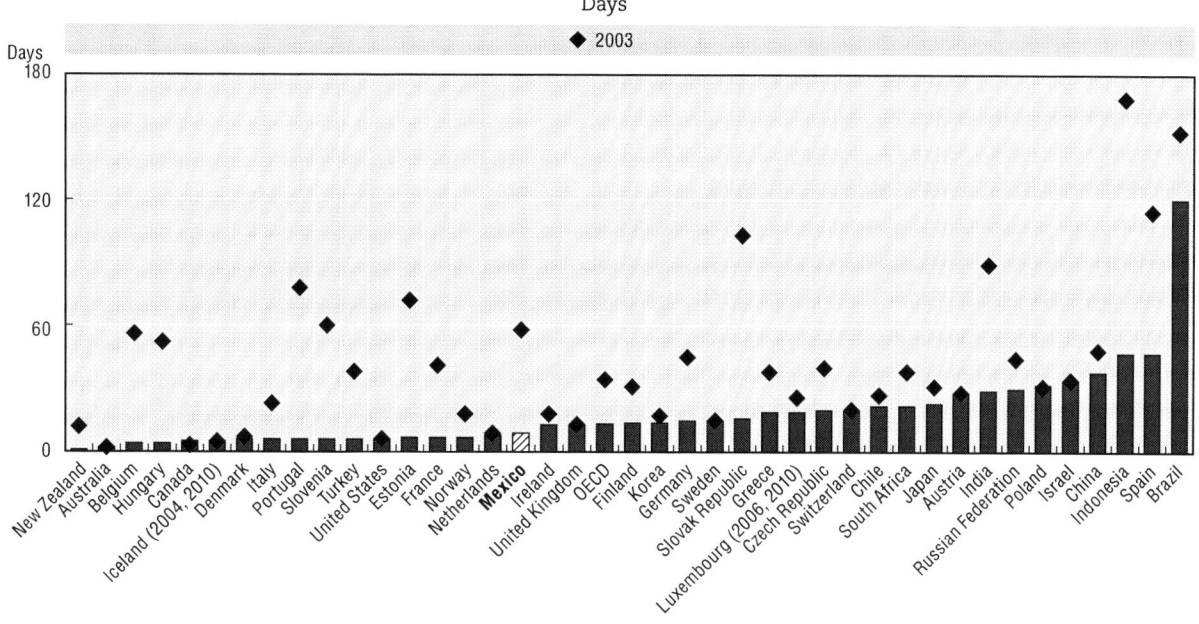

Note: The statistical data for Israel are supplied by and under the responsibility of the relevant Israeli authorities. The use of such data by the OECD is without prejudice to the status of the Golan Heights, East Jerusalem and Israeli settlements in the West Bank under the terms of international law.

Source: OECD (2011), *STI Scoreboard*, based on World Bank (2011), *Doing Business Database*, June.

Figure 2.18. **Time taken to open an enterprise in Mexico, 2006-09**

Average number of days

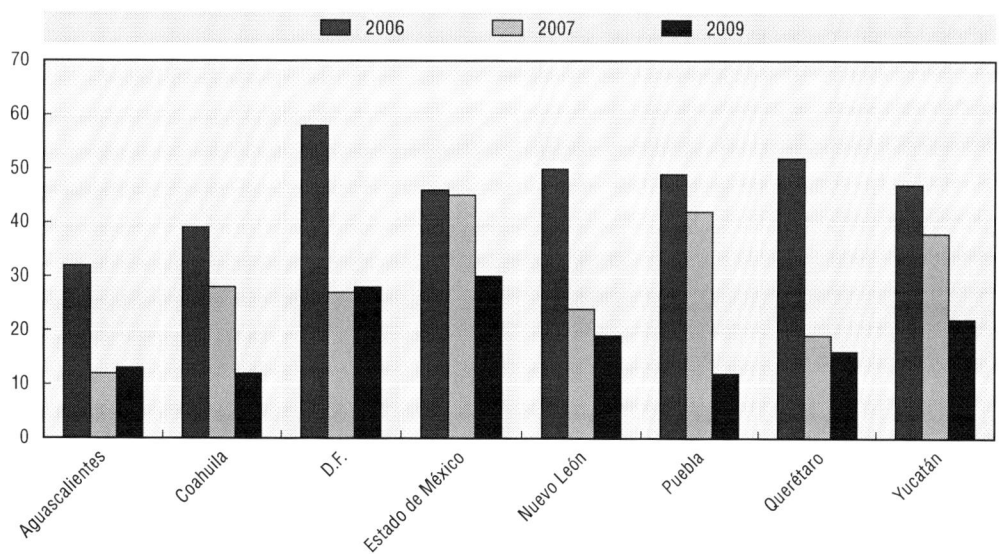

Source: Mexican Ministry of Economy.

an assessment of "Doing Business" indicators in major centres in each state (World Bank, 2012). One of the challenges is the lack of capacity of local and state governments to implement regulatory changes. The federal government has therefore introduced a tool kit that was developed with OECD assistance to promote priority actions that States can take. The municipal one-stop shops for the co-ordination of municipal procedures, for example, have now been implemented in 186 municipalities. In addition, State Commissions for Regulatory Improvement (CEMERs) have been introduced in 16 of the 31 states.

Box 2.1. **Good practice policy initiative in Mexico: The State Commission for Regulatory Improvement**

The government's commitment to better regulation is reflected in the establishment of the Federal Commission for Regulatory Improvement (COFEMER), which is developing a broad range of regulatory tools and processes including regulatory impact assessments. Greater transparency in the regulatory process and increased public consultation are part of the Commission's agenda. The aim is to enhance the government's capacity to create high quality regulation and to improve the quality of existing regulations. A complete review of legislation affecting private enterprises was initiated in 2009 using a process adhering to OECD good practice. In 2010, the government eliminated more than 16 000 standards, regulations, resolutions, and circulars and at least 2 000 steps of red tape. These reductions in red tape steps were largely in response to the government's "*Most Useless Step*" contest, which asked businesses and other stakeholders to submit their suggestions about unnecessary steps that could be eliminated. According to the Ministry of Public Administration, federal procedures have been reduced by a third and internal government regulations by 47% thanks to the work of COFEMER.

In planning its future work, the Federal Commission for Regulatory Improvement has identified 4 649 procedures (3 596 for businesses, 1 053 for citizens) of the federal registry, which have been classified according to the life cycle of businesses (see Table 2.2 below). Many of the business lifecycle procedures have been reviewed, but more are left to review, including those relating to starting a business (e.g. creating a corporation, obtaining permits and licences), operating a business (e.g. accessing government support, taxes and duties, importing and exporting, property rights and labour rules), and closing a business (e.g. cancellations of licenses, registering the commercial dissolution, etc.). The cost of these procedures to the economy has been estimated at approximately 4.8% of GDP, based on information provided by the Ministry of Economy during the OECD study mission. Reducing regulatory burdens would improve competitiveness and accelerate growth. COFEMER has agreed to consider reform of 27% of the procedures in the Federal Registry of Procedures and Services by the end of 2012, which would lead to an estimated reduction of 25% in the total costs to the economy (from 4.8% of GDP to 3.6% of GDP). Over half of the entrepreneurship-related procedures targeted in the Regulatory Improvement Programme will improve business operation and 42% will affect the ease of starting a business. The monitoring system created in COFEMER, requires government offices and agencies to report twice yearly on their progress in implementing reforms and to produce a complete evaluation at the end of 2012.

This model shows to other countries the importance of autonomy and political independence for policy makers to achieve quick progress on a specific objective. In this sense, the establishment of a national commission specifically devoted to the task of administration simplification and endowed with significant powers has been instrumental to Mexico's strides on simplifying business rules and regulations.

Table 2.2. **Procedures of the registry of procedures and services and the business life cycle**

Business life cycle		
Starting a business	Operating a business	Closing a business
Creating a corporation	Obtaining government supports	Cancellation of licenses, concessions
Providing information for public records	Taxes and duties	Registering the name of the liquidator
Notices delivery		Deposit the final balance sheet in public ministry
	Imports and exports	
Financing	Extension and modification of concessions, permits are licenses	
	Property rights	
	Business with government	
	Labour	
757 procedures	2 757 procedures	82 procedures

Source: Federal commission on Regulatory Improvement.

2.8. Foreign direct investment

Mexico is an attractive location for foreign investment, and a growing number of international companies have taken advantage of the foreign trade agreements that Mexico has signed in recent years, including NAFTA. As Figure 2.19 shows, the stock of foreign direct investment inflows in Mexico represented approximately 29% of GDP in 2010. This is above the average for OECD countries and above Brazil for example. The significance of FDI for SME development is that inward investors represent a potential market for Mexico's SME suppliers and a potential source of new technology and management know-how if linkages can be built with them. Public policy has recognised this opportunity with the National Supplier Development Programme.

Figure 2.19. **FDI stocks, 2010**
As a percentage of GDP, 2010 or latest available year

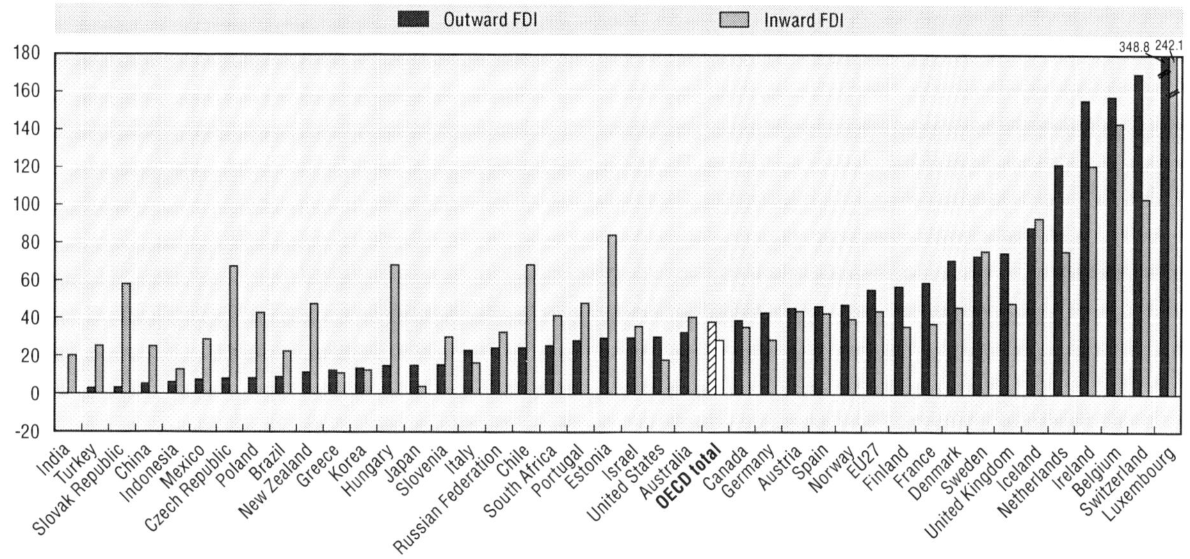

Note: The statistical data for Israel are supplied by and under the responsibility of the relevant Israeli authorities. The use of such data by the OECD is without prejudice to the status of the Golan Heights, East Jerusalem and Israeli settlements in the West Bank under the terms of international law.
Source: OECD, Factbook 2011.

2.9. The innovation system

One of the main priorities for the Mexican economy is to encourage larger numbers of innovative start-ups and raise the innovative capacity of SMEs. This will be favoured by effective national and local innovation systems consisting of networks of private firms, higher education institutions, research institutes, technical consultants and so on, from which SMEs can draw innovation inputs and supply innovation outputs.

Although innovation is not just about R&D, it is certainly one of one the major drivers of effective innovation systems. In this respect, there is a need for Mexico to invest greater resources in R&D. In 2009, government R&D expenditure stood at 0.25% of GDP and business R&D stood at 0.18%, significantly below the OECD median values of 0.72% for public R&D and 1.12% for business R&D. The radar diagram in Figure 2.20 focuses on the composition of business R&D and shows that it is relatively concentrated in medium-high and low-technology manufacturing and low knowledge services compared with

Figure 2.20. **Structural composition of BERD, 2009**

As a percentage of total BERD

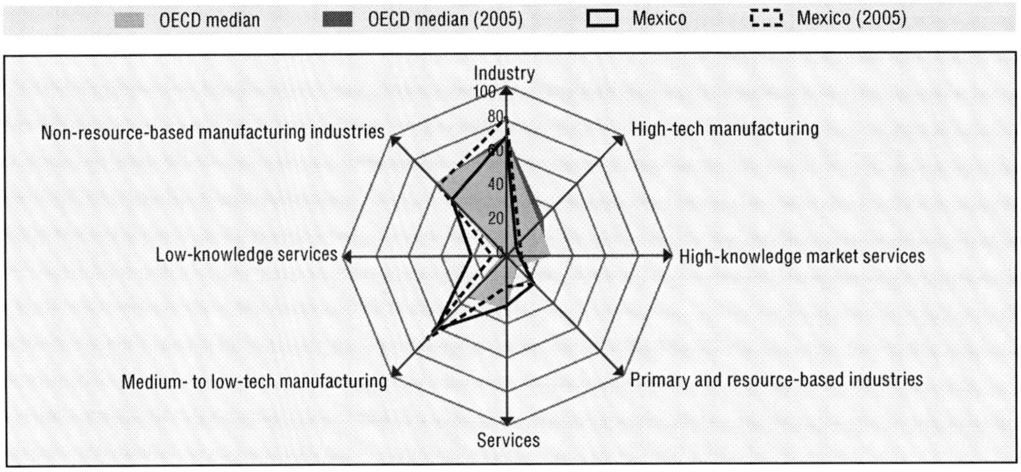

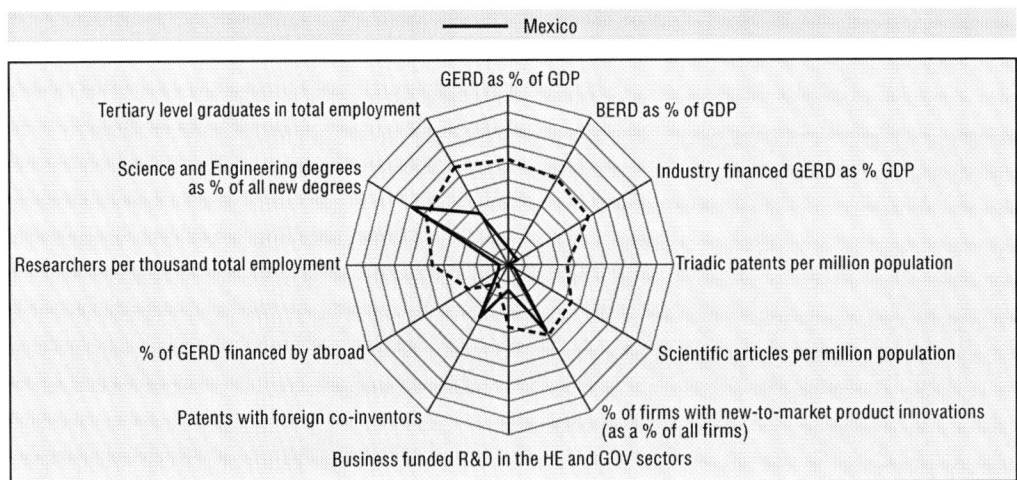

Source: OECD (2012), Science, Technology and Industry Outlook 2012.

OECD averages, with a relative dearth of business expenditure on R&D in knowledge-intensive services and high technology manufacturing.

Figure 2.21 compares innovation in Mexico with the OECD average for a broader range of innovation-related indicators. For 9 of the 12 indicators shown, Mexico's performance is significantly below the OECD average. The gap tends to be widest in the case of indicators related to expenditure on R&D and patenting activity. For example, Mexico has only 5.5 researchers per thousand employees, compared with an average of 46.8 in OECD countries. In contrast, the employment of science and engineering graduates, the introduction of new-to-market product innovations, and co-patenting with foreign firms are all strong in Mexico.

Figure 2.21. **Main innovation indicators in Mexico**

Source: OECD (2010b), Science, Technology and Industry Outlook 2010.

In addition, there are regional differences in innovation-related links between SMEs and universities. For example almost one half of research activity in higher education institutions is concentrated in just four large public sector institutions. As a consequence, the extent of the challenge facing policymakers in building the conditions for successful SME innovation is not uniform across the country.

Table 2.3 shows annual numbers of patent applications submitted and awarded in Mexico by Mexican nationals and foreigners. Throughout the period, foreigners accounted for the vast majority of patent activity, representing 93.5% of patents applied for and 97.6% of those awarded in 2010. This suggests a weakness in domestic innovation capacity.

Table 2.3. **Patents applied for and awarded in Mexico, 2001-10**

Number

	Applied for			Awarded		
	Nationals	Foreigners	Total	Nationals	Foreigners	Total
2001	534	13 032	13 566	118	5 360	5 478
2002	526	12 536	13 062	139	6 472	6 611
2003	468	11 739	12 207	121	5 887	6 008
2004	565	12 629	13 194	162	6 676	6 838
2005	584	13 852	14 436	131	7 967	8 098
2006	574	14 926	15 500	132	9 500	9 632
2007	641	15 958	16 599	199	9 758	9 957
2008	685	15 896	16 581	197	10 243	10 440
2009	822	13 459	14 281	213	9 416	9 629
2010	951	13 625	14 576	229	9 170	9 399

Source: IMPI, *Annual Report*, 2011.

These weaknesses in the innovation system have been recognised by the government and are the subject of important policy responses under the National Innovation Plan that can be expected to increase SME innovation. These measures include promotion of commercialisable research and academic-industry linkages by the Law of Science and Technology, the funding of SME innovative projects through the Innovation Fund, the gazelles programme and the national supplier development programme of the SME Fund, and a series of new programmes operated by the National Council for Science and Technology (CONACYT) such as INNOVATEC, INNOVAPYME, PROINNOVA, PROLOGYCA, and PROSOFT.

These actions have been associated with recent improvements in innovative conditions for SMEs and start-ups. For example, the World Economic Forum's *Global Competitiveness Index* ranked Mexico 55 out of 142 countries in 2011-12 on innovation and sophistication factors, an improvement of 14 places over the previous year (World Economic Forum, 2011).

2.10. Transparency and the rule of law

The 2004 OECD Istanbul Ministerial Declaration on Innovative and Internationally Competitive SMEs emphasised "the need for a conducive business environment where the rule of law is paramount". SMEs are not unique in requiring well-defined "rules of the game" and a strong legal system for start-up and operation, yet they are disproportionately vulnerable to situations of unpredictability and confusion created in the absence of such a system. Furthermore, SMEs tend to suffer more from illegal practices and corruption than large firms because they are weakly placed to resist demands for under-the-counter payments. Some may therefore resort to operation in the informal sector.

Figure 2.22 shows Mexico's position on Transparency International's Corruption Perception Index compared with a selection of other countries. A high score represents a perception that government is relatively free from corruption. With a score of 33, Mexico is clearly perceived to have a corruption problem.

Figure 2.22. **Freedom from corruption index in selected OECD and non-OECD countries, 2005-10**

Index of 0 to 100

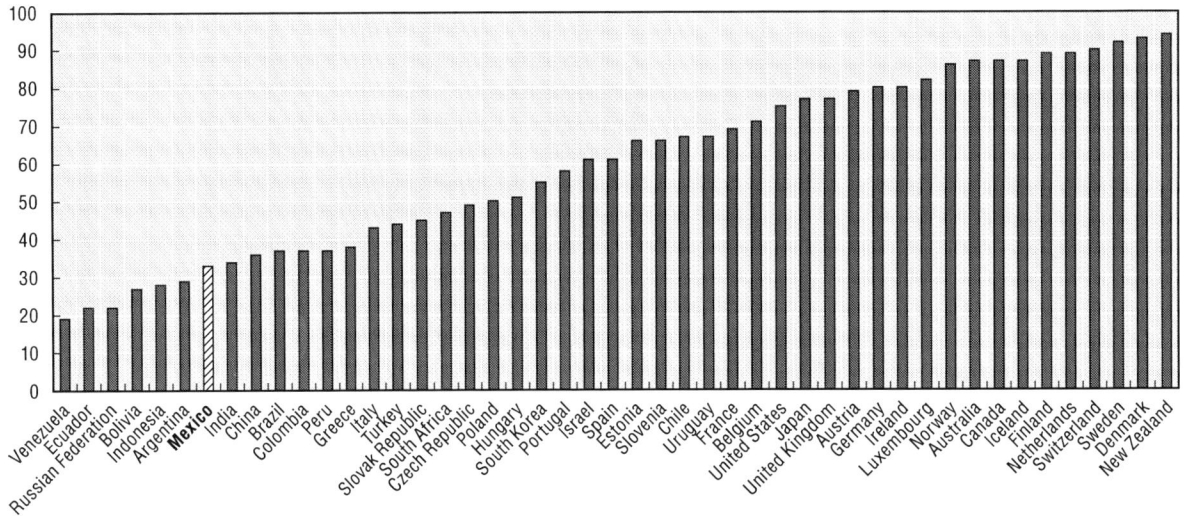

Notes: The score for "Freedom from corruption" is derived primarily from Transparency International's Corruption Perceptions Index (CPI) for 2008, which measures the level of corruption in 180 countries. The CPI is based on a 10-point scale in which a score of 10 indicates very little corruption and a score of 0 indicates a very corrupt government. In scoring freedom from corruption, the Index converts the raw CPI data to a scale of 0 to 100 by multiplying the CPI score by 10.
Source: Heritage Foundation (2010), Index of Economic Freedom.

This impression is confirmed by Figure 2.23, which shows a so-called "graft index" describing the proportion of times that a firm was asked or expected to pay a bribe when applying for six different public services, permits or licenses. In Mexico this applied to almost 14% of responding businesses compared with an average of about 6% for Latin America and the Caribbean and 8% for upper middle income countries.

Figures 2.24 and 2.25 present so-called "bribe taxes", which describes the extent to which specific regulatory and administrative officials require bribe payments. The proportion of firms reporting the need to pay bribes is higher in Mexico than in Latin America and Caribbean and upper middle income countries in general. This is likely to hamper business start-up and SME development.

Figure 2.23. **Incidence of graft index, 2010**

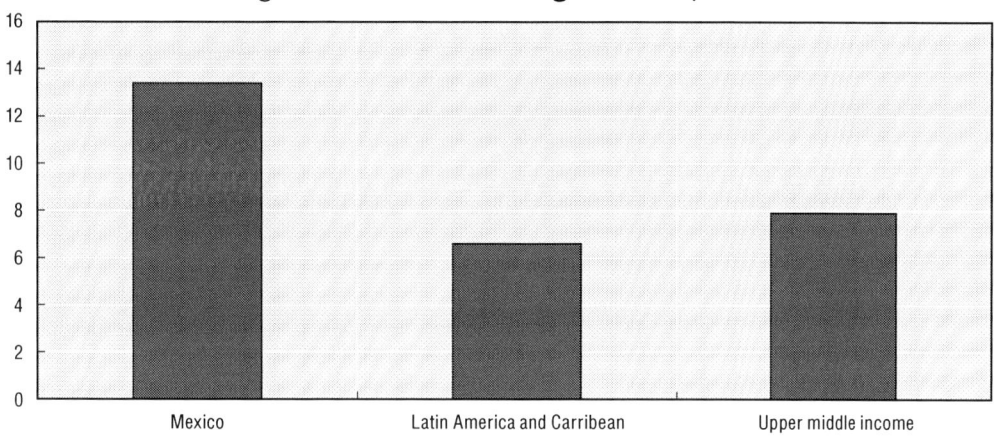

Note: Regional and world averages of indicators are computed by taking a simple average of country-level point estimates. For each economy, only the latest available year of survey data is used in this computation.
Source: World Bank *Enterprise Survey*, 2010.

Figure 2.24. **Proportion of firms expected to give gifts to tax inspectors or for government contracts, 2010**

Percentage of firms

In meetings with tax inspectors

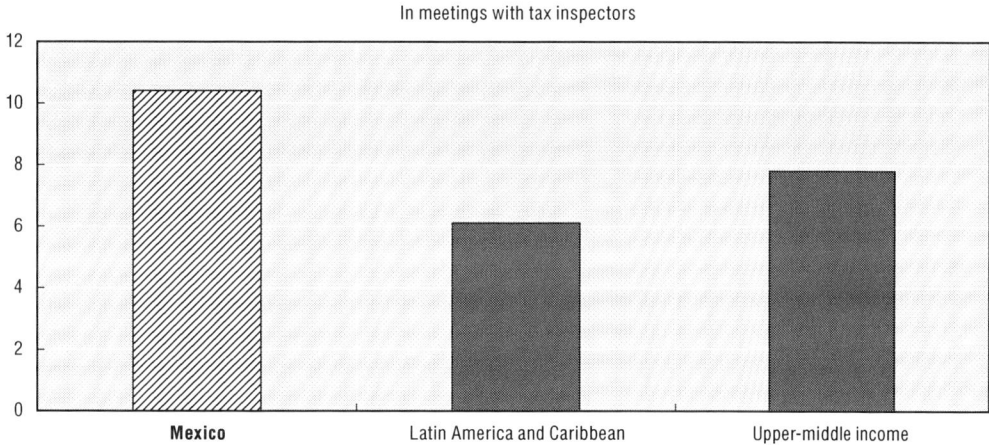

In securing a government contract

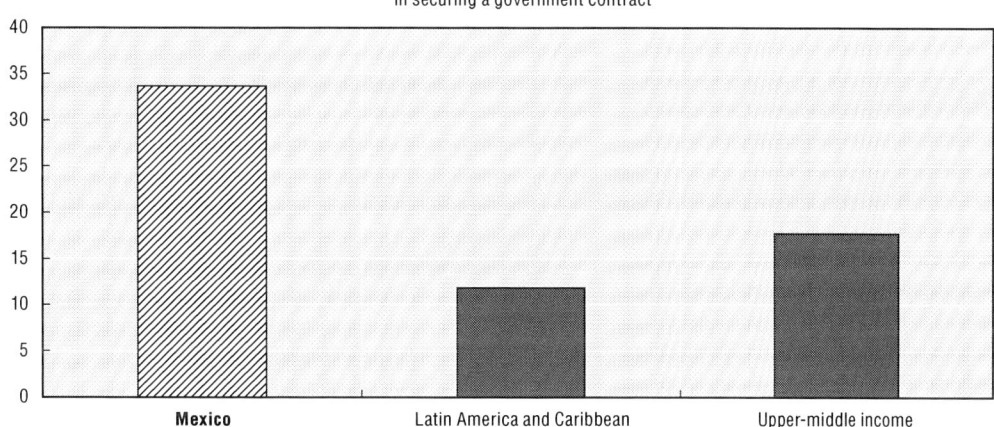

Note: Regional and world averages of indicators are computed by taking a simple average of country-level point estimates. For each economy, only the latest available year of survey data is used in this computation.
Source: World Bank *Enterprise Survey*, 2010.

Figure 2.25. **Proportion of firms expected to give gifts for specific licenses and permits, 2010**

Percentage of firms

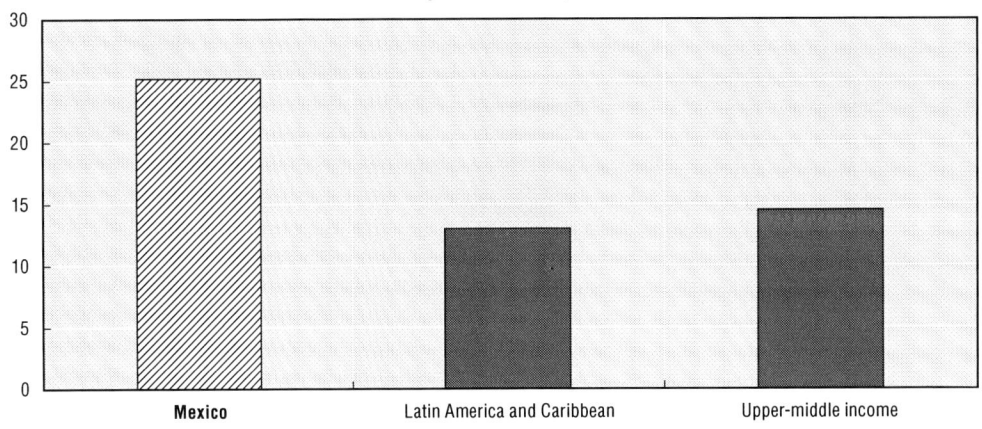

To get a construction permit

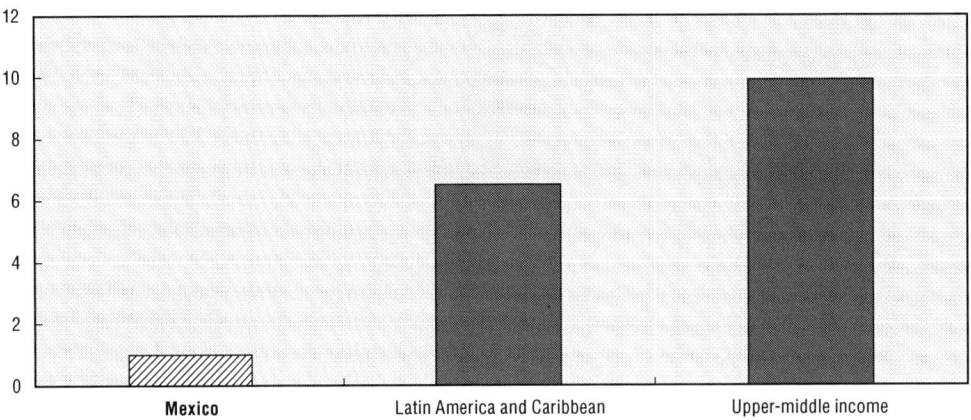

To get an import license

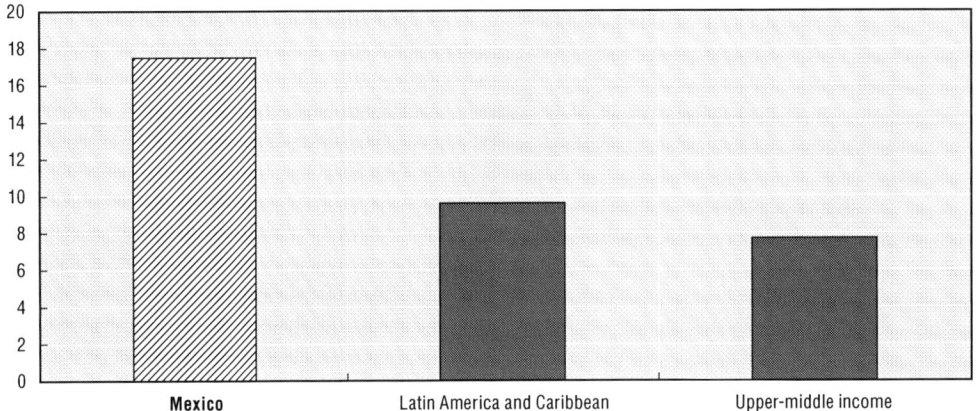

To get an operating license

Source: World Bank Enterprise Survey, 2010.

2.11. Conclusions

Mexico is well down the road of structural reform. As a result, most of the framework conditions conduce to entrepreneurship and SME development are at least partially in place. Furthermore, the government has shown awareness of the need for further reforms in relevant areas and has often been very active, such as in the case of regulatory barriers.

The key challenges to maintain the rate of progress achieved in recent years concern developing human resources, improving access to finance, reducing the burden of tax and social security, reforming business law and regulation and strengthening the innovation system.

With respect to human resources, the priorities are to boost spending per child in general education, to upgrade workforce skills and upgrade management competencies, and to introduce enterprise education in formal education with appropriate support for the provision of teaching materials and teacher training.

Government interventions have made significant impacts on improving the supply of debt finance, notably through the introduction and scaling up of loan guarantees, and is now stimulating the emergence of an SME equity market, and new fiscal incentives for private saving into equity funds could be important in this respect. These types of supply side interventions will continue to play a fundamental role in supporting SME development in the short and medium terms. In the long term it is also important to stimulate competition in the banking industry with the objective of increasing the motivation of financial institutions to seek profitable opportunities in SME lending, for example through facilitation of the creation of small co-operative banks. However, the solutions to the finance problem will need to go beyond supply-side interventions. One important priority is to shift the underlying SME culture towards borrowing from formal institutions, by improving awareness of formal finance opportunities among entrepreneurs and increasing their ability to put together sound proposals for external finance through appropriate advice, training and consultancy. Given the predominance of micro and informal enterprises in the Mexican SME population, and the impediments this implies for viable investment projects, developing credit history and protecting investors, significant progress will also be required in encouraging enterprise formalisation and increasing the productivity and profitability of the micro-enterprise sector.

In the area of tax and social security, a major step forwards in simplifying the tax system and reducing opportunities for tax avoidance and evasion was taken with the adoption of the alternative minimum tax on business income. This should be complemented by further reforms to reduce tax complexity. Reducing further the financial burdens of tax and social security payments would also act as an incentive to further enterprise start-up and SME development.

Regarding business law and regulation, much has been achieved in Mexico. Progress has been particularly important in reducing the number of days to set up a business for example and in the actions of the Federal Commission on Regulatory Reform. A priority now is to extend the better regulation commitment throughout the country, including by encouraging the extension of the SARE business registration system in as many localities as possible and the introduction of State Commissions for Regulatory Improvement (CEMER) in all states. Another priority is to review and reform the country's labour laws. These steps are important not just because of the opportunity to reduce the time and cost burdens of compliance on SMEs but also to reduce the scope for corruption and to reduce the incentive for entrepreneurs to operate in the informal sector.

Improving national and local innovation systems can also make an important impact on increasing the scale of innovative entrepreneurship and innovative SMEs, thus favouring those enterprises with the greatest potential for productivity growth and job creation. The positive initiatives taken over the last 12 years include the new science and technology laws and special programmes for SME innovation through the Innovation Fund and the SME Fund. These measures will help Mexico to exploit its strengths in its leading universities and public research centres and its FDI inflows of technologically competent foreign director investors. The priority for the future is to address low R&D spending by the business and government sectors and to strengthen networks for knowledge flows between universities and industry.

In the case of some of these framework conditions, improvements made today are likely to take some time to feed through into better economic performance because the problems are deep-seated and changes rarely happen overnight. This is the case for example for reducing the level of informality in the economy and changing attitudes towards borrowing from banks. However, policy interventions in these areas will reap substantial rewards and reduce the need for direct programme interventions in the longer term.

Box 2.2. **Specific recommendations on framework conditions for SMEs and entrepreneurship**

Invest in human resource development

- Roll out enterprise education across formal education institutions, including training and support measures to entrepreneurship teachers.

Facilitate access to finance

- Increase the outreach of the loan guarantee system to the SME population as an effective tool for improving access to finance and building formal debt markets in the short and medium terms.

- Increase competition in the banking sector to stimulate bank entry into profitable new markets in SME lending in the longer term, including through the promotion of small co-operative banks operating in loan sizes between those of large established banks and micro finance institutions.

- Introduce new fiscal incentives for private saving in equity funds targeted at investments in innovative start-ups and SMEs.

Simplify tax and regulation

- Simplify the design and operation of the tax system, applying the principle of Think Small First, and ensure that information about tax allowances is actively distributed to entrepreneurs through a variety of media.

- Continue the process of regulatory reform and spread it to the state and local levels, including through monitoring the time and cost involved in starting a new business in locations across the country and setting realistic targets for improvement.

- Review and reform labour laws focusing on encouraging enterprises to register and employ workers in the formal sector.

Reinforce innovation systems and local clusters

- Expand measures aimed at public and private investment in R&D and creating inter-firm and university-industry knowledge networks.

> ### Box 2.2. **Specific recommendations on framework conditions for SMEs and entrepreneurship** (cont.)
>
> **Facilitating access to finance**
>
> ● The case of the Small Business Investment Company (SBIC) programme in the US is described in Annex A.3. A series of privately-owned and managed investment funds make small subordinated loans and equity investments in early-stage and growth-oriented SMEs through the programme raising part of the finance from the sale of securities guaranteed by the US Small Business Administration.
>
> **Simplifying tax and regulation**
>
> ● Ukraine's Quick Regulation Strategy is described in Annex A.5. It illustrates an approach to the simplification of business regulations at local level through assistance to municipalities in seven cities under the direction of the State Committee on Regulatory Policy and Entrepreneurship.
>
> **Reinforcing local clusters**
>
> ● The PROFO initiative in Chile is described in Annex A.8. It provides incentives for SMEs in local clusters to work together through subsidised partnerships of at least 5 firms for joint initiatives such as accessing technological ideas, receiving consultancy support and participating in events for marketing.

References

Bruhn, M. (2008), "License to Sell: The Effect of Business Registration Reform on Entrepreneurial Activity in Mexico", *Policy Research Working Paper*, Series 4538, The World Bank.

OECD (2006), *The SME Financing Gap (Vol. 1) Theory and Evidence*, OECD Publishing, *http://dx.doi.org/10.1787/9789264029415-en*.

OECD (2010a), *Education at a Glance 2007: OECD Indicators*, OECD Publishing, Paris.

OECD (2010b), *OECD Science, Technology and Industry Outlook*, OECD Publishing, *http://dx.doi.org/10.1787/sti_outlook-2010-en*.

OECD (2011a), *OECD Economic Surveys: Mexico 2011*, OECD Publishing, *http://dx.doi.org/10.1787/eco_surveys-mex-2011-en*.

OECD (2011b), *Taxing Wages 2010*, OECD Publishing, *http://dx.doi.org/10.1787/tax_wages-2010-en*.

OECD (2011c), *OECD Science, Technology and Industry Scoreboard 2011*, OECD Publishing, *http://dx.doi.org/10.1787/sti_scoreboard-2011-en*.

OECD (2012), *OECD Science, Technology and Industry Outlook 2012*, OECD Publishing, *http://dx.doi.org/10.1787/sti_outlook-2012-en*.

World Bank (2012), *Doing Business 2012: Doing Business in a More Transparent World*, IFC/World Bank.

World Economic Forum (2008), *The Global Competitiveness Report 2008-2009*, World Economic Forum, Geneva.

World Economic Forum (2010), *The Global Competitiveness Report 2010-2011*, World Economic Forum, Geneva.

World Economic Forum (2011), *The Global Competitiveness Index*, Geneva, Switzerland.

ANNEX 2.A1

Technical details on taxation on corporate income figures

This annex gives technical information for the figure on taxation on corporate income.

For Australia, New Zealand and the United Kingdom, all with a non-calendar tax year, the rates shown are those in effect as of 1 July, 1 April and 5 April, respectively.

In Belgium, the effective CIT rate can be substantially reduced by a notional allowance for corporate equity.

In Chile, individuals and legal entities that are not resident or domiciled in Chile are taxed on any income derived from Chilean sources with a general tax rate of 35% (lower rates apply for some types of income and are available under double taxation agreements).

In Estonia, since 1 January 2000, the corporate income tax is levied on distributed profits.

For France, the rates include a surcharge, but do not include the local business tax (*taxe professionnelle*) or the turnover based solidarity tax (*contribution de solidarité*).

For Germany, the rates include the regional trade tax (*Gewerbesteuer*) and the surcharge.

For Hungary, the rates do not include the turnover based local business tax, the innovation tax, the financial institutions' surtaxes, the energy suppliers' surtax and the crisis taxes.

In Israel, within the VAT law, financial institutions pay taxes on the combination of their wages and salaries and their profits. These amounts are deductible from profits in the assessment of corporate income tax.

For Italy, these rates do not include the regional business tax (*Imposta Regionale sulle Attività Produttive*, IRAP).

In Poland, there is no sub-central government tax; however local authorities (of each level) participate in tax revenue at a given percentage for each level of local authority.

In Portugal, since 2009, two general tax rates are applied at a Central Government Level. A general tax rate of 12.5% is applied for the first EUR 12 500 of taxable income and a 25% tax rate is applied for the remaining amount of taxable income (when the total taxable income exceeds EUR 12 500).

For Switzerland, church taxes, which cannot be avoided by enterprises, are included.

For the United States, the sub-central rate is a weighted average state corporate marginal income tax rate.

Netherlands applies to taxable income over EUR 200 000.

Chapter 3

Strategic policy framework and delivery arrangements for SME and entrepreneurship promotion in Mexico

This chapter examines the strategic framework and delivery arrangements for SME and entrepreneurship policies and programmes and identifies future challenges. It reviews the strategic statements on which policy formulation is based. The structures and organisations involved in its delivery are also assessed, including the SME Fund, which is one of the major sources of programme funding in Mexico, and its approach to policy delivery through intermediary organisations together with the major delivery structures such as the Mexico Emprende Centres and the National System of Business Incubators. The programme portfolio is also examined in terms of the mix of expenditures, matched funding, numbers of businesses served and estimated job impacts across different stages of the enterprise life cycle and types of programme interventions.

3.1. The strategic framework

3.1.1. Description of the framework

The legal basis for the Mexican government's SME and entrepreneurship programmes derives from the Law for Development of the Competitiveness of Micro, Small and Medium Enterprises (SME Law) published in December 2002. This sets a broad cross-government target of "More and better jobs, more and better enterprises, and more and better entrepreneurs". By virtue of the 2002 SME Law, the Ministry of Economy has responsibility for the design and implementation of SME and entrepreneurship programmes. This responsibility is delegated to the Under Ministry for SMEs.

The 2002 SME Law also provided for the creation of a National Council for Competitiveness of SMEs. This was to be an inter-ministerial, inter-governmental body, including representatives of major sector and employer organisations and academia (31 members in total). Its mandate was to promote, analyse and monitor schemes, programmes, instruments and actions in support of SMEs. However, the Committee convened only once between 2007 and 2011.

The main policy actions for SMEs and entrepreneurship in the last six years have been promoted under the SME pillar of the Economy Sectoral Programme (ESP) 2007-12, which was designed by the Under Ministry for SMEs and links back to the objectives of the National Development Plan (NDP). However, at least eight other ministries have action plans that affect the development of SMEs and entrepreneurship (Agriculture, Education, Environment, Energy, Social Development, Tourism, etc.). The Under Ministry for SMEs has the responsibility to co-ordinate these actions with those of the SME pillar of the ESP. It also collaborates with Public Trusts in the delivery of various SME and entrepreneurship financing and innovation projects.

The priority of the SME pillar of the ESP was to provide a comprehensive support system that would (Secretaria de Economia, 2008):

1. contribute to the creation of jobs by promoting the creation of new businesses and the consolidation of existing SMEs, including meeting the special needs of micro-enterprises; and

2. encourage the creation of more and better jobs in the population of low-income entrepreneurs by promoting and strengthening productive projects.

Actions under the first objective were to:

● promote entrepreneurship education in schools;

● strengthen the national system of business incubators;

● design and support seed and venture capital schemes accompanied with advice and support to newly-created SMEs;

● provide specialised training and consulting to enable micro-enterprises to consolidate as companies;

- develop new distribution and marketing channels for micro-enterprises and promote a greater number of productive partnerships among micro-enterprises;
- strengthen the national system of guarantees and improve access to finance schemes;
- develop models of commercial modernisation and technological innovation among all size segments of SMEs;
- support fast-growing enterprises with business acceleration and franchise programmes;
- establish technology parks to speed up technological innovation;
- attract SMEs to tractor enterprises through supplier development, government procurement and other support mechanisms; and
- establish a national one-stop shop system for access to SME support services through development of Mexico Emprende Centres.

Actions under the second objective were to strengthen the productive capacity of social enterprises and the productive projects of low-income entrepreneurs through support for management, training and consultancy, innovation and technological development, financing and marketing.

These directions have guided the Ministry of Economy's SME and entrepreneurship support programmes over the past six years.

From all evidence, the formulation of the ESP was founded on good practice. At the outset, the Under Ministry for SMEs completed a review of the effectiveness of existing SME programmes, consulted with entrepreneurs and SME sector stakeholders and took into consideration the recommendations of the OECD review of SME policies implemented in the preceding period (OECD, 2007).

This exercise led to a reformulation of policy with respect to the core SME and entrepreneurship support measures supported by the SME Fund. Funding for certain programmes, such as the Centres for Productive Articulation and Innovation Laboratories was discontinued. Funding for other programmes, such as the PYMExporta Centres, was transferred to ProMexico following its creation as the national agency for exports and investment promotion at the end of 2007. New programmes were created. In addition, the former network of Business Development Centres (BDCs) was replaced with a new system of standardised Mexico Emprende Centres providing a one-stop shop for the provision of business support services. The overall goal of improving the SME competitiveness was maintained but a stronger emphasis was introduced on job creation as an outcome, as per the priorities of the NDP 2007-12. Furthermore, entrepreneurship promotion was incorporated into the policy framework together with new activities for the promotion of SME innovation.

The new strategic framework behind the SME Fund was also reorganised in order to increase customisation to the needs of different clients and to be clearer and more coherent. The result was a 5 x 5 model on two dimensions: enterprise segment and intervention type. The enterprise segment dimension classes enterprises by their size and development stage, distinguishing between new entrepreneurs (women and men in the process of creating, developing or strengthening an enterprise), micro-enterprises, SMEs, gazelle enterprises (young and fast-growing SMEs with potential for above average job generation) and tractor enterprises (large enterprises with operations in Mexico that can be at the centre of productive supply chains). This method of organising policy support enables better precision in meeting client needs. On the intervention type dimension, support has been regrouped into five categories: financing; training and consultancy services; management; marketing and commercialisation;[1] and innovation and technology development. This has enabled a clearer vision of the distribution of support and more coherence between actions.

At the same time, the 13 core programmes of the previous period were reorganised into five cross-cutting programmes matching the enterprise segments: the New Entrepreneurs National Programme; the National Programme for Micro-enterprises; the National SMEs Programme; the National Programme for Gazelle Enterprises, and the National Programme for Tractor Enterprises. The result of this reorganisation is the 5 x 5 SME and entrepreneurship policy framework of the SME Fund illustrated in Figure 3.1. It shows the "pathways" or "moving walkway" approach that has been adopted, emphasising the progression of entrepreneurs and enterprises from the point of becoming interested in starting a business, to start-up, to early-stage development, to consolidation and growth.

Figure 3.1. **Organising framework of SME Fund actions 2007-12**

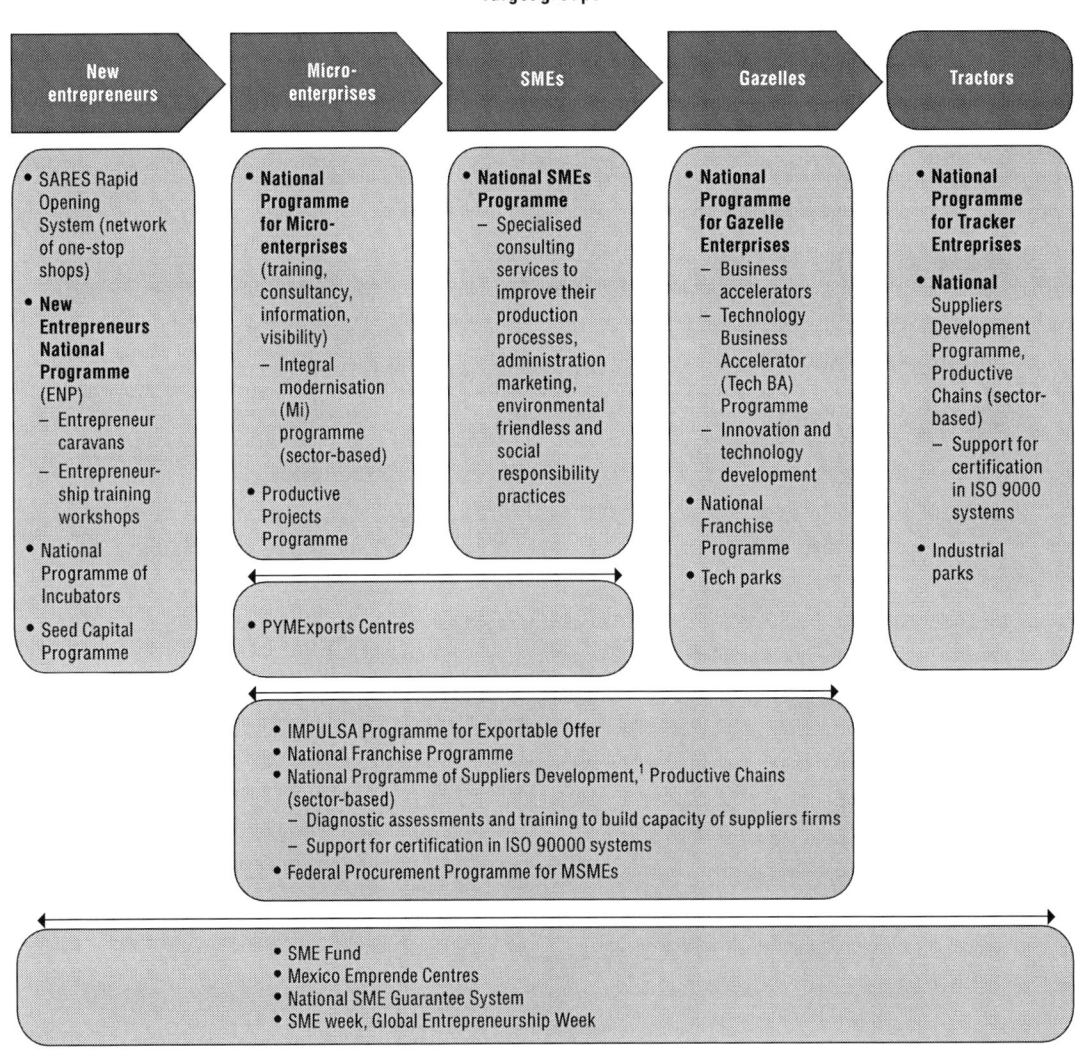

1. The National Suppliers Development Programme is intended to feed into the Tractors programme, but the beneficiaries are SMEs, which are being upgraded to act as suppliers to tractor enterprises.
Source: OECD elaboration based on information from Mexican Ministry of Economy.

In addition, State governments have powers to design their own programmes and the possibility to provide matching funding to SME Fund programmes and to participate in their implementation as intermediaries. In this respect, the Association of State Economic Development Secretaries (AMSDE), which consists of ministers from the 32 States, meets annually with the Under Ministry for SMEs to agree the amount of SME Fund resources to be allocated to each State and the conditions to be met by the State in order to receive the funding. In 2010, MXN 1.2 billion (USD 95 million) were allocated to the States, an average of MXN 37.5 million (USD 3 million) per State.

There is a State Committee on SMEs and Competitiveness in each State, which includes representatives from chambers of commerce and industry, business associations, state governments and the Federal Ministry of Economy. These committees are in charge of the administration of SME Fund projects at the State level, including the evaluation of project proposals coming from intermediary organisations within the State. If the State Committee is not convinced of the benefit of a specific programme for its state, then no matching resources will be released for projects and an unfavourable judgement of the project will be given to the Federal Ministry of Economy, leading in most cases to a decision not to provide any support.

State governments and development agencies cannot design their own SME policies and programmes through the federal budget. If they have policies or programmes that are inconsistent with the SME Fund programmes, they must finance them independently. This rarely happens because it is easier to take advantage of the cost-sharing of national programmes.

3.1.2. Strengths

One of the key strengths of the current policy framework is that it establishes a clear vision for the SME and entrepreneurship actions of the SME Fund, organised by five types of intervention and five life cycle stages of entrepreneurship.

The resulting framework is also comprehensive in covering the intervention areas identified as priorities for governments in the OECD Bologna Charter on SME Policies and the OECD Bologna Process, to which Mexico subscribes, and providing support to SMEs and entrepreneurs across a broad cross-section of sectors, including tourism, trade and services as well as manufacturing.

An important strengthening relative to earlier policies is the new emphasis on promoting entrepreneurship as well as established SMEs. This is in line with recent advances in policy knowledge and learning regarding the complementarity of entrepreneurship-focused policy and SME-focused policy and the incremental value of adopting an entrepreneurship policy approach (Lundström and Stevenson 2002, 2005; Stevenson and Lundström, 2002). In particular, the New Entrepreneurs National Programme includes initiatives to motivate interest in entrepreneurship among the population in order to facilitate a pipeline of new, competent and growth-oriented future entrepreneurs such as the *Caravan dos emprendedores* programme, which reaches out to people living in remote locations through travelling mobile units increasing awareness of entrepreneurship and attracting entrepreneurs into the national system of incubation.

Another important development has been the formulation of the National Programme for Micro-Enterprises in order to address the need to increase micro-enterprise productivity, upgrade the entrepreneurial and managerial skills of micro firm owners and bring more of these enterprises into the formal economy where they can have more opportunities to grow. This development responds to previous OECD recommendations.

Although gazelles had previously received support through the former Innovation and Technology Programme (particularly, the Accelerators Programme) and the Suppliers Development Programme, the new SME policy framework gives them an increased visibility, in line with recent knowledge about their disproportionate impacts on economic growth and job creation. Furthermore, the approach is proactive in seeking to select potential high-growth enterprises, but is balanced by broader support for innovation and training for the SME population as a whole, which mitigates the risks of poor performance in identifying potential growth enterprises.

A further strength is that State governments and state-level stakeholders are involved in the promotion and selection of projects for support by the SME Fund. This increases the degree of local tailoring of programmes whilst contributing to policy coherence.

3.1.3. Areas for improvement

Despite these good practices, there are three main opportunities for improvement of the SME and entrepreneurship policy framework in the future.

A policy statement on SME and entrepreneurship development

There is currently no high-level and integrated policy statement on SME and entrepreneurship development actions in Mexico. The introduction of such a statement would help to guide and co-ordinate the various government ministries, agencies and funds involved. It is true that SME and entrepreneurship development objectives are documented in the SME pillar of the ESP and that the President's annual report on implementation of the NDP states progress against SME milestones. However, these communications do not set out the action lines of programme design and operation. At the same time, while the operational guidelines of the SME Fund include its objectives, targets and mechanisms, this relates only to one component of SME and entrepreneurship policy and not to its sum. It excludes, for instance, government procurement, regulatory improvement and support for innovation systems.

A succinct, high-level policy document would identify the main SME and entrepreneurship policy actions expected to be delivered across government, provide a framework to fit them together and increase clarity on the objectives of policy and how to address trade-offs, such as those that exist between SME competitiveness and job creation. It would also set out the responsibilities and specific objectives of each ministry, agency and fund and the actions they undertake. It would also be useful in providing leadership and guidance to state and municipal governments in their own SME and entrepreneurship development approaches.

Given that the definition of SME policies depends on the National Development Plan, such a policy statement will need to be introduced at the time of the next revision of the National Development Plan in 2013.

Stronger linkages between SME and entrepreneurship policy and innovation policy

There are already important connections between the SME and entrepreneurship and the innovation policy areas in Mexico. For example, the 5 x 5 framework of the SME Fund contains a channel for technology and innovation actions aimed at SMEs, while the scope of the Innovation Fund extends to the support of SME innovation projects. This is consistent with the policy evolution evident in many OECD countries over the past decade as they have increasingly recognised the cross-over between SME and entrepreneurship policy and innovation policy.

Notwithstanding these existing linkages, there is potential for increased synergy. The National Innovation Programme approved in 2011 aims to support strategic sectors with high innovation potential and put in place six pillars for action: 1) building the domestic and international demand for Mexico's innovation (products, services and business models); 2) strengthening the regulatory and institutional framework, including technology transfer offices; 3) investing in human capital; 4) strengthening business innovation and the culture of innovation in society; 5) financing innovation; and 6) generating strategic knowledge. It will do this in such a way as to build the linkages among actors in the innovation ecosystem, including SMEs. The Under Ministry of SMEs should collaborate closely with the Under Ministry of Trade and Industry and CONACYT, which have the lead on implementing the policy and co-ordinating across government in the innovation area, in order to help develop this agenda and secure appropriate activities for the commercialisation of innovation through new start-ups and SMEs, focusing in particular on pillar 4 of the National Innovation Programme.

Reinvigoration of the National Council for Competitiveness of SMEs and establishment of an SME Advisory Committee

The National Council for Competitiveness of SMEs was set up with the mandate to promote, analyse and monitor SME support programmes but has regrettably met only once during the past five years. Such councils, in place in many countries, play an important role in ensuring cross-ministerial alignment of policies and measures targeting SME development and provide a forum for input and advice from private sector stakeholders on policy design. The Council has recently been reconvened, and the Ministry of Economy should commit to organising regular meetings.

In parallel, many countries have established formal SME Advisory Committees consisting of SME owners and their representative associations, to provide input and advice to the government on SME challenges, needs and responsive policy initiatives. Such a committee is not in place in Mexico. While there is a private sector Council of Communication providing the business sector with a voice in affairs of national interest, its membership is mainly comprised of large firms. The Ministry of Economy could explore the potential of forming a similar Council to as act as an advisory body to government on SME policies and programmes.

3.2. The delivery system

The SME and entrepreneurship strategy in Mexico is supported by a policy delivery structure that seeks to ensure the funding of programmes through the SME Fund. This finances the bulk of SME and entrepreneurship support programmes and is co-ordinated with and complemented by other support across government. It achieves outreach to beneficiary firms and entrepreneurs through a system of intermediary organisations, employed by the SME Fund to formulate and implement projects on behalf of government.

3.2.1. SME Fund

The creation of the SME Fund has enabled Mexico to make a step change in the scale and quality of services delivered to SMEs and entrepreneurs. It was created in 2004 by combining four previously separate enterprise support funds and is now the most important instrument for the provision of federal support services to SMEs and entrepreneurs in Mexico.

The SME Fund supports projects in the five categories of support and five enterprise segments described above. In addition, the Ministry of Economy uses the SME Fund to finance national promotional activities, such as the annual Small Business Week.

The Fund's rules of operation and procedures manual are published annually and made available on its website: *www.fondopyme.gob.mx*. The Ministry of Economy is required to prepare an annual report to Congress on the SME Fund with evaluations of its results, impacts and processes. The evaluation plan is approved by the Treasury.

There have been a number of refinements in the administration of the SME Fund over the past six years to improve its ease of access and transparency to the intermediary organisations that deliver projects with SME Fund participation. This includes the introduction of an electronic information system and web-based platform that enables project proposals and all project reporting documentation to be submitted online and project applicants to track the progress of project approval. Each year, a clear set of Fund operating rules and procedures are posted on its website, as well as specific guidelines and handbooks for the operation of particular SME Fund programmes and reporting templates.

However, the SME Fund rules of operation have become more complex and difficult to comply with in recent years, causing many problems to intermediary organisations and business service providers, especially with the closing of projects and the required proofs to verify that the resources were appropriately and correctly utilised. From 2012, the Minister of Economy has publicly promised a new system of SME Fund transparency that will optimise processes to avoid the recapture of information and duplication of functions involved in processing SME Fund applications.[2]

Potential reforms that can contribute to this effort include:

Changing from an annual cycle of certification of intermediary organisations and service providers to a longer 24- or 36-month cycle. This would reduce the costs and efforts involved in certification, and would be justified if supported by appropriate monitoring and reporting during the life of the contracts.

Further simplification and reduction of the reporting and verification requirements for delivery intermediaries. The opportunities for further simplification should be explored, while at the same time maintaining the necessary accountability, transparency and confidence in the use of public funds. One example could be the introduction of bi-annual rather than quarterly reporting. Furthermore, the reporting requirements have been increasing each year and becoming wider, for example extending from requesting information on the number of jobs to detailing the duration of each job. This additional information is useful and, indeed, further information such as the qualification and skill level of the job would help provide a better picture of support, but this level of analysis may be more properly suited to formal evaluation of project outcomes and impact rather than project monitoring.

Moving from standard rules to the differentiation of reporting requirements for different types of activities (e.g. high-tech, intermediate and traditional businesses). This reform would adapt reporting to the different business development processes involved for different types and sizes of businesses, for example high tech firms that need long time periods to prove the viability of business ideas compared to traditional businesses that can be trading and directly employing people in much shorter time periods.

Shortening the time required to process project proposals from receipt of the initial project proposals through assessment and approval and disbursement of project funding. Some intermediaries have had to use bridging funds to enable projects to progress because of the delays in receiving programme funding. Others, such as state governments and municipalities, have not become intermediaries because of the delays involved and have sought to find other ways to provide direct support to companies, albeit with less resourcing. In addition, the programme funding often arrives late in the financial year and yet still has to be spent in that same financial year.

Shifting to multi-annual funding. Because SME Fund budget decisions are made on an annual basis, projects are funded one year at a time, and must be closed before the fiscal year end. Delays in approving project renewals for the next fiscal year mean that host organisations might not have their projects approved for the coming year in time to ensure continuity of programmes and services. Longer term and more timely provision of programme funding would allow intermediaries to plan and schedule their activities more effectively.

Better follow-up to monitor the impact of support and assistance on the client firms. Without overburdening the intermediary organisations with compliance, it is necessary to improve the system of data collection with better quality data on the clients they serve.

3.2.2. The system of intermediary organisations

The majority of SME Fund projects are delivered through intermediary organisations, such as State governments, chambers of commerce, business associations and universities. Organisations wishing to act as intermediaries may submit bids for projects. Bids are then selected for funding on a competitive basis. There are two types of bid: those in response to direct propositions made to intermediaries by the Under Ministry of SMEs for core SME support projects such as the Mexico Emprende Centres (MECs) and business incubators and those for other projects that respond to the main programme categories and objectives stipulated in the SME Fund rules of operation but which have not been specifically invited, for example offers to provide diagnostic and consultancy services to innovative SMEs. As a rule of thumb, intermediary organisations cover a portion of the costs. In some cases, the beneficiary SMEs and entrepreneurs also contribute through fees and service charges, such as for consultancy services.

Intermediary organisations upload their funding bids on the SME Fund website, indicating the suppliers they will use to deliver the services. Once the Ministry of Economy has approved the list of programmes and/or projects, the central Treasury releases the project funding to the intermediary organisation. Once the project is completed, the intermediary organisations submit a project completion report online, providing proof that the service was delivered, the agreed-to objectives were met, and any suppliers were actually paid. If the agreed objectives are not fully met, such as the minimum number of jobs to be created in assisted enterprises, the intermediary must return a portion of the funding.

The SME Fund currently makes use of approximately 600 intermediary organisations. They include universities and technical institutes; business chambers and associations; labour unions; state and municipal governments; civil associations; corporate societies; financial trusts, such as the national development bank (NAFIN); non-bank financial institutions (NBFIs);[3] commercial banks; public agencies and trusts; local civil associations involved with Science and Technology promoted by CONACYT,[4] the National Committee for Productivity and Innovation (COMPITE);[5] the Mexico-United-States Foundation for Science (FUMEC);[6] the

Capitalisation and Investment Fund for the Rural Sector (FOCIR); the Technological Innovation Fund (FIT); the National Fund for Support of Solidarity Enterprises (FONAES); and ProMexico,[7] among others; as well as private sector training and consultancy firms.

The resulting SME Fund delivery structure as operated through the intermediaries includes:

- 200 Mexico Emprende Centre SME service centres (primarily hosted by chambers and business associations);
- 500 incubators (70% hosted by universities and technical institutes);
- 50 business accelerators (served primarily by private sector organisations);
- 8 international technology business accelerators (5 in the US, 2 in Canada, and 1 in Spain);
- 31 Technology Parks;
- more than 35 non-bank financial institutions (NBFIs) and several commercial banks delivering the National Guarantees Programmes;
- 150 private sector training firms working under franchises to deliver entrepreneurship training programmes to potential entrepreneurs;
- 986 financial advisors to assist SMEs with their loan requests;
- a National System of SME consultants, consisting of thousands of private sector consultants who are linked to incubators, accelerators, supplier development programmes, the franchise programme and the Mexico Emprende Centres;
- a System of Technological and Business Assistance (SATE), organised by FUMEC to provide consulting services to high-technology enterprises;
- 13 Investment Clubs (more commonly known as business angel networks in other countries);
- an Entrepreneurial Capital Fund of Funds for SMEs (e.g. Mexico Ventures);
- public trusts and other federal agencies.

The eventual target is to have 1 000 points of federal service. This is not an unreasonable target for a country with the population size and regional dispersion of Mexico. SMEs operate locally and it is therefore important to have local access points for information, training, advisory and consultancy services, and linkages to local financing sources and specialised technical assistance. For example, Canada, with a population only 30% of that in Mexico, has over 500 federal points of service for SMEs, not including the SME support offices provided by the provincial governments. Some of these points of service are government offices, such as the network of Canada Business Service Centres, others are government-funded or supported non-governmental or community based organisations that provide entrepreneurship training, advice and financing to SMEs, and others, such as university enterprise centres, technology transfer centres, and incubators, are co-financed by the federal or provincial governments.

Taking into consideration all the actors involved in the delivery process and the benefits to SMEs, a recent independent evaluation of the SME Fund concluded that its benefits exceed its costs (Centrode Estudios Económicos, 2011). One of the reasons for the success is that the Fund has created a system of intermediary organisations, including chambers of commerce, business associations, universities and state governments, that are able to help design, deliver and co-fund policy.

In common with many other OECD countries, the policy choice has been taken in Mexico to deliver SME and entrepreneurship programmes through third-party intermediary organisations, as opposed to the alternative of establishing a single government or arm's length body to manage the implementation of the SME policy and programmes, such as an SME Agency, similar to the US Small Business Administration (SBA).[8]

The use of a set of third-party intermediaries offers three important benefits:

1. The use of a diversity of intermediaries helps to achieve a wide outreach of support to different types of beneficiary SMEs across the sectors and regions of the country, exploiting the connections of the intermediary organisations to their client groups, without requiring the establishment of a large network of government offices.

2. The system builds capacities in the non-government sector and creates a private sector market for SME support services, rather than crowding-out these actors.

3. Innovation can be promoted across the system by permitting new ideas to emerge and be tested and encouraging the sharing of good practices across the intermediary network.

In Mexico, the critical consideration was the need to rapidly secure wide outreach of SME and entrepreneurship support across different SME segments the country, and it has been effective in doing this.

There are nonetheless co-ordination and management issues as well as potentially large transactions costs inherent in managing a large network of third-party delivery organisations such as this. In particular, the level and quality of service is much easier to control in a government-operated and managed system than in a third party arrangement with many intermediary organisations.

To maximise the effectiveness of a system operating through a large number of diverse intermediaries, it is important for the government to monitor the quality of service delivery and ensure the competence of the third-party agents to act on the government's behalf as well as to secure effective cross-referral of enterprises among the different service providers. Efforts are being made in Mexico in all of these areas, and this work should be pursued further without creating administrative blockages.

Public investments have been made in the intermediary organisations with the aim of achieving quality and homogeneity in the services they provide. These efforts should continue, emphasising in particular the training and certification of business development services staff. Evaluations of the effectiveness of different intermediary organisations and intervention approaches are undertaken, but could be strengthened in their robustness and used increasingly for concentrating support on the most effective providers and upgrading the system. A particular effort is also needed on improving the referral of enterprises to relevant intermediaries and support. This can build on the redesign of the SME Fund programme structure towards a "moving sidewalk" where new entrepreneurs are nurtured into the system and then handed on from one project (and intermediary organism) to another as they take the next step in the business development process.

Given the use of many different delivery agents, there are co-ordination issues with respect to the hand-over of SMEs and entrepreneurs to other programmes and providers, and more attention should be paid to helping them move to the next stage of development. In this respect, it would be useful to create regional and local networks of service providers and convene regular meetings to share experiences and status reports among them. It would also be very useful to have a client information tracking system that could monitor the conversion rates of individuals and firms from one entrepreneurial pathway of programme support to another.

3.3. The SME Fund portfolio and mix

The SME Fund has been providing substantial and increasing resources to SME development in recent years, both for productive projects and for loan guarantees, and this is required to meet government objectives for economic development and poverty reduction. Furthermore, to secure appropriate levels of SME and entrepreneurship support in the future, Congress amended the 2002 SME Law in late 2011 to stipulate that the SME Fund budget cannot be less than in the previous year. This is an important legislative change since it will provide the foundation for policy planning and consistency in SME programmes.

As well as the overall magnitude of funding, it is also important to consider how it is distributed across the policy portfolio in terms of the five target enterprise segments and the five support categories of the SME Fund. This permits an overview of policy priorities and the extent to which they appear appropriate to needs. In this section we examine the distribution of the SME Fund budget across enterprise segments and support categories together with the distribution of matching funding by partners including State governments and business associations, showing the degree to which the various programme actions are able to lever additional resources, and the distribution of the estimated job impacts of SME Fund projects.

3.3.1. Ministry of Economy SME Fund priorities

Table 3.1 shows the distribution of budget allocations for productive projects across the SME Fund portfolio during 2009-11, i.e. covering all expenditure excluding loan guarantees, which represented 70% of SME Fund resources in 2011. It is clear that SMEs, rather than nascent entrepreneurs, micro firms or gazelles, have absorbed the largest share of the productive projects funding, at 46% of the total. However, the share of the Fund allocated to new entrepreneurs and micro-enterprises increased within the period, which is in line with Mexico's need to develop new entrepreneurs for job creation and to upgrade and formalise micro-enterprises. As Mexico advances its economy, it may be appropriate to earmark more

Table 3.1. **SME Fund budget allocations for productive projects by enterprise segment and support category, 2009-11**

As a percentage of the total productive projects budget

	Financing	Training and consulting	Marketing/ commercialisation	Business management	Innovation/ technological development	Proportion of SME Fund by enterprise segment	Total (pesos)
I. New entrepreneurs	-	10.2	-	-	-	10.2	990 127 478
II. Micro-enterprises/franchises	-	7.8	0.7	-	-	8.5	820 048 217
III. SMEs	30.3	7.9	0.1	8.0	0.1	46.3	4 480 772 955
IV. Gazelles	-	4.6	0.4	0.2	6.2	11.3	1 090 715 936
V. Tractor companies	-	6.3	3.0	1.0	0.3	10.6	1 028 477 749
VI. Organisation of SME events/ other activities/promotion tools	-	3.7	1.2	0.2	0.0	5.1	497 244 655
VII. Others	1.8	0.0	0.0	6.2	0.0	8.0	775 000 000
Proportion of SME Fund by support category	32.1	40.5	5.3	15.6	6.6	100.0	
Three-year total (pesos)	**3 103 562 765**	**3 922 689 120**	**511 485 083**	**1 508 989 430**	**635 660 592**		**9 682 386 990**

Notes: Figures are rounded to one decimal place. The figures exclude SME Fund spending on loan guarantees.
Source: Mexican Ministry of Economy.

resources for supporting gazelles and SME upgrading in the supply chains of "tractor" enterprises because of their strong potential to contribute to innovation and growth.

The largest share of support by type of policy intervention (41%) has been allocated to training and consulting, with nearly one-half of that targeted at new entrepreneurs and micro-enterprises. About one-third of the budget was allocated to financing support programmes, although it should be recalled that loan guarantees are excluded from the Table and represent substantial additional expenditure. About 15% of the SME Fund productive projects budget was allocated to business management.

By contrast, innovation and technological development projects were allocated less than 7% of the total budget; almost all of this being allocated to gazelles. This raises an important policy question about whether sufficient priority is given to supporting innovation in growth enterprises, which are so critical to job creation and economic growth, although it should be noted that the Technological Innovation Fund provides an additional funding source for SME innovation projects. The smallest budget allocation has been for marketing/commercialisation support, which accounted for just over 5% of the budget during 2009-11.

3.3.2. Matching funding priorities of SME Fund partners

Ministry of Economy SME Fund allocations are matched by various partners including State and municipal governments, universities and the private sector. As shown in Table 3.2, these matching funds made up approximately 36% of the total productive projects budget during the period 2009-11. The largest single contributors to this portion of the budget were State governments and the private sector (which covers some of the costs of business services it receives).

Table 3.2. **Distribution of the SME Fund and matching funds for productive projects according to enterprise segment, 2009-11**

As a percentage of the total productive projects budget

Category	National Ministry of Economy	State government	Municipal government	Academic sector	Private sector	Other	Overall distribution
I. New entrepreneurs	10.2	0.2	0.0	8.0	0.9	51.7	9.9
II. Micro-enterprises	8.5	2.7	12.0	0.0	13.7	3.6	8.2
III. SMEs	46.3	16.2	12.1	0.1	27.8	23.3	37.3
IV. Gazelles	11.3	32.1	33.0	90.3	27.6	16.2	18.7
V. Tractor enterprises	10.6	41.9	39.8	1.1	22.1	1.2	15.2
VI. Organisation of SME events/ other activities/promotion tools	5.1	6.8	3.1	0.5	7.9	4.1	5.6
VII. Others (according to the rules of operation)	8.0	0.0	0.0	0.0	0.0	0.0	5.1
Total funds (pesos)	9 682 386 990	1 652 800 060	70 059 076	420 454 743	2 402 050 025	855 563 453	15 083 314 347
Share of total	64.2	11.0	0.5	2.8	15.9	5.7	100.0

Notes: Calculated from data provided by the Ministry of Economy. The column percentages indicate the distribution of each partners' funding to each of the enterprise segments and activities. Each column adds to 100%. Figures are given to one decimal place. There may be rounding errors. These data exclude spending on loan guarantees.
Source: Mexican Ministry of Economy.

One of the objectives set out in the ESP 2007-12, was to increase the leverage ratio of the SME Fund from a factor of 1.7 in 2006 to a factor of 3.0 by 2012. However, during the period 2009-11, the leverage ratio stood at only 1.6. This may be related in part to complexities in the operation of the SME Fund discussed above in relation to application, auditing and payment procedures. Notably, the State governments' contributions declined by almost one-half from MXN 374.6 million (USD 29.7 million) in 2007 to MXN 193.4 million (USD 15.3 million) in 2011, while the municipal governments' commitments, although smaller in scale, declined from MXN 83.7 million (USD 6.6 million) to MXN 20.9 million (USD 1.65 million). This suggests that the Ministry of Economy should either adjust its leverage objective downward or take more proactive steps to advocate and facilitate increased funding commitments from State governments and other partners.

In terms of revealed priorities, the budget choices of the matching funding partners, as shown in Table 3.2, reveal a stronger involvement of State and municipal governments in projects related to tractor enterprises and gazelles, while the academic sector tended to prioritise gazelles projects.

3.3.3. Businesses served and job impacts of SME Fund projects

The monitoring information on the SME Fund collected by the Under Ministry for SMEs includes details of the number of enterprises served. Table 3.3 reveals that during the period 2009-11, some 235 921 existing businesses and 26 862 new businesses were served (i.e. an annual average of 78 640 existing businesses supported and 8 954 new businesses created). This represents substantial activity. At the same time, however, this represents only 2% of all new businesses created and 2% of the stock of existing SMEs in any year, implying that there is much room for further expansion of programme reach.

Table 3.3. **Business served by SME Fund productive projects**

	Existing businesses served					New businesses served				
	2009	2010	2011	2009-11	2009-11	2009	2010	2011	2009-11	2009-11
	Number			(number)	(per cent)	Number			(number)	(per cent)
New entrepreneurs	1 200			1 200	0.5	6 107	8 467	10 047	24 621	91.7
Micro-enterprises	13 479	14 654	18 471	46 604	19.8		296	130	426	1.6
Small and medium-sized enterprises	16 134	24 521	8 305	48 960	20.8	1 221	424		1 645	6.1
Gazelles	4 687	2 658	1 256	8 601	3.6	13	17	4	34	0.1
Tractors	10 193	9 668	8 936	28 797	12.2	20	116		136	0.5
SME events/promotion	34 228	45 512	20 454	100 194	42.5					
Other		995	570	1 565	0.7					
Total	**79 921**	**98 008**	**57 992**	**235 921**	**100.0**	**7 361**	**9 320**	**10 181**	**26 862**	**100.0**

Note: Column percentages represent the distribution of businesses and jobs across the each of the enterprise segments/activities for each year. Data for 2011 represent projected goals.
Source: Mexican Ministry of Economy.

A central purpose of the Fund is to make a contribution to employment. This can happen in two ways, both shown in Table 3.4. The first is by providing support to maintain existing employment and the second is to stimulate the creation of new jobs. The distinction between created and maintained jobs is potentially important since a plausible case can be made that dynamic economies are characterised by their ability to create or generate new jobs, rather than by their ability to retain or maintain existing jobs.[9] It is estimated that some 170 064 jobs were maintained, and 105 268 new jobs created during the period 2009-11.

It is interesting to note that in the early years of the operation of the Fund, the vast bulk of jobs were maintained rather than created. However, as the Fund has developed, the proportion of total jobs created has risen. In the years up to and including 2006, created

Table 3.4. **Estimated jobs maintained and created by SME Fund productive projects**

Category	Jobs maintained					Jobs created				
	2009	2010	2011	2009-11 (number)	2009-11 (per cent)	2009	2010	2011	2009-11 (number)	2009-11 (per cent)
	Number					Number				
New entrepreneurs	1 198			1 198	0.7	16 002	29 635	36 565	82 202	78.1
Micro-enterprises	9 258	14 028	28 651	51 937	30.5		1 816	860	2 676	2.5
Small and medium-sized enterprises	12 727	28 363	23 413	64 503	37.9	8 880	3 050	790	12 720	21.1
Gazelles	1 741	29 731	9 584	41 056	24.1	343	3 162	553	4 058	3.9
Tractors	728	1 014	8 571	10 313	6.1	2 160	787	665	3 612	3.4
SME events/promotion	1 057			1 057	0.6					
Other										
Total	26 709	73 136	70 219	170 064	100.0	27 385	38 450	39 433	105 268	100.0

Notes: Column percentages represent the distribution of businesses and jobs across the each of the enterprise segments/activities for each year. Data for 2011 represent projected goals.
Source: Mexican Ministry of Economy.

jobs were less than 5% of total jobs but jobs created had risen to about 60% during the period 2009-11. This is an important and desirable change, although there must be some caution attached to the reliability of these estimates since they come from monitoring records rather than more rigorous evaluation. A relatively high proportion of the jobs created were in new enterprises although SME growth was also significant. Surprisingly, gazelles have been responsible for only a small share of new jobs created from 2009-11.

It is also possible to calculate approximate cost per job estimates for the SME Fund for the period 2009-11. These estimates are shown in Table 3.5. At first sight, and in terms of job impacts alone, these data appear to suggest that the new allocations of one-fifth of the 2009-11 SME Fund budget to new entrepreneurs and micro-enterprises is warranted, given their impact on creating and maintaining employment compared with the costs incurred. The data also suggest that programmes for gazelles are relatively cost effective in terms of total job impacts. When focusing on job creation alone, initiatives for new entrepreneurship appear to offer the greatest cost efficiency. However, these estimates need to be treated with some caution because they are based on monitoring data rather than more robust evaluation data and because they consider only job impacts and not the extent to which other objectives of policy are being achieved, such as productivity growth. These issues are discussed in Chapter 6.

Table 3.5. **SME Fund expenditure on productive projects and estimated results, 2009-11**

Category	Ministry expenditure (MXN millions)	Total public expenditure (MXN millions)	Jobs maintained	Jobs created	Total public cost (MXN) per job	Ministry (MXN) cost per job	Ministry cost (MXN) per job created
New entrepreneurs	990	1 470	1 198	82 202	17 623	11 871	12 045
Micro-enterprises	820	904	51 937	2 676	16 554	15 015	306 428
SMEs	4 481	4 956	64 503	12 720	64 180	58 027	352 280
Gazelles	1 091	2 162	41 056	4 058	47 927	24 183	268 851
Tractors	1 028	1 765	10 313	3 612	126 726	73 824	284 607
SME events/promotion	497	644	1 057	0	609 387	470 199	-
Other	775	775	0	0	-	-	-
Total	9 682	12 676	170 064	105 268	46 039	35 165	91 975

Note: Data for 2011 represent projected goals.
Source: Mexican Ministry of Economy.

3.4. Conclusions

One of the major achievements of the Mexican government over the past 12 years has been the introduction of a sound policy framework to support SMEs and entrepreneurship and increase their contribution to economic growth and poverty reduction. "More and better jobs, more and better enterprises, and more and better entrepreneurs" are the objectives of this new SME and entrepreneurship policy agenda. They were first given serious weight through the actions under the Entrepreneurial Development Plan 2001-06, as promoted and co-ordinated by the Under Ministry of SMEs in the Ministry of Economy, and through the creation of the SME Fund by the Under Ministry. During the period 2007-12 these measures were further reinforced within the strategic framework of the Economy Sectoral Programme. This extended policy to cover nascent entrepreneurship and micro-enterprises and increased the scale of support to SMEs and entrepreneurship as a whole.

The rationale for the SME and entrepreneurship policy strategy adopted by the Mexican government is clear and appropriate and addresses the intervention needs highlighted elsewhere in this report. Thus attention is paid to stimulating entrepreneurial ambitions and activities in the population, raising productivity levels in the micro-enterprise sector, and supporting innovative SMEs, gazelles and exporters, as well as improving practices in established and traditional SMEs. The strategy also emphasises addressing the need to improve entrepreneurial skills and management capabilities and address market failures in the provision of financing to SMEs. The strategic orientations of the SME pillar of the Economy Sectoral Plan (ESP) 2007-12 and the actions of the SME Fund and complementary programmes match well with these priorities and reflect a sound diagnosis of policy needs. The coverage and integration of policy are illustrated by the five-by-five and moving walkway framework and portfolio of the SME Fund.

The policy efforts for SMEs and entrepreneurship are not limited to the SME Fund but operate across government, including for example actions for innovative entrepreneurship through the Innovation Fund, support for credit guarantees by the NAFIN public development bank, support for small enterprise development by particular ministries such as Tourism and Agriculture, the creation of a PMYExporta Centre network and the establishment of ProMexico as an agency for exporting and internationalisation. Effective co-ordination arrangements have been put in place across these actions under the co-ordination of the Ministry of Economy and the Under Secretariat for SMEs, which are playing a major role in ensuring appropriate policy design and coverage of the key intervention areas of policy and in securing synergies.

Programme delivery structures and organisations have also been established and reinforced in parallel with the increasing importance of SMEs and entrepreneurship in the policy agenda. During the period 2007-12, the Under Ministry for SMEs has created an extensive infrastructure of business support services that permits outreach to the diverse categories of SMEs and entrepreneurs and territories across the country through an intermediary network that now comprises some 600 organisations that design, fund and deliver actions in partnership with federal government, including sub-national governments, universities, business associations, private training providers and business incubators, financial intermediaries and other actors. The measures have been associated with the creation since 2010 of 200 Mexico Emprende Centres, reaching out to SMEs and potential entrepreneurs and acting as first-stop-shops for government services, a doubling in the number of business incubators since 2007, the creation of 50 business accelerators and 31 Technology Parks, the training and accreditation of 1 000 financial advisors and the creation of a national network of accredited SME consultants. All this has enabled the delivery of large scale programme support for SMEs and entrepreneurs, as required by the scale of the target group in Mexico.

For the future, there are three main opportunities to strengthen the strategic framework for policy and its delivery arrangements.

3.4.1. A strategic policy document on SMEs and entrepreneurship

One of the missing elements in the policy framework is a distinct high-level policy document laying out a national strategy for SME and entrepreneurship development. The strategy should present a comprehensive and cohesive articulation of the objectives and targets of policy across government and the set of policy and programme actions that translate them into impacts. A strategic policy statement would increase the visibility of SME and entrepreneurship support, help to co-ordinate the Federal government agenda and guide State and municipal governments in their efforts, as well as help to track how well policy is achieving its ends. It would bring together the relevant regulatory policies and reform initiatives, policies affecting SMEs' access to public procurement contracts, and the entrepreneurship and SME-related priorities of other ministries and agencies. For each action area, the statement would clarify the rationale in terms of the market or other failures to be addressed, the quantifiable objectives and targets for the policy and each of its measures and all of the organisations involved and their respective responsibilities.

3.4.2. Develop the intermediary system

One of the major challenges for a policy delivery system that works through a network of multiple and diverse intermediary organisations is ensuring quality and consistency. A critical tool for achieving this is the creation of output-based performance criteria for the drawing down of funding, and the use of robust evaluation practices to assess the performance of the various intermediary organisations and their various projects. Emphasis needs to be placed on selection processes that allocate funding to the most effective and efficient intermediaries, i.e. those with the greatest impacts, and that stimulate competition among intermediary organisations in order to reduce their inefficiencies and promote innovation and adaptation in the design and implementation of programmes.

A further important tool for the upgrading of an intermediary organisation network is the creation of mechanisms for good practice exchange and networking among participant organisations. This should extend to business service suppliers, which should be subject to national standards for the quality of business processes and be offered appropriate training for managers and staff.

Steps should also be taken to improve co-ordination among the various intermediary organisations so they can become more effective in referring (or handing-off) assisted entrepreneurs and SMEs to the appropriate programmes that will help them move to the next stage of development and/growth. Developing a centralised management information system and populating it with better tracking data on assisted clients will produce much value-added in this endeavour.

3.4.3. Streamlining the operating procedures of the SME Fund

There is scope to increase the effectiveness and financial leverage of the SME Fund through simplification of the Fund's rules and operating procedures with respect to the reporting and compliance processes for intermediary organisations. In particular, the reporting burden needs to be reduced and the predictability of financing increased. The

> ## Box 3.1. **Specific recommendations on the strategic framework and delivery arrangements for policy**
>
> **Create a high-level strategic document and joint actions with innovation policy**
>
> - Produce a high-level, integrated and stand-alone SME and entrepreneurship policy statement to guide and co-ordinate those ministries, agencies and public trusts involved in SME and entrepreneurship policies and actions.
>
> - Increase consultations with stakeholders on policy design and implementation by reinvigorating the National Council for Competitiveness of SMEs and establishing a formal SME Advisory Committee, consisting of private sector SMEs, entrepreneurs and their associations.
>
> - Strengthen linkages between SME and entrepreneurship policy and innovation policy by joint actions between the Under Ministry for SMEs, the Under Ministry of Technology and Innovation and CONACYT that support the commercialisation of research by knowledge-intensive start-ups and SMEs.
>
> **Develop the intermediary system**
>
> - Improve the collection by intermediary organisations of data on the clients they serve for purposes of evaluation and referral. Review the Registry of Beneficiaries to determine the additional categories of information that would be useful for policy evaluation purposes, such as completion rates of training programmes, change in employment and value added of supported enterprises, subsequent access of related public programmes.
>
> - Prioritise competitive selection processes for intermediary organisations.
>
> - Introduce mechanisms for good practice exchange on business processes and product development among intermediary organisations.
>
> - Use appropriate performance management targets and evaluation to level-up quality in intermediary organisations and business service suppliers, identifying areas for improvement and upgrading or weeding-out poor performers in the long run.
>
> - Stimulate intermediary organisations to provide more help to assisted SMEs to move to new programmes and intermediaries that can support them in their next stage of development.
>
> **Accelerate the reform of the operating procedures of the SME Fund**
>
> - Accelerate the process of simplifying the reporting and compliance requirements of the SME Fund, in consultation with intermediary organisations and other project deliverers, and improve turnaround time on project approvals and closures.
>
> - Change from an annual cycle of certification of intermediary organisations and service providers to a longer 24- or 36-month cycle.
>
> - Move from standard rules to differentiated reporting requirements for different types of activities (e.g. high-tech, intermediate and traditional businesses). Reconsider the appropriateness of performance targets for different types of activities.
>
> - Shift to a multi-year funding formula for the SME Fund to enable multi-year funding commitments for programmes and projects. Build performance milestones into the project funding contracts and monitor annual progress against these milestones.
>
> **Management of a network of intermediary organisations**
>
> - Australia's Enterprise Connect initiative is described in Annex A.1. It offers an example of the management, co-ordination and capacity building of a networked model of intermediary organisations for policy delivery.

Ministry of Economy has committed to taking appropriate actions to enhance the transparency and administration of the Fund, which should be followed through as expeditiously as possible. This should include seeking approval from the Treasury for a multi-year budget cycle for the SME Fund. These measures will facilitate the involvement of intermediaries in the delivery of SME Fund programmes, assisting both in outreach to beneficiary firms and entrepreneurs and in securing co-funding and co-design of initiatives.

Notes

1. The word "commercialisation" in the context of the policy framework is used more in the sense of "marketing" or getting products to markets, than it is in the sense of commercialising technological innovations.

2. See: *www.economia.gob.mx/mexico-emprende/notas-relevantes/6764-se-mejora-la-attencion-para-emprendedores-y-empresas*.

3. The micro-finance sector is composed of more than 600 NBFIs, such as micro-finance companies, limited purpose financial companies (Sofoles), multiple purpose financial companies (Sofomes), credit unions, and others. The NBFIs work closely with the national development banks and public trusts to ease credit for SMEs than cannot access credit from commercial banks. They are involved with SME Fund projects through the national system of guarantees.

4. CONACYT is a public agency responsible for the elaboration of science and technology policies in Mexico. Its objectives are to increase the country's scientific and technologic capacity and the quality, competitiveness and innovation of enterprises. It participates in the SME Fund on innovation-related SME projects and other funds operated by Under Ministry of Trade and Industry.

5. COMPITE provides targeted counselling for micro-enterprises and SMEs to help them apply more efficient manufacturing methods to improve their productivity.

6. FUMEC's purpose is to promote bi-national collaboration in science and technology between Mexico and the United States and to improve the competitiveness of key Mexican sectors, including the emergent high growth entrepreneurial sector. It is a partner in SME Fund programmes to accelerate the growth of SMEs.

7. ProMexico is a public trust under the Ministry of Economy and responsible for promoting exports from Mexico and attracting foreign direct investment into Mexico. It provides services to SMEs if they are already involved in exporting or part of consortia that are integrated into export supply chains in the agri-business sector. ProMexico supports these firms to participate in trade fairs, buyers' missions and sourcing forums, and provides access to consulting and financial services, rental of space for showcasing products, and information on potential markets. It also promotes the purchase of Mexican products by multinationals. Its budget comes directly from the Treasury, but it also submits projects to the SME Fund to support certain SME-related activities. This is a new mechanism of co-ordination between federal government, local and state government and private sector.

8. In fact, even the SBA delivers many of its SME support programmes and services through third-party organisations, which it funds to operate Small Business Development Centres, Women's Business Centres and micro-loan funds for example.

9. The original work by David Birch on job creation in the US observed that the regions which created net new jobs were those that had high rates of job creation, rather than low levels of job destruction. Indeed Birch found that job loss rates varied comparatively little, with there even being evidence that the more successful regions had higher, rather than lower, rates of job loss than the less successful regions.

References

Centrode Estudios Económicos (2011), *Evaluación Específica De Costo-Efectividad 2010-2011 del Fondo de Apoyo Para la Micro, Pequeña y Mediana Empresa*, Pedregal de Santa Teresa, El Colegio de México, México.

Lundström, A. and L. Stevenson (2002), *On the Road to Entrepreneurship Policy*, Swedish Foundation for Small Business Research, Stockholm.

Lundström, A. and L. Stevenson (2005), *Entrepreneurship Policy: Theory and Practice*, Springer Publishers, New York.

OECD (2007), *SMEs in Mexico: Issues and Policies*, OECD Publishing, *http://dx.doi.org/10.1787/9789264031791-en*.

Secretaria de Economia (2008), *Decreto Por El Que Se Aprueba El Programa Sectorial De Economía 2007-2012*, 14 De Mayo, Presidencia de la República, Diario Oficial (Primera Sección), Estados Unidos Mexicanos.

Stevenson, L. and A. Lundström (2002), *Beyond the Rhetoric: Defining Entrepreneurship Policy and Its Best Practice Components*, Swedish Foundation for Small Business Research, Stockholm.

Chapter 4

Federal SME and entrepreneurship programmes in Mexico

This chapter reviews the SME and entrepreneurship support programmes operated by federal government. It examines the key programmes across the five types of support of finance, training and consultancy, business management, marketing, and innovation and technology, and how they address the needs of the five enterprise segments, namely nascent entrepreneurs, micro-enterprises, SMEs, gazelle enterprises and tractor enterprises. It also examines cross-cutting programmes for promoting entrepreneurial culture, government procurement from SMEs and women's entrepreneurship.

4.1. Finance

The Mexican government operates an integrated set of access to finance programmes for new and small firms that weave together as a systematic support structure able to alleviate the financing problems experienced by enterprises at different stages of development.

Figure 4.1 shows how this finance support has evolved during the last 12 years. The emphasis was initially on the provision of grants. However, in the early years, the policy effort shifted towards loans. Grants are now only granted in exceptional circumstances, such as scrapping bonuses for the replacement of inefficient equipment or support for reconstruction in companies affected by natural disasters. While for a time there was significant emphasis on direct loan funding, the recent trend has been to replace loans with guarantees in order to increase the leverage of public resources and stimulate the growth of a financial intermediary system that takes more of the risk. Loans are used only in cases when the market conditions are not conducive to the participation of commercial banks. Most recently, efforts have been placed on promoting the capitalisation of companies and stimulating the formation of private equity capital markets through mechanisms such as risk capital and the participation of SMEs in bond markets. The Ministry of Economy has also supported a very innovative factoring programme whereby suppliers in the value chains of large companies can obtain prepayment of their invoices. The platform processes 10 000 transactions a day, involving 70 000 suppliers and 40 financial intermediaries.

Figure 4.1. **Recent evolution of access to finance programmes in Mexico**

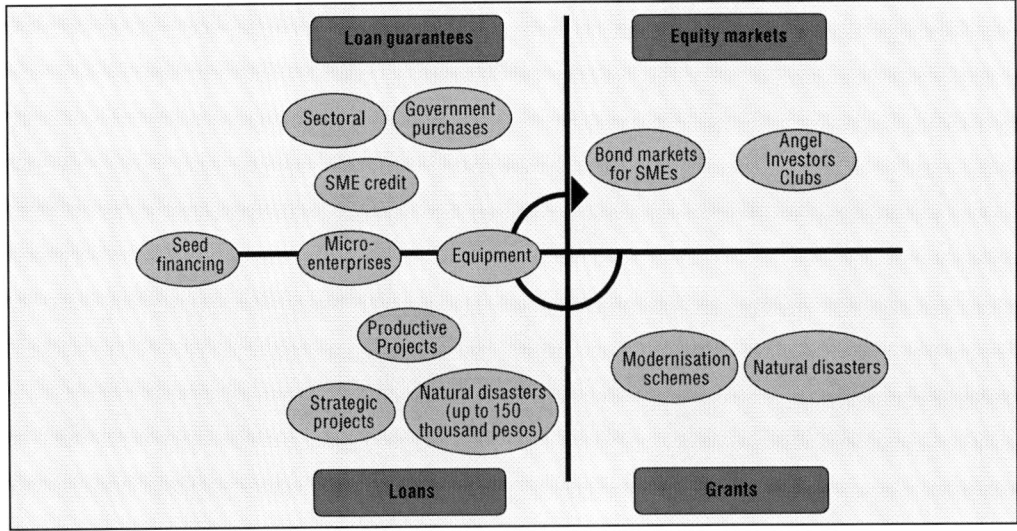

Source: Ministry of Economy.

Table 4.1 illustrates how the main components of current provision of financing support are targeted by the key enterprise segments.

Table 4.1. **Main finance programmes, by target groups of enterprises**

	New entrepreneurs	Micro-enterprises	SMEs		Gazelles
Debt					
Programme	Seed Capital Programme (enterprises up to one year old)	Equipment Financing Programme (enterprises of more than one year old)	National Guarantee System	SME Productive Projects Project	National Franchises Programme (growth enterprises that are at least two years old)
Amount of loan (pesos)	MXN 50 000-300 000 (traditional incubator); MXN 100 000-500 000 (intermediate technology incubator); MXN 350 000-1 500 000 for high technology incubator)	MXN 30 000-150 000	**Size bands:** *micro-enterprises:* up to MXN 50 000; up to MXN 100 000; up to MXN 500 000; up to MXN 1 million; *small enterprises:* up to MXN 500 000; up to MXN 1 million; up to MXN 5 million; up to MXN 15 million	Up to MXN 2 million	Up to MXN 250 000 towards the cost of the franchise fee
Terms	85% of the project (12% interest rate)	10% interest rate; loan processing fee of 2.5%	10% interest rate (2010)	Up to 70% of the project cost; up to 50% of working capital (12% interest)	50% of franchise fee (interest free)
Repayment (grace period)	Traditional and intermediate technology incubator – 42 months (6 months); high-technology incubator – 48 months (9 months)	48 months		48 months	36 months
Equity			Angel Investor Clubs (to invest in innovative SMEs, exporting SMEs, or SMEs integrating into supply chains)		Entrepreneurial Capital Fund of Funds
Terms			Investments of MXN 2 to 20 million (USD 1.5 million). Investment is guaranteed up to 70%; ceiling of USD 500 000		35% of the capital; maximum of USD 30 million
Investment period			3-5 years		Up to 10 years

Source: OECD based on information provided by Mexican Ministry of Economy.

4.1.1. Loans

Seed Capital Programme

The Seed Capital Programme was launched in 2006 to provide loans for the creation of new businesses operating within or graduating from the national business incubation system. It aims to fill the finance gap caused by a lack of credit history and collateral for debt finance. Before making an award, an assessment is made of the technical, commercial and financial viability of proposed projects through evaluation committees operating in each State. In the initial phase of the programme, the loans were managed by incubators. However, incubator staff did not have the necessary skills and experience in collecting credit, which caused many administrative problems. Consequently, management of the loans was moved to Non-Banking Financial Institutions (NBFIs).

The loan terms depend on the project's technology, with loan amounts ranging from MXN 50 000 to MXN 1.5 million (USD 2 400-70 000) over periods of 42 to 48 months. The average size of loan since the beginning of operation of the programme has been about MXN 290 000 (USD 12 800).

The programme budget (to cover administration and loan losses) increased from MXN 44.8 million (USD 1.9 million) in 2006 to MXN 150 million (USD 6.4 million) in 2010.

However, only about 40% of accredited incubators presented projects to the programme in 2010, although the proportion has been increasing, and only 1 012 of the 8 467 enterprises in the incubator system in 2010 submitted proposals for funding (about 12%). On average, about 45% of proposals are approved. Table 4.2 shows basic activity levels of the programme by year.

Table 4.2. **Metrics for the Seed Capital Programme, 2006-10**

	SME Fund expenditure (MXN million)	Entrepreneurs' investment (MXN million)	Number of projects supported	Average loan amount per project (MXN)	Number of incubators participating	Average number of seed capital projects per incubator
2006	44.80	8.96	154	290 000	44	3.5
2007	120.00	24.00	530	230 000	91	5.8
2008	46.63	9.33	201	230 000	66	3.0
2009	90.99	18.20	355	260 000	191	1.9
2010	149.33	40.00	532	340 000	202	2.9
Total	451.75	100.49	1 772	290 000		

Note: Since 2011, a new mechanism to operate the Seed Capital Programme started with commercial banks.
Source: Mexican Ministry of Economy.

The Seed Capital Programme has been successful in increasing the reach of bank financing to an important market that the banking system has not served well in the past. There are nonetheless two significant opportunities to increase the benefits flowing from the programme. Firstly, there is scope to increase the penetration of the programme among incubators and enterprises. This will require better marketing of the programme to incubator managers and enterprises, as well as prior coaching to incubated enterprises to assist them to make higher quality business proposals. Secondly, seed capital programmes in other countries often supply not just loans but also equity capital for growth-oriented start-ups. This is the approach taken in Brazil and Chile, for example, whereas the Mexican programme confines itself to an offer of subsidised credit and lacks any element of growth capital. In the case of high-tech incubators, there is an opportunity to introduce such an element of funding through equity capital in addition to loans.

Finally, it should be noted that in case of defaulting loans, the programme's interest rate soars to 24%, twice the regular rate. While it is important to set a significant disincentive for late repayments, an interest rate premium of this degree is too much of a handicap for a start-up company that is already likely to be experiencing cash-flow issues.

SME Productive Projects

The aim of this programme is to promote the establishment of small enterprises in needy regions of the country, particularly rural areas by providing loans to entrepreneurial projects that cannot obtain adequate financing through commercial banks. The loan can be used for financing equipment, infrastructure, and up to 50% of working capital, to a maximum of MXN 2 million (USD 81 000) per project. The interest rate is 12% for a term of 48 months with a reduction to 6% if the client makes monthly payments on time. To be eligible, the enterprise must be registered and at least one year old and the client firm must contribute 30% of the value of the investment project.

The programme is administered through the Public Trust Fund for Capitalisation and Investment Financing for the Rural Sector (FOCIR), which channels the funding through at least one NBFI partner in each State. The NBFI performs the project assessments and takes responsibility for recovering collateral in the case of defaults.

From 2007 to 2011, the SME Fund invested an average of MXN 540 million (USD 21.9 million) per year in the programme, funding a total of 4 593 projects. The losses on these loans are reasonable, at an estimated default rate of between 10 and 20% and there appears to be scope to increase the scale of the programme.

Financing franchise activity

The National Programme of Franchises was launched by the government in 2007 with the aim of creating relatively large SMEs following good business process models as part of a franchise. Entrepreneurs wishing to start a new business as a franchise can access an interest-free loan from a partnering financial institution to cover up to 50% of the costs of the franchise fee (to a maximum of MXN 250 000, USD 19 800), which must be repaid over a 36-month term. Existing Mexican enterprises that want to expand using the franchising model can also benefit if they have been in operation in at least two locations for at least two years.

During the period 2007-11, the programme supported 1 627 franchising outlets of which 638 were new enterprises. The businesses tend to be concentrated in food and beverage and retail, while there are also businesses in technology fields. Fourteen specialised consultants were accredited to provide services to the sector. This programme helps to exploit an important opportunity for SME creation and improvement.

4.1.2. Loan guarantees

National Credit Guarantee System

The national credit guarantee system is the main policy tool to increase credit financing to SMEs in Mexico. It serves to substitute collateral with government guarantees. One of the two funding channels used by the programme involves an innovative public auction system that gives financial institutions the opportunity to bid for the right to obtain guarantees. The selection of winning bids is made based on the proposals of banks on the volume of loans the government guarantees will leverage and the interest rate they will charge on these guarantees. The other channel provides guarantees in a non-competitive manner to banks and non-bank financial institutions. In a typical year about one-half of the bank financing flows through the auction system and about one-half through straight counter guarantees. Approximately one third of the value of SME Fund is allocated to financing the national credit guarantee programme, which is administered by NAFIN, the public development bank.

The core benefit of a government loan guarantee programme is that it results in loans being made by commercial banks to small enterprises when, without the guarantee, these loans would not be made. Unlike most programmes in OECD countries, the Mexican programme also seeks to ensure that the loans are made at interest rates that are lower than would be charged on fully commercial loans. Therefore, for the SME, the benefit is that credit becomes available and at lower rates. For the commercial banks, lending to risky operations becomes more secure, in the knowledge that they will be paid in part in the event of a default. In the longer term, successful schemes also enable SMEs to develop a credit history, which will impact favourably on their longer-term ability to access commercial loans, and introduce banks to new and profitable markets (OECD, 2009a). This facilitates the development of a private credit market, which should reduce the need for public intervention in the longer term.

One of the innovative elements of Mexico's national loan guarantee programme is the allocation of guarantee funds to commercial banks through auctions of backing for entire loan portfolios. Under the auction channel, the guarantee fund provides a fixed sum from the SME Fund for which banks make bids. Their bids comprise both the value of loans they will make (i.e. the multiplier offered by the bank) and the interest rate they will charge the SMEs to borrow. Based upon these bids, the programme managers make a decision on the allocation of the money. It is then up to the individual banks to decide which SME loans to make as part of their commercial offerings and which to offer under the Guarantee Fund.

The Ministry of Economy's auction in the fall of 2011 called for bids on MXN 1 billion (USD 79 million) and offered a guarantee of 3.8% against first losses (i.e. predicted largest losses as opposed to total potential losses). There has been much interest from the private sector in accessing the guarantee programme, and thirty-seven intermediaries are now involved in its delivery, signalling the success of the auctions. This should not be taken for granted, as elsewhere in Latin America credit guarantee funds have failed due to burdensome regulations and delays in the provision of public guarantees (Ferraro and Goldstein, 2011).

The Mexican choice of channelling a large volume of support through an auction system follows a number of pilot projects involving the testing of different models of loan guarantees (Canales, 2011). The auctions were deemed the most efficient and effective vehicle given the large scale of guarantee support that needed to be delivered and in light of the lack of resources within the government and its agencies to make individual loan decisions under a counter-guarantee model. By backing entire loan portfolios and creating competition in this way among banks on loan coverage and interest rates, the programme operates in a much different way than government-backed SME guarantee systems in most countries around the world (European Commission, 2006; Beck et al., 2008; OECD, 2009a).

Under the second channel, the national credit guarantee programme issues lines of credit to non-bank financial institutions (NBFIs) in order to guarantee loans under a range of other programmes. This includes, for example, the Equipment Financing Programme under the Modernisation and Integration (Mi) Programme for micro-enterprises, and schemes offering loan guarantees for software developers and suppliers to tractor enterprises. Recent further examples include support for the guarantee fund for financing of SME export activities in Jalisco state started in 2011, and the scheme for Financing Exporters in the Automotive and Auto Parts Industry introduced during the global financial and economic crisis. In these ways, the system seeks to achieve good coverage across the regions, sectors and special situations. The Ministry of Economy is to be commended for its efforts to strengthen non-bank financial institutions (NBFIs) in their role in delivering of guarantee products to special markets.

The amount of Mexican government investment in the national guarantee system increased more than seven-fold between 2002-06 and 2007-12, from a total of MXN 1.2 billion (USD 95 million) to MXN 11.9 billion (USD 942 million) (Table 4.3). Furthermore, the programme has leveraged MXN 263 billion in bank financing during the last five years, over 30 times the guarantee amount. In 2006, for each peso provided in guarantees, banks were lending 62 pesos (Storey, 2008); in 2010, this ratio dropped to 1 peso in guarantees to 30 pesos of bank lending, but it remains higher than the leverage ratio of approximately 1 to 10 in Chile, which operates a similar scheme.

The number of supported businesses more than doubled between 2002-06 and 2007-12, from 157 877 to 381 230. Furthermore, the guarantee system is delivering finance access to

Box 4.1. **Good practice policy initiative in Mexico: The National Credit Guarantee Programme**

Mexico has introduced a system of auctions for guarantees to banks against losses on their SME loan portfolios. The banks make bids specifying the degree to which they will leverage the public investment and the interest rate they will charge. This helps keep down public costs, increase coverage, reduce interest rates and create competition in the banking sector. The auction system has been regularly filled.

In addition to the auctions to banks, the national credit guarantee programme also provides straight counter guarantees to banks and credit lines that permit Non-Bank Financial Institutions (NBFIs) to provide more differentiated and targeted guarantees.

The budget for the national guarantee fund has been increasing steadily since 2002 (the only exception being 2006), to attain the amount of MXN 2.3 billion in 2010. This has had a positive impact on the volume of SME lending, which reached the peak of MXN 77.6 billion in 2009.

The guarantee programme has resulted in improved credit conditions for SMEs. Bank credit requirements have been softened (e.g. banks will now accept simple bank statements instead of audited statements) and the interest rate for the broad range between MXN 250 000 (USD 19 800) and MXN 4 million (USD 317 000) is competitive in the market (10% in 2010, 2% lower than the rate applied by most public programme in the same range of loan size), although according to data from the Ministry of Economy, the interest rate for small-size loans (up to MXN 250 000, USD 19 800) exceeded 21% in 2010.

The system of auctioning guarantees among commercial banks has allowed authorities to achieve a high leverage ratio of nearly thirty times greater credit offered than the guaranteed amount, significantly higher than in many other countries, and to limit their loan losses to a maximum of 3.8%.

Obtaining finance through the programme should also help SMEs develop a credit history and so that they can benefit in the future from non-guaranteed bank loans, although it is not possible to show progress on this with certainty as there has been no tracking of guarantee clients to determine the medium and longer-term impacts on access to non-guaranteed financing.

Mexico's Credit Guarantee Programme shows the importance for governments of developing good and trustworthy relations with banks when setting up such programmes. A delay in the payment of guarantees, complex or burdensome regulations, or regulations that change too often over time, can discourage banks from being part of the programme.

Table 4.3. **Activities of the National Credit Guarantee system, 2007-12**

In MXN millions

	Invested	Credit leveraged
Subtotal: 2002-06	**1 209**	**47 896**
2007	825	21 854
2008	1 136	63 751
2009	1 935	77 656
2010	2 300	67 390
2011	3 002	74 285
2012	2 794	19 275
Subtotal: 2007-12	**11 992**	**324 212**

Note: For 2012, results are up to March.
Source: Ministry of Economy.

micro-enterprises as well as larger SMEs; in 2010, 57.6% of guarantee beneficiaries were micro-enterprises, 29% were small enterprises and 13.4% were medium enterprises (Presidencia de la República México, 2010). This is a welcome response to the recommendation of the previous OECD SME policy review in Mexico to enlarge and strengthen the guarantee programme (OECD, 2007).

The core features of the Mexican programme vary somewhat from those in many other countries. Table 4.4 provides an illustration of the diversity of approaches elsewhere in the OECD. There are a number of key differences between the Mexican programme and those described in Table 4.4:

- None involve a bidding procedure as is in place in Mexico, and none seek to lower the commercial bank interest rate. Instead much more typical is the imposition of a supplementary charge to banks for the offer of guaranteed loans in order to finance the risk premium.

- In most OECD countries, loan guarantee programmes are clearly targeted upon specific groups that are disadvantaged. These may be racial groups or possibly those living in certain areas but generally they share the common characteristic of being unable to demonstrate their ability to repay a loan from a commercial bank by being able to provide sufficient collateral to satisfy the bank, whereas in Mexico the objective is to increase the amount of credit available to micro-enterprises and SMEs in the economy in general.

- The Mexico programme is of relatively large scale. Up to 100 000 loans have been made under this programme. In the UK, by contrast, a country of approximately one-half the size of Mexico, the number is closer to 2 000. In Canada, there were only 7 466 guarantees in 2011 while in the US, 53 706 loans were made under the 7a) program in 2011. However, this large scale is justified by the greater scale of market failure in Mexico than the comparator countries at the current juncture in the development of Mexico's finance markets. It nonetheless implies the need for longer term work to reduce the market failure at source in Mexico by promoting greater competition for SME lending activity in the private banking sector, for example by encouraging the establishment of new banks and reducing regulations that limit banking competition.

- Whereas it is usual for government guarantee programmes to have explicit exit plans, there appear to be no plans to exit from the market for public guarantees in Mexico. The objective of most guarantee programmes is to provide experience for banks in lending to higher risk customers and demonstrating the opportunities for selective profitable lending to the sector, rather than seeking to compensate in a permanent manner for a private finance gap. For that role to be effective in Mexico it is important that a clear life-span is specified for its guarantee programmes.

Apart from the lack of exit plans, the differences between the Mexican national loan guarantee programme and those in other OECD countries are not to be seen as weaknesses, but rather as appropriate adaptations to the Mexican context, in terms of the more limited access of Mexican SMEs and micro-enterprises to bank credit. Thus while it is larger in scale than loan guarantee programmes in many other OECD countries and aimed at the total SME population rather than specific target groups, this largely reflects the relatively underdeveloped private finance market for SMEs and micro-enterprises in Mexico. Rather than seek to scale down the programme at this point in the development of finance markets, the immediate challenge is to help bank finance to reach out to a higher proportion of the more than 4 million SMEs in Mexico, given that the guarantees currently

Table 4.4. **International comparisons of loan guarantee schemes**

	United States	Netherlands	Denmark	Belgium	France	Germany
Delivery agent	SBA Express	BBMKB	Vaekstkaution	SOWALFIN	SOFARIS	Burschafts-banken
Guarantee	Up to 50%	Up to 50% for all businesses except for start-ups and innovative companies where limit is 75%	66.67% for loans of up to EUR 350 000; 50% for loans from EUR 350 000 (USD 486 500) to EUR 700 000 (USD 973 000)	Up to 75%	Varies – generally around 50% (average of 45% for 2001). Up to 70% for start ups	Up to 80% (average between 50 and 80%)
Maximum loan size	USD 250 000	EUR 1 million (USD 1 4 million)	EUR 700 000 (USD 973 000) but minimum size EUR 10 000 (USD 14 000)	EUR 2.5 million (USD 3.475 million)	No limit on loan size but SOFARIS' risk is limited to EUR 750 000	EUR 1 million (USD 1.4 million)
Cost of loan	Premium of 1% on loans of USD 150 000, 2.5% on loans of USD 150 000-700 000 and 3.5% for loans over USD 700 000: an annual fee of 0.25% of the balance of the guaranteed sum is also charged	One off commission of 2 to 3.6%	3% per annum in first two years, 1.5% thereafter	1% per annum on guaranteed exposure (paid as once-off and upfront fee)	Annual fee of 0.45-0.60% on the outstanding amount	0.75% commission on amount guaranteed; premium of 1% per annum (can be 1.2% for first operation, then 0.8%)
Interest rate	Fixed by lender but between 2.25 and 4.7% above Base	Fixed by Government (usually equal to a low risk rate, but the commission is passed on by lenders to borrowers)	Fixed by lender	Fixed by lender	Fixed by lender (subject to restrictions ensuring it is a market rate)	
Length of loan	Maximum 7 years	Maximum 6 years (but 12 years for property lending)	3-10 years	Maximum 10 years but lenders can request longer	Length of loan guarantee matches length of underlying loan	Up to 15 years but average of 10 years
Target firms	Vast majority of SMEs	Firms up to 100 employees; special conditions for start-ups and innovative companies	SMEs in six focussed areas	All SMEs	All SMEs in all phases of their existence; there are 10 different guarantee funds managed by SOFARIS	All with a focus on start ups

Source: Graham, T. (2004), "Review of the Small Firms Loan Guarantee", H.M. Treasury, London.

covers only 70 000 to 80 000 per year (on the generous assumption that these are always different firms and not repeat borrowers).

On the other hand, a concern is that some of the public funding may be used to underwrite loans that banks would have made even without a guarantee. Evaluation is needed to assess this issue, as discussed in Chapter 6, in order to maximise the efficiency of the public spending.

Furthermore, in the longer run, consideration must also be given to the timing of a downscaling of the public guarantee programme as the private market picks up. As the programme builds the experience of private banks in lending to SMEs and demonstrates the opportunities for profitable lending, the public sector should start to withdraw. Indeed, it is useful that a clear time horizon is put into place now as regards the expected duration of the programme, although the timing for any withdrawal should be carefully considered in terms of the "readiness" of the financial system to serve SME needs, since withdrawing too soon could lead to a sharp fall in lending to SMEs.

At the same time, complementary actions should be taken to increase the readiness of the financial system to lend without guarantees. In particular, attention needs to be paid to making improvements to the quality and coverage of credit bureau data across the SME sector, improving facilities for registering collateral for bank loans, building on the recent amendment to the commercial code providing for a unified Registry of Movable Property Collateral, and stimulating banks to serve the SME market by increasing competition within the commercial banking sector, which can be expected to encourage firms to seek new opportunities for profitable investments.

4.1.3. Equity markets

The Mexican government has recently expanded its emphasis on developing equity and quasi-equity markets. These offer an additional investment financing route for start-ups and SMEs, and one that is particularly appropriate to more innovative start-ups, for which loans are not so well suited given their high upside as well as downside risks. Key recent policy measures in this domain in Mexico are the creation of Angel Investors Clubs, venture capital funds and a mechanism to bring high-potential SMEs to the bond market.

Angel Investors Clubs

Business angels are wealthy people, often former entrepreneurs, who are ready to invest "informal" equity into new or growing firms and to give management advice. They can meet the equity needs of early-stage and growth-oriented enterprises that are below the amounts attractive or feasible for formal venture capital companies, and thus fill an obvious financing gap. In Mexico, support is provided through Investor Clubs that foster networks among informal investors and entrepreneurs. In 2011, there were 13 government-supported *Angel Investors Clubs*, offering equity investments in the range of MXN 2 million to MXN 20 million (USD 81 200 to USD 846 300).

The initiative uses consultants to evaluate entrepreneurial projects and present them to potential investors, as well as facilitating the pooling of their investments. In this way, the Clubs reduce operating costs for individual members, augment their investment capacity and enable diversification of portfolios through facilitating the pooling of investments, hence increasing the supply of finance to entrepreneurs. A further feature of the Clubs is a specific and tailored investment guarantee created in 2006 called PYME Option, which covers up to

70% of investments in early stage SMEs engaged in innovative, high value added or export oriented activities, to a maximum of USD 500 000 over a three- to five-year period. Beyond contributing to the operational costs and equity guarantees, the Ministry of Economy invests in building capacity. For example, in 2010, MXN 1.05 million (USD 42 600) was channelled into the development of an angel investment handbook and helping high-potential SMEs to formulate business plans in order to seek angel investments.

This programme is an innovative form of institution building that directly confronts the difficulties that investors face in identifying appropriate SME investment opportunities, and puts the Mexican government firmly inside of the international trend over the past decade to introduce such initiatives. However, while this represents an international good practice, the problem lies in there being only 13 such clubs in the country. Generally, investor networks are local initiatives, because investors like to be in relatively close proximity to their investee firms, even though there are a growing number of online networks to link investors with entrepreneurs seeking early-stage equity capital (such as the US-based Angel Investment Network). To meet the important latent demand for informal equity capital, steps should therefore be taken to introduce further incentives to stimulate private interest in informal equity investment and to support formation of new investors Clubs, based on the practices of the best performing of the existing 13. The government might also consider other models for escalating the provision of risk capital, such as the Small Business Investment Company described in the international learning example in Annex A.3.

Entrepreneurial capital fund of funds

The previous OECD review of SME policies in Mexico (OECD, 2007) recommended that more resources should be allocated to creating a venture capital market and that increased incentives should be used to stimulate private venture capital. Since then, the government has made significant progress, although venture capital remains more limited in Mexico than in China and Brazil (World Economic Forum, 2010).

First, the government is investing in capacity-building for entrepreneurs, SMEs, and investors to increase knowledge on both the supply and demand sides about the mechanisms and value of formal equity investment. In 2009, for example, the Ministry of Economy's SME Fund invested MXN 1.32 million (USD 53 600) in the development of venture capital courses in partnership with the Mexican Association of Venture Capital (AMEXCAP) and NAFIN.

Second, at the beginning of 2011, the NAFIN public development bank created a fund-of-funds with support from the SME Fund. This organisation, the Mexico Ventures I, L.P, operated by the Corporación Mexicana de Inversiones de Capital and Sun Mountain Capital, makes investments in other venture capital funds, rather than investing in firms directly. Its objective is to increase the availability of private sector venture capital to early-stage innovative SMEs with high growth potential. The MXN 850 million (USD 34.5 million) of government investment made during 2011-12 is expected to leverage MXN 6.5 billion (USD 514 million) of private venture capital investment in growth-oriented SMEs.

There are nonetheless limits to the capacity of this fund, given that it is obliged to invest in venture capital funds that have already been in operation for at least 5 years and that these funds in turn invest in growth stage SMEs with between 3 to and 5 years of operation. The Ministry of Economy is therefore designing in parallel a new venture capital fund together with AMEXCAP with an investment focus on initial and early stage SMEs (with 1 to 3 years in operation).

Furthermore, the incipient stage of development of the formal equity market in Mexico suggests that more needs to be done in this field. For example, the NAFIN support to private funds could be expanded and NAFIN could search for partnerships with US venture capital funds to promote investment in Mexican SMEs. The creation of public venture capital funds could also be considered as long as they operate with commercial discipline and professional management. In addition, the government should consider backing up the supply side of equity markets in Mexico through the introduction of tax credits for people who invest in venture capital funds supporting high-growth potential and innovative SMEs, as is the case is many other OECD countries.

Bond markets for SMEs

In 2011, the Ministry of Economy allocated MXN 50 million (USD 4 million) to launch the Debt Programme in alliance with the Mexican Stock Exchange and AMEXCAP. Its aim is to enable companies to issue bonds that can be quoted on the Mexican Stock Exchange. The programme offers middle-sized SMEs funding to carry out the necessary corporate governance process, introduce an appropriate software infrastructure, and obtain legal and advice services for listing. Some 124 companies registered in the first call and 10 were selected. A second call is being closed in 2012 with an additional MXN 100 million (USD 8 million) funding support, and the Under Ministry of SMEs is evaluating the timing schedule to launch a third call with an additional MXN 50 million (USD 4 million). This represents an important extension of financing into a new niche area.

4.2. Training, consulting and management support

4.2.1. Young entrepreneurs training workshops

The Young Entrepreneurs Model is a 150-hour entrepreneurship training workshop on how to start a business and developing a business plan combining online and classroom sessions. It serves to foster a stronger entrepreneurship culture and "entrepreneurial mind-set" in the country, provide business know-how to trainees and build demand for the new entrepreneurs seeking to enter the national system of business incubation.

The programme is delivered through a network of 153 approved franchises (normally held by private consulting and training firms), which have benefited from the investment made by the Under Ministry of SMEs in the design and development of training methodologies and modules and training of trainers. In this way, the workshops have so far provided entrepreneurship training for 70 000 people. The methodology has also been transferred to at least 67 universities and technology institutes to integrate into their education programmes, and is offered to Mexican nationals in five states of the US (Arizona, California, Illinois, New York and Texas).

One of the issues for the Ministry of Economy is controlling for the quality of the training delivery. The training is generally contracted out to private firms that have been approved by the Ministry of Economy, which is one control, but without follow-up monitoring on the quality of training delivery, and the impact on client enterprises, it is difficult to measure the success of the training against its objectives. Programme planning would benefit greatly from more tracking data on the impact of the training on outcomes for the trainees, going beyond the current impact measures of the number of registered trainees and the number of franchised training organisations. For example, data may be gathered on the percentage of workshop registrants who complete the training, the percentage who start a business following the training (in one of the incubators or otherwise), and the one and two year survival rates for these businesses. It would also be useful to know if conversion rates from "training to start-up" differ by demographic or other variables.

4.2.2. National system of business incubation

Various experiences from OECD countries show that incubators assist in the creation and development of SMEs (improving their chances of survival and growth), and are particularly important for innovative businesses (OECD, 2004). In Mexico, there is a national system of publicly-supported incubators, which are part funded by the SME Fund at a rate of between MXN 25 000 and 65 000 (USD 2 000-5 100) per participant. The incubators offer a wide range of support services to emerging entrepreneurs, including feasibility studies of market opportunities, business modelling, access to information and consultants, linkages to financing and technology, and provision of office space and equipment.

In November 2011, there were 500 business incubators located in 190 cities across the country, often based in universities and technical institutes. This represents a substantial expansion of the number of incubators since 2007, from 254 to 500, in line with the recommendations made in the *OECD Review of SME Policies in Mexico* for the period 2001-06. The expanded incubator network has an improved reach to more rural areas of Mexico in particular.

The three types of incubators that can be supported under the SME Fund are described in the *SME Fund Operations Manual* (and incubator handbook) as:

- traditional incubators, which assist the start-up of enterprises in traditional sectors with well-known material and input requirements, such as shops, services and light industries (incubation period of six to eight months);

- intermediate technology incubators, which assist start-ups that require knowledge inputs from specialised institutions, large firms and strategic innovation networks (incubation period of 12 to 18 months); and

- high technology incubators, which assist start-ups in the domain of information technology, biotechnology, microelectronics, wireless technologies, robotics and automation, new materials, etc. (incubation period of up to 24 months).

Most host organisations choose to operate a traditional incubator because the costs and technology needs are lower. Furthermore, high technology incubators need to be located in knowledge-intensive centres and networks, which is not always possible in rural areas. Of the 500 incubators, 217 are traditional (44%); 262 are intermediate technology (52%); and 21 are high technology (4%). As a point of comparison, 39% of the 1 100 incubators in the US that are members of the National Business Incubators Association (NBIA) focus on technology enterprises (without reference to whether they are intermediate or high-technology) and 54% are mixed-use (Knopp, 2007). However, high-technology firms account for less than 2% of incubated enterprises in Mexico; a low proportion by international standards.

The number of businesses that have been incubated has escalated rapidly in line with the expansion in the number of incubators. The headline results are shown in Table 4.5. A total of almost 35 000 enterprises were incubated from 2007 to 2011 (an average of 16 incubated enterprises per incubator). It is further estimated that there is an average of 3.6 jobs per incubated enterprise. This evidence suggests that the incubation system is an effective generator of new enterprises and new jobs.

Table 4.5. **National business incubation system monitoring metrics**

	Number of business incubators	Number of incubated businesses	Average number of enterprises per incubator	Average number of jobs per business
2007	286	4 900	17	3.3
2008	400	5 000	13	4.0
2009	450	6 092	14	4.0
2010	500	8 467	17	3.5
2011	500	10 000	20	3.5
Total	**500**	**34 459**	**16**	**3.6**

Source: Mexican Ministry of Economy.

The selection of business projects for incubation is one of the critical factors in an incubator's success. In Mexico, the selection is undertaken by a private committee based on an assessment of the applicant's skills, knowledge and experience; the innovativeness of the project (product or service); and the potential of the proposed business idea. The applicant agrees to start a business as a condition of being admitted to the incubator, but if the project does not go forward as planned and does not result in a start-up, then the incubator has to return the funding allocated for that project to the SME Fund. Thus, making good decisions about who should be admitted as an incubator client is very important.

A second critical factor in incubator success is provision of training and consultancy to hosted entrepreneurs. In Mexico, selected applicants normally receive a 66-hour training programme to learn how to prepare a business plan, incorporate technology, and so on, preparing them for the work to be done while in the incubation phase. One of the routes used to attract applicants to incubators is the 150-hour Entrepreneurship Development Workshop, and an option would be to require all incubated entrepreneurs to undertake this training before qualifying to enter an incubator. Each incubator is linked to a network of external consultants through the national system of SME consultants and financial advisors, who can provide specialised consultancy to the entrepreneurs during the process of starting the business.

On completion of the incubation process, the nurtured businesses can stay in the incubator for 12 to 24 months, depending on the type of incubator. Furthermore, they are not cut off from services once established in their own premises; they can continue to access appropriate SME Fund-related programmes and services, such as from the Mexico Emprende Centres, the National SMEs Programme, and the business accelerator programme.

The national incubator programme appears to be well managed and achieving its objectives. For example, Ministry of Economy monitoring has estimated that the incubators have lengthened the average life of newly created firms, with 70% of them surviving an initial period of two years compared to a national average of around 50% (OECD, 2007). Even though selection bias is not taken into account in this comparison, an impressive number of new enterprises and jobs appear to have been created.

For the future, the priorities are to strengthen the system through increasing the standardisation of services, increasing quality levels and filling gaps in support to knowledge-intensive start-ups. With respect to standardization, there is significant variation in the services provided across incubators. Two-thirds supply only the core services required for SME Fund support, but others offer useful additional specialised services such as networks of graduated businesses and a few have not yet achieved the full service offer formally required to participate in the programme. Greater standardisation in the package of services should be introduced in order to deliver against internationally accepted standards, for example by ensuring that entrepreneurs consistently have access to mentors and networks of alumni enterprises.

A second issue to be addressed is that there are some significant differences in the qualifications and experience of incubator managers. This is likely to affect their ability to market to potential clients and to provide effective services. For example, managers in university-hosted incubators are often appointed from within the ranks of senior academics and do not necessarily have practical knowledge to bring to the task, and interns are sometimes used to do the work of consultants. Yet, the experience and capacities of incubator managers and their management practices has been shown to be fundamental to the success of incubators in many countries, and can be more important to success than any other single factor (Price Waterhouse Coopers, 1999; Buy and Mbewana, 2007; Lewis et al., 2011; Ramluckan and Thomas, 2011, Smilor, 1987).

More assistance should therefore be provided to build the capacity of incubator staff to provide a higher level of support and service to the incubated enterprises. A standard list of qualifications and experience for incubator management should be developed and enforced, as well as minimum standards for the range of services. This could ultimately lead to the development of occupational standards for an incubator manager, and professional development and upgrading opportunities for existing incubator managers, which might be co-ordinated through the National Council of Standardisation and Certification of Labour Competences (CONOCER).[1] Mexican education institutions should examine the possibility of developing and offering a diploma programme in incubator management that would match with these occupational standards, and support them in providing informed incubator services, such as in basic legal advisory services, product development, market identification, patents, copyrights, etc. Networks for good practice sharing across incubators would also support upgrading. The recent action of the Ministry of Economy to create the National Council of Business Incubators to enable incubator host organisations to share their knowledge and experience is to be commended in this respect. It could benefit from close collaboration with the US-based National Business Incubators Association.

Thirdly, there is a need for continued public investment in the incubator network. The official target is for incubators to be self-financing after three years. International experience suggests that this might be an unrealistic objective for many incubators, although private sources of revenue certainly need to be incorporated in incubator funding flows. In addition, the SME Fund requires 2.5 employees to be created per incubated enterprise, but this is a high expectation for a newly-created business and is likely to hold intermediary organisations back from hosting incubators since they will not receive full payment from the Fund if they do not meet the job creation objective. Even dropping the average requirement to two employees would be helpful in encouraging incubation.

In the meantime, there are constraints to the capacities of many of the incubators to scale up their services in order to meet the potential demand. There are particular

---

1. CONOCER operates a National Competences System and is the only institution in Mexico that can grant valid national and official certificates that recognise prior work and life experience. For a new occupational standard, a Competences Management Committee is formed to define and develop the competence standards for the sector.

difficulties with respect to the capacities of high-technology incubators. Only 4% of the current incubators are high technology incubators, reflecting the greater investments in capital and skills needed to incubate this type of enterprise. Greater funding needs to be allocated to high-technology incubators to increase the formation of knowledge and growth-intensive start-ups.

4.2.3. Modernisation and integration programmes for micro-enterprises

Modernisation and Integration (Mi) programmes aim to help micro firms in traditional sectors to modernise their production processes and integrate into markets. To be eligible, enterprises have to register, showing that they have traded for six months.

The programme is in three parts.

- Training is provided for 10 hours in groups of 20, with the training provider then visiting the business to provide additional firm-specific guidance.
- The enterprise is linked with funding sources for equipment loans at 10% interest rates for sums of between MXN 30 000 (USD 2 375) and MXN 150 000 (USD 11 876). The Ministry of Economy uses the intermediary SOFOLES to administer the finance.
- Specialist consultancy is provided *in situ* at the premises of the entrepreneur on a one to one basis. The cost of the consultancy is MXN 1 600 (USD 127) but there are subsidies which can reduce this cost in some cases to zero for the individual enterprise.

A central benefit of the programme is that it encourages firms to migrate from the informal to the formal sector since only registered firms can participate. A second potential benefit to the enterprise is a possibility to access loans at interest rates below those from commercial banks. Furthermore, the provision of groups training and one-to-one advice should help the micro-enterprise to become more productive, which should raise their likelihood of survival and enhance their productivity.

Box 4.2. Good practice policy initiative in Mexico: Modernisation and Integration (Mi) Programmes

Micro-enterprises in Mexico are supported by a set of Modernisation and Integration (Mi) programmes each focused on a particular type of traditional industry. They combine training and consultancy to upgrade workforce skills, production processes, product quality and marketing with access to financing to buy equipment to meet modernisation requirements.

The programmes are structured in four stages: 1) promotion to attract micro-enterprises to participate; 2) organisation of the micro-enterprises into training groups of up to 20 for modularised training; 3) provision of consulting services to smaller groups of 5-8 enterprises and six hours of one-on-one customised consulting at each business site focused on areas where improvements could be made in their operations; and 4) access to financing for modernisation improvements (particularly for acquisition of new equipment).

A number of "Mi" programmes have been initiated including:

- *Mi Tortilla*, which aims to work with 8 000 tortilla-makers in four regions (about 10% of the total) and is currently dealing with approximately 1 000 new participants each year.
- *Mi México Paradores Turísticos*, which seeks to promote microenterprise development in the area of the *paradores* (touristic villas). The Marquesa National Park was the first location for the roll-out of this project.

Box 4.2. **Good practice policy initiative in Mexico:
Modernisation and Integration (Mi) Programmes** *(cont.)*

● *Mi Estética*, which has been developed in co-operation with the Mexican Chamber of Physical Beauty to advise beauty shops on technical subjects and implementing working programmes for better management, technological and commercial practices. This has reached 350 enterprises.

● A Mi-programme developed jointly with the federal government lottery company *Pronósticos para la Asistencia Pública* with the goal of placing a lottery sale point or terminal in 5 000 micro-enterprises to allow them to generate additional income.

The aim of these programmes is to raise productivity, competitiveness and enterprise formality by reaching out to as many micro-enterprises as possible and encouraging them to form groups in order to receive training on topics including how to organise sales, how to manage inventory, how to improve customer service and other basic skills. The target is traditional enterprises, such as tortilla shops, small print shops, and other "everyday" enterprises.

The training modules are developed by consultants and experts. They last 10 hours and cover administration, customer services, financial management, and marketing. Much of the training is now facilitated through the Mexico Emprende Centres. The Ministry of Economy subsidises 80% of the cost of training and 90% of the cost of consultancy.

In the consultancy component, the micro-enterprises are helped with introducing new technology, increasing their productivity, diversifying their products, modernising their marketing and premises, implementing new administrative techniques, reducing energy consumption to become more efficient. In the case of tortilla shops, a further aim was to help in meeting the hygiene norms set by the Ministry of Economy, which often requires the purchase of new tortilla-making machines.

As an outcome of the training and consultancy, each participating micro-enterprise develops an action plan for improvements in each area of their business (administration, production, marketing, etc.) and turns this into a request for financial assistance. The programme is also a powerful instrument for the regularisation of the informal economy, since in order to qualify for support, an enterprise has to be registered with the Federal Registry of Taxpayers (RFC). If an interested enterprise is not legally registered, the programme will help them with the formalisation process and then admit them.

An evaluation of the *Mi Tortilla* Programme has revealed very positive impacts: participating enterprises experience a 31% increase in sales, a 21% reduction in service time, and all of them diversify their products. The cost of providing the training and consulting services was about USD 1 000 per tortillary.

The Mi programme shows to other countries that innovation and modernisation are processes that concern all types of business, including micro-enterprises on the brinks of informality. In this case, however, given the lack of basic business skills of most micro business owners, it is essential that the programme keeps a composite approach combining training, coaching and financing. A scheme that only relies on one single form of support is unlikely to achieve success in the case of businesses faced with various types of disadvantage.

The efforts of these programmes to modernise sectors in which micro-enterprises are dominant by providing sector-tailored training and consultancy to individual enterprises using business improvement methodologies and tools, including using "standards" to improve quality, are impressive.

The biggest challenge for the future is to increase the number of beneficiaries relative to the total population of micro-enterprises. While the programme aims to serve 10 000 micro-enterprises per annum, there are 3.7 million micro-enterprises in Mexico in total. The challenge for those delivering the programme is to raise awareness of the benefits of the programme and to persuade the micro-enterprise that there are benefits from switching to greater formality. The decision facing the owner of the micro-enterprise is whether these benefits exceed those of registration – where the latter increases the likelihood of becoming eligible for tax payments.

It would also be useful for refining the programme to have data on the proportions of micro-enterprises that complete the different steps of support from training through to consultancy and equipment financing.

4.2.4. Mexico Emprende Centres

Mexico Emprende Centres (MECs) were introduced in 2010 as an ambitious innovation in the delivery of information, training, consultancy and access to financing to SMEs and nascent entrepreneurs. They replace the former Business Development Centre (BDC) network with a more consolidated and nationally branded single point of entry and one-stop shop.

There are two types of operation: in 2011, there were some 71 full Centres, in larger buildings, and some 140 smaller Kiosks. Each offers a basic menu of information, products and assistance services (some of which can be accessed online) through a portal, a call centre and facilities to receive visits. Each conforms to a unified look and feel. The numbers of Centres and Kiosks is expected to rise. The goal is to have 300 Centres and Kiosks by the end of 2012 in order to fully cover the many regions of the country.

The Centres and Kiosks are linked to a network of trained and accredited external consultants who perform a business diagnosis and work with the enterprise to produce an improvement plan. The specific services offered are access to finance, business management, commercialisation, consultancy, training and linking to government programmes, such as financing, exporting, incubation, etc. By the end of 2010, 1 100 accredited financial and business consultants were attached to the networks of the MECs (Presidencia de la República México, 2010).

To receive services from an MEC, the entrepreneur has to register (this can be done online), have a registered enterprise if they are already in business, and become a member of the chamber or business association that is host to the MEC (if applicable).

In the majority of cases the Centres are operated by the business organisations with the largest memberships in each city. Thus the National Chamber of Industry Transformation (CANACINTRA), the Confederation of National Chambers of Commerce, Services and Tourism (CONCANACO), and the Employers' Confederation (COPARMEX), together manage 90% of the full-scale Centres and over 80% of the kiosk modules. In addition, CONCAMIN (the Confederation of Industrial Chambers), CANAFIRMA (National Chamber of the Pharmaceutical Industry), CANACAR (National Chamber of Cargo Autotransport) and CCE (Entrepreneurial Coordinator Chamber) play a significant role. Three-quarters of the funding comes from the SME Fund, amounting to MXN 100 million (USD 8 million), while the remaining one-quarter comes from the intermediary organisations co-participating in the scheme.

The rationale of the Mexico Emprende Centre programme is to enable the government to reach out to entrepreneurs across the country with public and private services that will improve the business prospects of participant firms. The system of complementing

Centres with Kiosks promotes the availability of business services in relatively peripheral areas. They work in such a way as to achieve a minimum degree of standardisation and certification in the supply of business development services, as demonstrated by the standard training in business consulting that the staff of the centres receive, and to enhance the role of private suppliers, rather than crowd them out, by tasking them with the delivery of public policies. An implicit assumption is that micro-enterprises have highly imperfect knowledge about their own markets, particularly overseas, and about their own opportunities for productivity improvements and of access to finance. The programme seeks to make their clients better informed and link them to public and private services that will help.

From May 2010 to the end of October 2011, the MECs had served over 46 000 existing SMEs and almost 28 000 potential and new entrepreneurs, and received over 500 000 web visitors. Table 4.6 shows the main monitoring information gathered on MEC activities. For example, approximately 70 000 entrepreneurs were assisted through an advisor and 60 000 accessed the Harvard ManageMentor® Plus online course (the entrepreneur's "virtual university").

Table 4.6. **Mexico Emprende Centre monitoring metrics**

Services provided	Entrepreneurs, SMEs and clients served		
	24 May to 30 December 2010	First ten months of 2011	Accumulated total to 30 October 2011
Established businesses assisted through an advisor	18 955	27 416	46 371
Potential and new entrepreneurs assisted through an advisor	4 382	23 222	27 604
Diagnostics applied (with links to a specialised consultant)	1 603	1 720	3 323
Linked to a business or financial consultant for preparation of an improvement plan	1 958	1 870	3 828
Japan International Cooperation Agency (JICA) Business Consulting Programme (for enterprises with more than 10 employees)	144	95	239
DIES (for family enterprises with fewer than 10 employees)	521	1 042	1 563
Financial consultancy	1 293	773	2 026
Linked to programmes of the Ministry of Economy	3 537	6 352	9 889
Harvard ManageMentor® Plus Course[1]	39 560	19 175	58 735
Online	38 830	17 039	55 869
With a facilitator	730	2 136	2 866
Tax Administration Service workshops in 52 venues	5 000	1 800	6 800
Mini MBA Workshops	0	568	568
Web page development	21	1 551	1 572
COMPRANET certification (to access government contracts)	0	150	150
Subscriptions to the COMPRANET Workshop	0	236	236
Call Center assistance	26 214	10 115	36 329
Visits to the Mexico Emprende website	246 006	256 574	502 580

1. The Harvard ManageMentor® Plus Course is an online reference tool that provides expert business advice and information on everyday management challenges, including management tools and methods to increase efficiency of work and improve business results. This programme is offered under license from Harvard Publishing.
Source: Mexican Ministry of Economy.

The MEC network is increasing the volume and quality of business development services provided to existing SMEs. Visibility of services has been increased through the creation of a uniformly branded one-stop entry point to SME programme assistance. Furthermore, the take-up response has been very favourable even though the operation of the Centres is still in the infancy stages. Different models and intermediary organisations are being employed to deliver the brand and the range of SME Fund services, which allows for some experimentation and innovation. Moreover, the new model, in contrast to the previous BDC network approach, enables the Ministry of Economy to have more control over the range and consistency of programme and service offerings provided by the network and to promote it as the nationally-branded single point of entry to business information and support for new entrepreneurs and existing SMEs. The MECs also play a role in the formalisation of the shadow economy, as they can be used to advertise public programmes that increase the incentive for entrepreneurs to formalise their activity.

At this point, the key challenge is to increase awareness of the existence of MECs among SMEs, particularly among micro-enterprises. This will require further efforts to brand the MECs and enhance their image as the best point of entry for enterprises. A new information campaign launched by the Ministry of Economy promoting the MECs on television and radio is seeking to achieve this greater awareness.

As demand for the MEC services expands, however, the Ministry will have to ensure that they are producing the expected services in the right way and to the quality standard required. In this respect policy should seek to address the following shortcoming in coming years:

● Co-ordination among the different MECs is only ensured through a common web portal where information on SME policy programmes is made available. There is no consolidated exchange of information about practices in the different centres and kiosks. The creation of a learning network where managers and employees can share experiences and good (and bad) practices will be important for achieving consistency and quality of service and in promoting innovation in approaches.

● As a core federal government programme, it is essential that staff based in the centres and kiosks meet a standard set of qualifications and are fully trained on the programmes, products and services offered and knowledgeable about the linked consultant network. They also need training in customer service, facilitation and referral skills.

● It is important to develop a system for monitoring the performance and efficiency of the centres and their management by the host intermediary organisations to assess variations in performance and identify where improvements must be made. In the medium term, low performing centres might well be weeded out of the programme.

● In order to expand outreach to new entrepreneurs and micro-enterprises, more widespread promotion will be needed to create awareness of the existence of the centres as the entry point to the SME support system, including information about the online and call centre access.

4.2.5. National networks of SME consultants and financial advisors

The National System of SME Consultants was set up in 2007 to create a body of skilled and accredited consultants able to support the delivery of SME Fund programmes, such as the consultancy services offered through the business incubators and MECs, and to provide services to SMEs more generally. One of the main tools used to develop the consultant network is the Integrated Programme for Training SME Consultants. This offers consultants 30 hours of modularised training in business diagnostics and consulting, including business plan development and financing. Over 1 000 consultants have been trained using the standard methodology developed in Mexico and another 2 000 have been trained in other methodologies, such as that of the Japan International Cooperation Agency (JICA) Business Consulting Programme. In 2011, the SME Fund approved an additional project to support the professional development of an additional 500 consultants.

Considerable effort has also been invested in training a network of accredited financial advisors to offer SMEs advice on how to access financing and provide them with linkages to the supply of financial products. SME Fund-supported training has led to the accreditation of over 986 financial advisors who can analyse the financial positions of SMEs and support them in preparing requests for financing. The scheme focuses on gazelles originating from the Business Acceleration Programme. About 70% of the assisted SMEs are successful in obtaining financing, and financial institutions experience fewer losses from these SME clients than is otherwise the case.

The core service provided by the financial advisors consists of:

● Diagnosis: Analysis of financial and legal documentation, horizontal and vertical analysis of the SME, financial indicators analysis, financial forecasts, simulation of the proposed credit, general recommendations about the best financing options, and analysis of the current SME profile debt.

● Finance application process: If finance is a feasible option for the SME, then the amount of financing to be applied for is determined according to the SME's payment capacity, and two possible financing options are identified.

● Follow up of granted credits: Three months after the credit is obtained follow up is carried out in order to analyse the end-use and impacts of the credit.

During the period 2009-11, MXN 4.5 million (USD 360 000) was allocated to this programme, benefiting 259 SMEs. Of these, 63 obtained some kind of credit, with a total value of MXN 377.1 million (USD 30 million).

These programmes are important in building the supply of capable business development service providers in Mexico.

4.3. Marketing and export support

4.3.1. PYMExporta Centres and Impulsoras offices abroad

The network of PYMExporta Centres has been operating since 2003 to provide a set of contact points offering services to SMEs to support them in the export process. The centres diagnose the capacities of SMEs to compete in export markets, and then develop an action plan based on their needs involving training, consultancy and support with international promotion. To be eligible, the SME has to be formal, in operation for at least two years, and have a potentially exportable product.

The centres are supported by the SME Fund and operate in collaboration with ProMexico, the agency in charge of the promotion of export opportunities and foreign investment. There are currently 24 registered centres, but many have not requested support from the SME Fund in recent years as this responsibility has gradually been passed over to ProMexico. The centres are normally housed in the economic development offices of state and municipal governments or in chambers of commerce and universities. An area for improvement is that some of the SMEs receiving assistance from the PYMExporta Centres are not at all ready for exporting activity and might better be served by other programmes.

Whereas the PYMExporta Centres support SME exports from offices in Mexico, the Impulsoras programme supports export services offices located abroad. There are currently four Impulsoras offices and associated service outlets, one in the United States, one in Canada, one in Central America and one in China. They help to identify the demand for products and/ or services in the international market, and then help with activities such as the establishment of business contacts and export consolidation actions including marketing, sales and distribution. The Impulsoras offices and the supported SMEs work closely with ProMexico, which provides care to individual SMEs, whereas the Impulsoras programme supports groups of companies that share a common need. Table 4.7 shows the combined key performance results for the PYMExporta Centres and Impulsoras programmes.

Table 4.7. **Key activities of the PYMExporta Center Network and Impulsoras Programme**

	2007	2008	2009	2010	2011
Number of projects supported	58	15	14	17	28
Budget (MXN)	79 286 445	35 777 193	34 393 717	47 835 607	81 060 787
Number of companies assisted	3 311	1 441	862	1 180	1 127
Number of companies consolidated	312	142	299	210	290
Value of supported exports (MXN)	26 500 000	41 187 380	76 875 392	43 243 500	38 663 391

Source: Ministry of Economy.

4.3.2. ProMexico

ProMexico was created in June 2007 to boost the government's activities for internationalisation of the Mexican economy. It currently operates 30 offices in 21 countries working both to support Mexican exports and attract foreign direct investment. It operates a series of actions to support individual SMEs, as itemised and costed in Table 4.8. However, ProMexico tends to work with SMEs that are export-ready or already in export markets, which may have left a gap in services for emerging exporters. PYMExporta Centres used to play a key role in this function, but there are now only a few active centres in the country.

Table 4.8. **ProMexico's services and estimated expenditure**

Services	Number of times provided	Number of beneficiaries	Budget (MXN)
National pavilions at exhibitions	353	249	11 146 811
ProMéxico magazine	70	32	8 400
Business meetings	176	120	1 480 200
Consultancy in international business	31	29	2 275 880
Advertising in Print Media	17	3	994 410
Promotion of export products	12	11	101 720
Agreements	3	n.a.	1 270 000
Sponsorship of green solutions	6	6	700 000
Specialised counselling	2 209	591	–
Training for practitioners in international business	35	35	7 170 310
Individual participation in international events	234	195	13 263 110
Technical assistance	87	86	4 758 901
Travel support	348	332	7 872 697
International business training courses	91	3 023	4 662 850
Export Projects	2	2	2 135 000
Distribution centres	11	8	603 333
Total	**3 685**	**4 722**	**58 443 621**

Source: ProMéxico.

4.3.3. National System of Orientation for Exporters

SMEs interested in exporting are supported through the National System of Orientation for Exporters (NSOE). This provides personalised and free advice and guidance to the local business community via 62 Exporter Orientation Module (EOM) offices located throughout Mexico. Foreign trade specialists based in the EOMs assist entrepreneurs in person or by telephone or e-mail for example offering advice on certificates of origin, trade promotion programmes abroad, export procedures, import permits, free trade agreements, and tariffs and non-tariff regulations and recommendations for exporting. If necessary, they hand-off SMEs to other agencies such as PYMExporta Centres or Mexico Emprende Centres. Services and business diagnostics can also be accessed on online through the Portal of the Exportable General Direction (http://189.203.204.246/DGOE).

4.3.4. Joint Commission for Export Promotion (COMPEX)

The role of the Joint Commission for Export Promotion (COMPEX) is to analyse, evaluate, propose and co-ordinate actions involving the relevant federal ministries and agencies, as well as state and municipal authorities and private sector business organisations sectors to strengthen Mexican exports. Its activities include agreeing actions with the relevant authorities to improve the legislative framework and facilitating access to marketing support programmes. One of the tasks for the Commission is to co-ordinate support for SME exports, which has become a shared responsibility of the Ministry of Economy and the Ministry of Foreign Affairs.

4.4. Innovation and technological development support

4.4.1. Technological Innovation Fund

A new thrust of government policy during the period 2007-12 has been the creation of the Technological Innovation Fund, which offers funding for Mexican SMEs to develop their innovative ideas. This reflects a major policy change because, prior to 2007, funding for innovation was directed primarily towards larger enterprises.

The Fund is administered as a public trust under the joint auspices and funding of the Under Ministry for SMEs and the National Council of Science and Technology (CONACYT). It provides a subsidy on eligible innovation expenditure with the balance being covered by the business. All the stages of the innovation commercialisation process can be supported, including prototype development, design, patents, pre-commercialisation pilot testing, and market readiness. The project can last 1, 2 or 3 years. Progress is reviewed at four stages and, where businesses fail to meet their specified milestones, monies may be withheld. Projects that are developing new or better products, processes, services or materials with a high level of innovation are supported with up to 50% of the project costs, and new business start-ups based on high value-added and capable of generating a sustainable competitive advantage through innovation, research and technological development are supported with up to 70% of project costs. Help is also provided in securing external finance.

Projects are selected through competitive calls for proposals issued one to three times a year. The eligibility criteria for each call are specified, enabling the sector focus of the programme to change each year. Awards are made following an evaluation of each proposal by sector specialists. Priority is given to seven technology areas: biotechnology, nanotechnology, health technology, agri-food, multimedia and mobile technologies, clean technologies, and advanced manufacturing systems (e.g. advanced automotive and aerospace).

Since 2007, 473 successful applications have been made to the Fund, which has had an outlay of MXN 1.2 billion. The success rate of applications over that time has been about 10% but application rates have fluctuated, being particularly low in 2009, but rising sharply in 2010. The application numbers have also varied because the eligibility criteria have changed and also because the low success rates in 2007-08 probably discouraged businesses from applying in 2009.

Programmes of this nature exist in a large number of countries such as Canada's Industrial Research Assistance Programme (IRAP) and the Small Business Innovation Research (SBIR) programme in the US. They help to overcome barriers related to obtaining funding for projects with a high level of uncertainty and risk. However, the difficulty in Mexico is that there is a shortfall in funding available. The 2011 calls for proposals received project requests from almost 800 SMEs totalling MXN 3 billion (USD 237.5 million) but only 70 proposals were funded, for a value of MXN 166 million (USD 13 million).

4.4.2. SME innovation instruments

The attention placed on SME innovation by CONACYT, the Under Ministry for SMEs and the Under Ministry of Trade and Industry has increased substantially in 2007-12 compared with 2001-06. This is reflected in the recent creation of two new SME innovation instruments:

- INNOVAPYME provides support for innovation in high value added SMEs. A subsidy of a value of up to MXN 21 million per annum can be offered to SMEs for research commercialisation independently or with a university or research organisation.
- PROINNOVA provides support for SME collaboration with universities and public research organisations for innovation in precursor technologies. It can cover collaborative innovation projects between SMEs and research organisations up to an amount of MXN 27 million per annum.

Together with the introduction of the Technological Innovation Fund, the introduction of these instruments demonstrate an increased attention to the issue of stimulating innovative SMEs in Mexico, which is merited given their potential to create jobs and increase growth.

4.4.3. Business Acceleration Programme

The Business Acceleration Programme stimulates innovation and technological development among gazelles and existing high growth potential SMEs that are ready for rapid growth in niche sectors with strong growth potential, such as cloud computing, mobile devices, and health technology. The programme is delivered by a non-profit organisation, the United States-Mexico Foundation for Science (FUMEC), but approximately 90% of the funding comes from SME Fund.

The programme is organised in a similar way to the Small Business Innovation Development Centres that exist in all US states. In 2011, there were 50 business accelerators, both national and international. They offer a range of forms of advice and assistance through:

- regional strengthening programmes focused on strengthening their innovation efforts and attracting investment capital, with support from the states;
- innovation, consulting and market driven networking; and
- pre-acceleration and acceleration of companies in a highly dynamic international ecosystems (delivered by TechBA, see Box 4.3).

Box 4.3. **Good practice policy initiative in Mexico: The TechBA Business Acceleration Programme**

TechBA is a particularly innovative international Business Accelerator Programme. It aims to develop and strengthen the technological, innovative and business management capacities of Mexican gazelle companies (young high-growth firms) in order to bring them to global markets. It propels their growth by facilitating interactions with companies in international environments that allow them to generate sales, strategic alliances and investments. It also strives to position these high potential SMEs as world class technological providers. One of the strengths of the programme is that it places Mexican companies in the centre of physical locations and networks outside of Mexico where there are strong markets and knowledge flows in their specific technologies.

The programme is run by the Ministry of Economy in an alliance with the United States-Mexico Foundation for Science (FUMEC), and operates in partnership with US organisations in order to ensure access to the entrepreneurial and financial ecosystems of key US technological regions. It operates five centres in the US – in Silicon Valley, Austin, Phoenix-Scottsdale, the Detroit region and Seattle – two in Canada – Montreal and Vancouver – and one in Madrid in Spain. Mexican firms are provided with office space in these locations, while they receive further consulting and are linked to successful firms in these ecosystems. By learning to operate in these environments, firms can master what it takes to perform at the global technological frontier.

TechBA works with innovative companies related to high technology sectors with a strong presence in global technology markets, such as information and communication technologies, aerospace and automotive sectors, life sciences, electronics (including microsystems and robotics), advanced materials, multimedia, animation, digital content and educational services, biotechnology related to the agricultural and food industries, and alternative energies and other green industries. Mexican companies selected for the programme spend three to four months in the pre-acceleration stage during which time they undergo market and competitive assessment, market exploration, and market readiness improvement. This is followed by a 10-month acceleration process when they make contact with the relevant industry players, develop their first sales, receive coaching on sales and channel development, and develop their growth strategy. In the final 12 months of the programme, they are helped to expand more internationally and attract investment and partnerships.

More than 600 firms have participated in various stages of the TechBA acceleration process. Between 80 and 100 firms have set up permanent offices internationally, although the majority remained headquartered in Mexico. These firms have generated roughly USD 168 million in sales. Further anecdotal evidence of success in the programme is illustrated by the example of an alliance with Microsoft through the TechBA in Seattle. This has involved the use of an international network together with expertise in Mexico that has helped some 45 companies to migrate to the cloud. Another example is the TechBA partnership with a Vancouver company to exploit mobile technology applications in which 80 Mexican enterprises are involved.

One of the strengths of this programme is its recognition that, especially in cutting edge areas, competencies may be very specific and unavailable domestically. It also demonstrates the importance of soft forms of support such as coaching and mentoring, rather than hard support such as financing, for those limited set of firms which have the potential to grow fast. Managing a process of rapid growth comes along with challenges for the entrepreneur with respect to business organisation and management decisions; as a result, it is on these areas that policy support should focus.

There are currently 1 600 Mexican technology companies in the portfolio. They are selected by external experts, who identify high-growth potential enterprises and evaluate their growth prospects. The experts visit the enterprises for a diagnostic assessment including the technology of the company, the growth objectives of its owners and its willingness to improve all areas of business management and co-operate with universities and research centres in innovation. They also conduct an inventory of local resources that could form the basis of an innovation network or cluster (e.g. business incubators, research expertise, etc.). The acceptance rate of firms into the acceleration process is 10-15%.

The acceleration services themselves are provided by a combination of private sector, non-profit and higher education entities. They offer innovation consulting and brokerage of connections into value chain linkages with tractor firms. Support is also offered from the Technological and Business Assistance System (SATE). This is a specialist network of advisors working in areas such as advanced manufacturing, information technology, interactive media, energy, sustainable technology, plastics, food, and automotive and aerospace industries.

One of the accelerator models is the international technology business accelerator: TechBA programme, profiled in Box 4.3.

The aim of the programme is to create gazelles. Among its strengths are its capacity to provide continued support to the most promising innovative start-ups from incubation, its focus on developing partnerships with tractor companies domestically and abroad, and its emphasis on the development of local business clusters rather than isolated firms.

A limitation concerns its small scale. The reasons for this are unclear, but it could be due to an insufficient number of third-party entities with the interest or capability to deliver acceleration programmes that are very labour intensive and specialised in nature. Given what appear to be positive results from the programme efforts should be made to scale-up existing high-performing accelerator models and to seek new delivery partners to expand the programme more widely across Mexico. In addition, the programme might be improved by increasing the role of management departments and business schools of universities in Mexico in developing the management skills of accelerated companies alongside their technical capabilities.

4.4.4. Technology Parks Programme

Another new focus of the SME Fund in the past six years is the development of technology parks such as the recently established Ibero American University Science Park. The aim is to provide favourable environments for the development of a core of innovative SMEs through high quality premises, access to common services and opportunities to develop innovation and production linkages with other firms and organisations in the parks and their neighbouring areas.

Since 2007, the programme has financed the construction or expansion of 33 technology parks in 19 states, with federal investment of MXN 915 million (USD 72 million), supplemented by matching funds from State governments, universities and the private sector. Some 480 businesses are currently hosted in these facilities.

Generally the parks are led by centres of knowledge creation such as universities and research institutes. At Monterrey Tech for example, there are several parks, only some of which are Ministry-funded. A range of services to enterprises are provided. Some provide services only to clients in specific target sectors, whereas others also provide premises for clients that are outside a narrow range of selected sectors. The basic template is a building with at least 840 square metres of space, several meeting rooms, space rented to entrepreneurs who have not start a business yet but need a small space to work, 480 square metres of exhibition space with some permanent exhibitions, and office spaces where pre-incubated entrepreneurs can have business meetings. Many of the parks also host business incubators, accelerators, foreign companies, spin-offs, laboratories and other facilities that contribute to generating a favourable ecosystem for entrepreneurship and innovation.

The Association of National Technology Parks plays a role in training of the technology park managers by offering courses and workshops on topics such as how to register patents and how to develop linkages.

The benefits of the programme are to promote innovation, growth and job creation in technology enterprises by providing advice, networking with universities and international markets and, in some cases, incubation facilities. Because the focus is upon sector-specific technology, the focus is upon advice and networking relevant to these sectors, such as accessing finance and protecting intellectual property. However different parks have different objectives, which have evolved in conjunction with the state and the federal government, as well as the university.

4.4.5. Business Clusters Programme

The Business Clusters Programme is promoting the development of innovation in two clusters, one in construction and one in information technology, both centred on an industry-specific innovation and technology development centre, with an investment of MXN 75 million (USD 6 million). It has an important impact on SME development in these sectors, although the sectoral coverage of the programme is currently limited.

4.4.6. Supplier Development Programme

The Supplier Development Programme (SDP) aims to harness the technologies and international linkages of large tractor companies to support the innovation and internationalisation of SMEs. The programme is described in Box 4.4.

**Box 4.4. Good practice policy initiative in Mexico:
The Supplier Development Programme**

The objective of the Supplier Development Programme (SDP) is to ensure that SMEs are integrated vertically into the supply chains of export-driven companies so that they can access to international markets and indirect exporting. The linkages are achieved in two ways. The first is a strategy to integrate new suppliers into the productive chains of large "tractor" companies. The second is a strategy to support large companies in developing the competitiveness of their current SME suppliers. In SDPs linking SMEs and tractor enterprises, local SMEs are supported through quality accreditation, technological upgrading, and organised events for established transnational companies to meet potential new local suppliers.

The creation of supply chains generally begins with the selection of 10 suppliers or distributors and one large firm that will be involved in development projects. Projects are put in place during nine months to upgrade the quality of the products and production processes of the SMEs up to the requirements of the large firm. A consultation methodology is applied by Ministry of Economy-accredited SDP consultants based on international standards. The consultants work to recruit large companies and SME suppliers, perform a

---

Box 4.4. **Good practice policy initiative in Mexico:
The Supplier Development Programme** *(cont.)*

diagnostic of the capacities of the supplier enterprises, help the SME owners develop an improvement plan and then to implement the plan. It often involves coaching SMEs through the ISO9000 certification process. Under the SDP, consultants receive standardised training to prepare them to give structured support to network candidates.

SDPs have been developed in 20 different cities, with groups of SMEs at various stages of development (e.g. size, growth phase) and operating in various sectors (e.g. aerospace, auto parts, electronics, agri-food, construction, tourism, retail). During 2010, 80 large "tractor" companies developed supply chain relationships with 5 674 SME suppliers. The benefits are clear. Building capacity of the supplier firms increases their efficiency, skills and management, and results in a mind-set change that enables them not only to supply the tractor firm but also move on to new markets on their own initiative. Also, the large companies see an increase in their competitiveness and their degree of implantation in and attachment to their local economies.

International supply chains are likely to grow in importance in coming years and this programme represents an approach that can raise awareness of supply chain opportunities amongst SMEs, achieve a match between suppliers and buyers, and facilitate their technological and quality upgrading and an increase in their physical capacities so that they become ready to supply international firms by offering appropriate advice, training, consulting, and financing.

After several years of implementation, Mexico has achieved a high degree of sophistication in this area and the SDP is a model for other economies, especially those engaged in the attraction of FDI but that have not yet been able to develop a strong base of local enterprises ready to take supply opportunities.

The SDP is an appropriate method to bring selected Mexican SMEs up to the standards necessary for them to act as reliable suppliers to larger firms and multinational enterprises. This strategy acts both to increase Mexico's attractiveness as a foreign direct investment (FDI) destination and increases the indirect export potential of products made by Mexican SMEs.

4.5. Promoting an entrepreneurial culture

The SME Fund has introduced a number of activities to promote an entrepreneurial culture among the Mexican population. One of the major initiatives introduced in the period 2007-12 is the *Caravan dos Emprendedores* (Entrepreneur Caravans). This involves mobile caravans that travel from city to city throughout the year with information about entrepreneurship and entrepreneurship support programmes, and around which two-day promotional events are organised. The caravan is often located in a university campus, for example. Presentations are given, speakers are invited from the local area and the questions of potential entrepreneurs are answered. This is an important tool to reach out to remote localities in particular. The caravans have been successful in reaching over 100 000 people and recruiting many Mexicans into taking the 150-hour entrepreneurship training workshop on how to start a business.

Similar regional entrepreneurship forums have been a component of entrepreneurship policies in other countries, particularly ones where the culture of entrepreneurship is weak and the objective is to stimulate interest in entrepreneurship and increase the business start-up rate. For example, regional entrepreneurship forums were built into the framework of Finland's Entrepreneurship Project with the goals of fostering a positive image of entrepreneurship, increasing regional co-operation in the promotion of SME activity and conveying the interests of public authorities towards enterprise support. Such promotional venues have a positive impact on creating interest in becoming an entrepreneur and taking the next step. In the case of Mexico, being able to offer these motivated potential entrepreneurs the opportunity to register for the entrepreneurship training programme is a valuable extension.

The second major promotional activity is the National SME Week, sponsored and co-ordinated by the Under Ministry of SMEs and business chambers. This is one of the SME Fund's signature events and most important promotional and networking activities. For a full week in November of each year, the SME Week exhibition includes lectures, panels, workshops, forums, and hundreds of enterprises, of all sizes, and service providers, including the Mexico Emprende Centres, showcasing their services and products. Thousands of Mexican entrepreneurs, business people, and students find ideas for new businesses or solutions to strengthen and increase the productivity of their existing business. SME Week 2011 attracted over 116 000 participants. Many other countries also hold national SME Weeks, such as the US, Canada, 37 European countries (participants in the European Small Business Week) and Australia. In Mexico, the event is rolled out regionally. During 2011, there were five regional versions of the National SME Week.

The SME Fund also supports a number of other promotional activities, such as awards to recognise entrepreneurial and innovation achievements. Recently, the National Entrepreneurship Award has been created. These are important in improving the image of entrepreneurship, disseminating role models and instilling entrepreneurial vocations.

4.6. Government procurement and SMEs

Research has demonstrated that SMEs face barriers in accessing government procurement contracts. Not only do SMEs find bidding for public sector contracts an expensive and complex process, but government procurement practices often do not create a level playing field for the competitive participation of smaller enterprises. The potential to use procurement to develop the SME sector by expanding the scale of market opportunities available to them and encouraging innovation is immense. Basically, SMEs need to be better informed about awarding processes and enabled to participate in awarding procedures at a low cost (both in terms of complexity and financial burden).

A significant development since 2007 is the federal government's decision to implement a policy allocating a portion of all federal government procurement contracts to SMEs. It was specified that 20% of federal contracts would be allocated to SMEs in 2009, increasing to 35% in 2012 (Presidencia de la República México, 2010). The government subsequently launched a government procurement internet portal for SMEs (*www.comprasdegobierno.gob.mx*) in order to provide information. The SME Fund also supports training programmes for SMEs on how to sell to the government that reached 15 752 enterprises in 2009. Since 2009, the government has also organised the EXPO Government Purchases exhibition, at which all ministries and state-owned enterprises showcase their areas of interest in purchasing goods and services from SMEs. Through the Federal Government Procurement Programme, NAFIN offers financial services, training, technical assistance and information for SMEs that want to access government procurement contracts.

These measures are having a significant impact on bringing SMEs into the federal government supply chain, which in turn promoting their competitiveness. It is planned that the federal government will increase its purchases from SMEs to MXN 83 billion (USD 6.57 billion) in 2012, up from MXN 61 billion (USD 4.8 billion) in 2010, for anything from pencils to desks to disks for computers.

Such a policy is consistent with strategies in a number of other countries. In the US, for example, Congress set a quota in 1996 for 23% of the value of federal government contracts to be awarded to small businesses, but other good practices also exist in the UK, Canada, Romania, Denmark, Korea and others.

The experience of other countries indicates that allocating procurement dollars to the SME sector does not necessarily mean that smaller firms will be able to access this market without some adjustments to simplify the process of submitting tenders and competing for government procurement contracts. These adjustments include simplifying the tendering documents and procedures, de-bundling large contract tenders into small lots that smaller firms will have the capacity to deliver on, implementing a SME supplier registration system that allows them to be pre-qualified as bidders, and providing information and training to SMEs on how to successful access procurement contracts. It appears that the Mexican government has put many of these structures in place. On the other hand, the ceiling on the definition of an SME for the purposes of government procurement quotas is quite high, covering businesses with up to MXN 250 million (USD 19 million) in annual sales. Within this, it would be useful to report data on the distribution of successful tendering by SME size categories to determine the extent to which the smaller firms are actually participating in the procurement system. In addition, the federal government should encourage state and local governments to adopt similar SME procurement programmes.

4.7. Women's entrepreneurship

One of the objectives of government SME and entrepreneurship policy is to promote a greater participation of women in national economic development; clearly stated for example in the operating rules of the SME Fund. However, there is very little evidence that gender considerations have been taken into account in the design of specific SME and entrepreneurship programmes, or that gender disaggregated data is collected from SME Fund intermediaries. In contrast, programmes are generally standardised for the use of all entrepreneurs (i.e. no special programmes are designed for women entrepreneurs); while it is estimated that percentage of women-led enterprise clients is often as low as 10%, depending on the sector and region, although 40% of the clients of business incubators are women (Secretaría de Economía, n.d.). One of the issues that needs to be addressed is that women's share of ownership of enterprises is much higher in informal enterprises (17.6%) compared with formal enterprises (Powers and Magnoni, 2010), and as owners of informal enterprises, a large share of women entrepreneurs in Mexico are not eligible for many government programmes.

The only programme specifically targeted to women entrepreneurs in Mexico appears to be the Microfinance Trust Fund for Rural Women, funded by the Under Ministry for SMEs. The aim of this programme is to promote self-employment and production activities among low income women in rural areas, and assist them in developing basic entrepreneurial skills and saving practices, and in particular to improve rural women's access to the products and services of microfinance institutions and organisations to support their production activities. Thus, it would appear then that Mexican SME programmes are not sufficiently addressing the needs of women entrepreneurs.

The OECD (2004b) recommends that governments should incorporate a women's entrepreneurial dimension in the formation of all SME-related policies by ensuring that the impact on women's entrepreneurship is taken into account at the design stage; periodically evaluating the impact of SME-related policies on the success of women-owned businesses and the extent to which these businesses are taking advantage of SME programmes; and improving the factual and analytical underpinnings of understanding the role of women entrepreneurs in the economy.

The creation of government offices of women's business ownership is one way to facilitate this. Such offices could have programme responsibilities such as supporting the development of women's business centres, organising information seminars and meetings and providing web-based information to women who are already entrepreneurs and have important insights into the changes needed to improve women's entrepreneurship. In evaluation studies of women's enterprise centres in Canada, clients of these centres report high levels of satisfaction and many advantages (Orser and Riding, 2006; Ference Weicker & Co., 2008; CWB, 2010; Orser, 2011). Women clients report that these centres offer a safe, warm and nurturing environment for them and that the counsellors provide advice from a "woman's perspective"; take their ideas and concerns seriously; are sensitive and knowledgeable about the gender-related challenges of business ownership; and demonstrate understanding and respect for the challenges that women entrepreneurs face, including the needs of women to juggle family and business (Orser, 2011). The nurturing relationships between the counsellors in these centres and the women entrepreneur clients lead to stronger relational aspects and enhanced trust. The emotional and motivational support they receive gives women self-confidence and encouragement. Women clients also find value in the opportunities to network with and learn from other women entrepreneurs. For more detail on the operation and impact of a women's enterprise centre, based on Canadian experience, see the learning model in Annex A.4).

Good data is also required to design appropriate policy measures for women entrepreneurship, including information on whether there are significant gender differences in entrepreneurial activity and access to relevant public programmes. Measures should be taken to improve the level of knowledge about the level of participation of women in the various public programmes and projects, to establish mechanisms to ensure the needs of women entrepreneurs are being met and that women-owned enterprises are given equal opportunity for accessing assistance programmes that will lead to increased productivity, innovation, and growth in their enterprises.

4.8. Conclusions

Mexico has substantially reinforced its SME and entrepreneurship programme support during 2007-12. Today it offers a comprehensive and integrated set of interventions that address the needs of existing and nascent businesses. Many of the government actions can serve as good practice models for policy development in other OECD member countries as well as in emerging economies, for example the national loan guarantee programme, the supplier development programme, the business acceleration programmes, and the modernisation programmes for micro-enterprises. Furthermore, the policy approach has evolved effectively over time in order to meet new priorities and respond to changing

Box 4.5. **Specific recommendations on programme improvement**

Continue the SME and entrepreneurship programme effort

- Maintain the policy budgets and structures that have been introduced for support across the different phases of the enterprise life cycle, from nascent entrepreneurship to micro-enterprises, mainstream SMEs and gazelles.

- Maintain good practice programmes such as the national loan guarantee programme, the Modernisation and Integration Programme, the Supplier Development Programme, and the Business Acceleration Programme.

Develop access to financing

- Promote the Seed Capital Programme more effectively to business incubators and incubated enterprises. Ensure that the incubator managers, consultants and staff have the qualifications to provide the necessary advice to incubated entrepreneurs on how to prepare higher quality, supportable funding proposals. Identify and overcome any other barriers to participation of incubated enterprises in the Seed Capital Programme.

- Assess the impact of the national credit guarantee programme on the performance of beneficiary SMEs and the level of deadweight of loan guarantees.

- Implement further actions to stimulate the growth of a private sector venture capital market, such as tax incentives to private investors in SME equity funds, expanded support to existing angel investment clubs and formation of clubs in new regions, and setting up public venture capital funds.

Extend the scope of micro-enterprise programmes

- Expand the Modernisation and Integration (Mi) Programmes to support more micro-enterprises.

- Introduce an initiative to increase the participation of micro-enterprises in government procurement through guidelines on their inclusion in public procurement programmes at federal, state and local government levels and a reporting system that identifies and encourages successful tenders from micro firms.

Upgrade business service support service provision

- Increase the marketing of the national business incubator network and Mexico Emprende Centres as points of entry of new and existing enterprises into the public SME support system.

- Provide training to upgrade the professional capacities of management, staff and consultants in business incubators and Mexico Emprende Centres, with particular attention to training on own products and services, customer service and referral of clients to other service providers.

- Create learning networks for networking, good practice exchange and mutual learning among the incubators in the national network and the Mexico Emprende Centres.

- Develop a standard set of qualifications certifying the competences of staff and management of the Mexico Emprende Centres and business incubators.

- Conduct an assessment of which business incubator models and types are producing the best outcomes and focus resources on the best performing incubators.

- Examine whether there is a gap in hands-on support for emerging SME exporters as opposed to export-ready enterprises.

Box 4.5. **Specific recommendations on programme improvement** *(cont.)*

Shift support towards innovative SMEs and start-ups

● Fill gaps affecting the incubation of knowledge-intensive start-ups and increase the proportion of business incubator funding going to high technology incubators. Increase marketing of the business incubator programme to the population of high potential start-ups.

● Reinforce programmes for the upgrading of management, production and marketing capabilities in innovative SMEs through an expansion of the Supplier Development Programme.

● Increase funding of the Technological Innovation Fund to enable funding to help meet the oversubscribed demand from viable SME innovation projects.

● Examine the potential for scaling-up existing high-performing business accelerator models and seek new delivery partners to expand the programme more widely across Mexico.

● Consideration the introduction of an innovation voucher scheme in Mexico to stimulate SMEs to take a first step toward collaboration with public research organisations and undertake simple technology upgrading projects.

Strengthen entrepreneurship skills provision in vocational and higher education

● Promote the integration of entrepreneurship-related curricula in public technical institutes and universities in order to strengthen an entrepreneurial culture and increase the level of entrepreneurial know-how among the next generation of entrepreneurs.

Promote women's entrepreneurship

● Pay increased attention to the growth of women-owned enterprises. Require all SME Fund delivery organisations to collect and report on the use of their services on a gender-disaggregated basis. Take actions to increase the accessibility of SME and entrepreneurship programmes and services to women, for example by operating a "women's desk" as an entry point for service.

---

economic conditions. The evolution is illustrated, for example, in the way that the access to finance programmes have shifted over time from subsidies to financial market building and in the extension of the scope of policy to cover new entrepreneurs, micro-enterprises and gazelles as well as mainstream SMEs. It is important to maintain these programmes and build on them in the future.

In parallel, efforts should be made to secure the continued evolution of programmes towards the priorities and needs of the future. Several opportunities have been identified in this chapter. One concerns the strengthening of access to financing interventions. Although policy has recently intervened to increase the availability of risk capital, more can be done to fill the gaps that remain in private equity and venture capital supply. The seed capital fund is also playing an important role in providing access to debt finance, but more promotion is needed to potential beneficiaries. Furthermore, while the loan guarantee scheme represents a good policy practice in current conditions, it is important to use evaluation to monitor the degree of deadweight and non-additionality in the use of publicly guaranteed funds by banks, and if necessary to introduce measures to reduce the volume of guarantees going to loans that would be made in any case. In the longer run, measures to increase competition among banks can be expected to inject private finance into the SME funding gaps, as banks seek new opportunities for profits, and reduce the need for government intervention.

Box 4.6. International Learning Models

Training and certification for business development service staff and management

- The activities of the National Business Incubators Association (NBIA) in the United States are described in Annex A.2. The NBIA supports specialised training for incubator managers and staff in its membership, leading to a NBIA Certificate in Incubator Management. Mexico can gain inspiration from and participate in these activities.

Stimulating innovative SMEs and start-ups

- Innovation Vouchers in the Netherlands are described in Annex A.6. This approach builds relationships and knowledge transfers between SMEs and public research institutions by providing SMEs with a voucher to spend on a research-based consultancy project from an approved organisation. It helps build a market for innovation services by giving the SME the responsibility of acting as an innovation purchaser.

- Brazil's Sector Funds are described in Annex A.7. They provide SMEs with subsidies for approved knowledge-transfer partnerships with universities funded through corporate licenses on natural resource exploitation.

Promoting women's entrepreneurship

- The example of the Women's Enterprise Centre, Canada, is described in Annex A.4. This initiative offers a network of one-stop-shop centres for women interested or involved in entrepreneurship offering advice, business planning assistance, mentoring/ matchmaking, networking opportunities, information, referrals and loan funds specifically for women.

A second key area of opportunity involves expanding activities for key enterprise segments that can have important relatively impacts on productivity and job creation performance. Great strides have been made by policy in strengthening and formalising micro-enterprises, for example through the modernisation programmes and Mexico Emprende Centres, but greater outreach is still required given the scale of the policy need. Innovative SMEs and knowledge-intensive start-ups are another key priority. There are some good practice programmes in Mexico that are addressing the barriers appropriately, but these programmes can be up-scaled to reach larger numbers of firms. In particular, blockages need to be addressed in reaching the target group, visible for example in the low proportion of business incubators focused on high technology and the limits to the Technological Innovation Fund that leave many viable SME innovation projects without funding. Initiatives for improving entrepreneurial attitudes are also having an impact on nascent entrepreneurship, but there is scope for new initiatives to promote the teaching of entrepreneurship skills and start-up support for graduates in universities and vocational education and training colleges. More attention is also needed to supporting women's entrepreneurship.

Monitoring and evaluation of programme impacts will be one of the fundamental tools to support the evolution to meet the new challenges, enabling the identification of the measures providing the greatest benefits and the shifting of resources towards them. Particular attention is needed to assessing the Mexico Emprende Centres and the national business incubators as part of a performance management approach that focuses resources on the better performers, complemented by actions to support the development of competences, certification and learning networks for their managers, consultants and staff.

References

Beck, T., L. Klapper and J.C. Mendoza (2008), *The Typology of Partial Credit Guarantee Funds around the World*, The World Bank Development Research Group, November, Washington, DC.

Buys, A.J. and P.N. Mbewana (2007), "Key Success Factors for Business Incubation in South Africa: The Godisa Case Study", *South African Journal of Science*, 103(9-10), September/October, pp. 356-358.

Canales, R. (2011), *From Ideals to Institutions: Institutional Entrepreneurship in Mexican Small Business Finance*, Yale School of Management, available at *http://ssrn.com/abstract=1763385*, New Haven, CT.

CWB (Centre for Women in Business) (2010), *Supporting Women's Enterprise: The Impact of Women-Focused Business Management Programming*, Mount Saint Vincent University, Halifax, Canada.

European Commission (2006), "Guarantees and Mutual Guarantees", *Best Report*, No. 3, Office for Official Publications of the European Communities, Luxembourg.

Ference Weicker & Co. (2008), *Impact Assessment of the Women Enterprise Initiative (WEI)*, prepared for Western Economic Diversification Canada, Vancouver, BC.

Ferraro, C. and E. Goldstein (2011), "Políticas de Acceso al Financiamiento para las Pequeñas y Medianas Empresas en América Latina", *Documento de Proyecto*, Comissão Econômica para a América Latina e o Caribe (CEPAL), Santiago de Chile.

Knopp, L. (2007), *2006 State of the Business Incubation Industry*, OH, National Business Incubator Association (NBIA) Publications, Athens.

Lewis, D.A., E. Harper-Anderson and L.A. Molnar (2011), *Incubating Success: Incubation Best Practices that Lead to Successful New Ventures*, Institute for Research on Labor, Employment, and the Economy, Ann Arbor, University of Michigan, Michigan.

OECD (2004a), *Effective Policies for Small Business: A Guide for the Policy Review Process and Strategic Plans for Micro, Small and Medium Enterprise Development*, OECD Publishing.

OECD (2004b), *Women's Entrepreneurship: Issues and Policies*, 2nd OECD Conference of Ministers Responsible for Small- and Medium-sized Enterprises (SMEs), "Promoting Entrepreneurship and Innovative SMEs in a Global Economy: Towards a More Responsible and Inclusive Globalisation", Istanbul, Turkey, 3-5 June, OECD, Paris.

OECD (2007), *SMEs in Mexico: Issues and Policies*, OECD Publishing.

OECD (2009a), *Discussion Pages on Credit Guarantee Schemes*, OECD Publishing.

Orser, B.J. and A.L. Riding (2006), "Gender-Based Small Business Programming: The Case of the Women's Enterprise Initiative", *Journal of Small Business and Entrepreneurship*, 19(2), Spring.

Orser, B. (2011), *Client Perceptions about Women-Focused Business Development Programs and their Implications for Entrepreneurship Policy*, University of Ottawa, Canada.

Powers, J. and B. Magnoni (2010), "A Business to Call Her Own: Identifying, Analyzing and Overcoming Constraints to Women's Small Businesses in Latin America and the Carribean", prepared for the Multilateral Investment Fund (FOMIN), Inter-American Development Bank, New York.

Presidencia de la República México (2010), *Cuarto Informe De Ejecución Del Plan Nacional De Desarrollo 2007-2012*, Gobierno Federal, available at *http://pnd.calderon.presidencia.gob.mx/cuarto-informe-de-ejecuci-n.html*, Mexico City:

Price Waterhouse Coopers (1999), "National Review of Small Business Incubators", *Final Report*, Department of Employment, Workplace Relations and Small Business, November, Canberra, Australia.

Ramluckan, S. and W. Thomas (2011), "Raising Businesses: How are South Africa's Government-Subsidised Small Business Incubators Doing at Nurturing Start-Up Enterprises", *Agenda*, No. 2, University of Stellenbosch Business School, Cape Town, South Africa.

Smilor, R. (1987), "Managing the Incubator System: Critical Success Factors to Accelerate New Company Development", *IEEE Transactions on Engineering Management*, 34(3), 146-155.

Storey, D.J. (2008) *Entrepreneurship and SME Policy in Mexico*, prepared for the Inter-American Development Bank.

World Economic Forum (2010), *The Global Competitiveness Report 2010-2011*, World Economic Forum, Geneva, Switzerland.

ANNEX 4.A1

Summary information on the major federal SME and entrepreneurship programmes

	Objective	Eligibility criteria	Main components	Activities
New Entrepreneurs National Programme	To contribute to the generation of employment, new entrepreneurs and new enterprises by promoting an entrepreneurship culture and providing entrepreneurial skills training and an incubation environment for new start-ups.	Anyone interested in learning more about becoming an entrepreneur; or operating a business for less than six months.	1. Entrepreneurship caravans/road shows. 2. Entrepreneurship training workshops. 3. National system of business incubation. 4. Seed Capital Programme.	Over 100 000 Mexicans have participated in the entrepreneurship caravans. From 2007-11, 34 000 enterprises have been incubated in one of the 500 business incubators. Incubated businesses create an average of 3.6 per jobs. Since 2007, almost 2 200 new enterprises have benefited from the Seed Capital Programme; enterprises with Seed Capital Programme funding create an average of about three jobs.
Micro-enterprises National Programme	To contribute to the conservation of formal jobs; stimulate the generation of new enterprises; and the strengthening of micro-enterprises through improvement of their processes (technical, marketing and management) and linkages to other support mechanisms and financing. Ultimately, the goal is to modernise (and formalise) micro-enterprises and help them grow into small enterprises.	Up to 10 employees and up to MXN 24 million (USD 1.9 million) in annual sales; registered in the Federal Taxpayer's Registry (*Registro Federal de Contribuyentes*, RFC); in operation for at least six months. The target is micro-enterprises in traditional sectors (e.g. tortillaries, small shops, bakeries, etc.).	1. Modernisation and Integration Programme (training and consultancy); 2. Equipment Financing Programme.	Improved identity for micro-enterprises; improved opportunity conditions; reduced production and waste costs (e.g. usage of water, electricity, etc.); and introduction of new technology. The goal for 2011 was to reach 10 000 micro-enterprises with training and consulting services. In the case of the MiTortilla Programme, the aim is to work with 8 000 tortillaries in four regions (about 10% of the total).
SMEs National Programme	To improve the competitiveness of SMEs through better access to information, consultancy services and financing.	Firms with 11-250 employees.	1. National System of Guarantees; 2. National System of SME Consultants; 3. National System of Credit/Financial Advisors; 4. Mexico Emprende Centres; 5. PYMExporta Centres.	From 2007-11, the Guarantee stimulated MXN 263 billion (USD 20.8 billion) of credit to benefit over 330 000 SMEs. Almost 1 000 credit/financial advisors are available to SMEs; thousands of SME consultants are linked to the Mexico Emprende Centres. In 2010, the PYMExporta Centres were supported with MXN 47.8 million (USD 3.8 million) from the SME Fund and 210 enterprises were helped in the export process. In 2011, about MXN 60 million (USD 4.75 million) were allocated from the SME Fund for these Centres.

Summary information on the major federal SME and entrepreneurship programmes *(cont.)*

	Objective	Eligibility criteria	Main components	Activities
Gazelle Enterprises National Programme	To encourage and promote growth of high growth potential businesses and increase their productivity, sales, and employment-generating capacity by providing them with consulting, marketing support, financing support, management support, and innovation support, as well as promoting the franchise model as a growth option.	At least three years old; have achieved a growth rate of at least 15% in sales in one of the last three years.	1. Business Acceleration (BA) Programme; 2. International TechBA programme; 3. Technological Innovation Fund (FIT); 4. Technology Parks; 5. National Franchise Programme (PNF).	In 2010, 2 658 "gazelle" enterprises were assisted. These firms created 3 396 new jobs. FUMEC assists about 250 enterprises in the business acceleration process each year. Tech BA facilities host over 200 Mexican SMEs in diverse technology sectors. From 2007-10, FIT provided support totalling more than MXN 760 million to approximately 400 Mexican SMEs to develop projects of technological innovation and boost growth in niche markets with high added value. 31 technology parks have been established. From 2007-11, the PNF supported 1 627 franchising outlets and 638 new franchises. These franchises created almost 12 000 new jobs.
Tractor Enterprises National Programme	To strengthen value chains in the sectors of the economy with potential to generate employment by developing Mexican SMEs as suppliers and facilitate industry transformation in key sectors.	Large enterprise that is a sector leader, generates growth, and is interested in developing its value chain.	Supplier Development Programme (SDP).	SDPs have been developed in 20 different cities. In 2010, 80 large "tractor" companies developed supply chain relationships with 5 674 SME suppliers.
National SME Week	To create a large scale public forum to provide information, training, advice and networks to entrepreneurs and SMEs.	Anyone can register.	Networking, seminars, training workshops, trade fair, exhibition of providers of financial and non-financial products and services for SMEs.	In 2011, an estimated 116 000 students, entrepreneurs, SMEs, financial institution and SME service providers participated in the week-long event.
Federal SME procurement programme	To contribute to the growth of the SME sector by integrating them into the government's supply chain.	SMEs with up to MXN 250 million (USD 19.8 million) in revenue.	Policy requirement to allocate 35% of federal government procurement contracts to SMEs; government procurement for SMEs portal; training for SMEs on how to sell to the government; annual exhibition on government purchases; NAFIN programme to offer financial services, training, technical assistance and information to SMEs seeking to access government procurement contracts.	15 752 SMEs were trained on how to sell to the government in 2009. In 2010, SMEs were awarded government contracts totalling over MXN 61 billion (USD 4.8 billion); the goal was to increase to MXN 83 billion (USD 6.6 billion) by 2012.

Chapter 5

The local dimension to SME and entrepreneurship policy in Mexico

This chapter examines how SME and entrepreneurship policies and programmes are adapted to differing needs across the states and regions of Mexico and how coherence is achieved between federal and state policies and programmes. Policy recommendations are offered on strengthening this local dimension to policy.

5.1. Introduction

It has been noted that there are substantial spatial variations in the scale and nature of SME and entrepreneurship activity across the states and regions of Mexico and in the opportunities for their promotion. These important spatial variations imply a need to differentiate policy design and delivery across the country. It has also been noted that state governments play an important role in designing, funding and delivering policies and programmes for SME and entrepreneurship development. These interventions need to be co-ordinated with those of federal government in order to maximise synergies and the achievement of both national and local goals. This chapter therefore examines how policies are tailored to meet differing local needs at state level and how federal and state policies are co-ordinated.

The points are illustrated through the cases of Queretaro and Morelos, two small states in Central Mexico with two very different industrial structures. Queretaro concentrates on traditional manufacturing and heavy industries and has higher than average GDP per capita. Approximately one-third of its workforce is engaged in manufacturing, which is dominated by automotive, auto parts and other heavy industry sectors. One-third of its employment is in services and the remainder is in the primary sector. By contrast, the economy of Morelos harnesses its immediate proximity to the Capital region for specialisations in tradable services. Tertiary sector activities contribute more than 50% of GDP. Tourism is prominent among them and generates 12% of state GDP. Manufacturing plays a distinctly smaller role in Morelos than in Queretaro, accounting for only 17% of state GDP in 2006, although chemicals and pharmaceutical production are important areas of focus. The state has a relatively low GDP per capita of 60% of the national level.

5.2. Policy tailoring

Framework conditions – such as economic structure, business stock, supply chains, access to finance, educational attainment and skill levels – vary significantly within countries and directly shape the potential for SME and entrepreneurship activity and the types of policy interventions required. Mexico's federal system of government, and its further decentralisation in recent years, provides substantial autonomy in economic development policy at the state level. This gives state government relative freedom to design and implement policies and programmes that are appropriate to local needs and fit into their wider economic development strategies. It is therefore not surprising that there is strong evidence of local tailoring of SME and entrepreneurship programmes in Mexico. There are also differences in regulatory arrangements at state and local levels in Mexico and substantial state and local compliance burdens on SMEs. Efforts are increasingly being made at local level to address these problems.

In addition to state governments having their own powers and resources, the operational arrangements of the SME Fund play an important role in permitting local tailoring of policy. This works at two levels. Firstly, state governments have the opportunity to co-fund the programmes and projects that are most relevant to their local problems, helping to secure a policy mix that fits with needs. Secondly, Fund programmes are delivered through intermediary organisations. There is therefore not a "one-size-fits-all" approach, since the intermediaries play a role in determining the specific nature of the interventions they are responsible for locally. State governments and local organisations such as chambers of commerce and universities can apply to act as intermediaries to deliver policies on behalf of federal government. Local tailoring is afforded both in the selection of the projects that they act as intermediaries for and in the way that they choose to deliver these projects.

Examples of how this system supports the adaptation of policy and programme to local circumstances are presented below.

5.2.1. Local interventions for innovative entrepreneurship

Queretaro's economy contains many large industrial businesses in established international supply chains that can constitute the focus for SME policy support. In particular, there are opportunities in the auto and auto parts sectors, in which the state has specialised since the 1960s, and more recently in the emerging aerospace sector (with the Canadian firm Bombardier as an anchor firm). The presence of international firms in these sectors has led the state government to place strong emphasis in its use of the SME Fund on implementation of the national Supplier Development Programme locally. The programme provides a vehicle to link SMEs into international supply chains through quality accreditation (including achieving costly quality management certifications such as AS9100 in aerospace, and ISO9001 in the auto industry), technological upgrading, and the organisation of events for established transnational companies to meet potential new suppliers. It has also been used to favour the transposition of knowledge of manufacturing processes from the existing automotive toward the expanding aerospace sector.

The detailed design of the approach in Queretaro is made by the state, which is therefore able to organise close co-operations with relevant support institutions that exist locally. Thus local supplier development efforts have been co-ordinated with local business incubators (particularly the high technology incubator) and with the technology centres of the National Council of Science and Technology (CONACYT) that are hosted in the state (focused on industrial automation, advanced manufacturing and electrochemistry and environmental technologies).

Building up the skills of SME workforces also requires local level intervention, in that the specific skills that are required depend on the industry, and the public sector can often play a role in developing training programmes that match local industry needs. Unfortunately, this type of activity is often underdeveloped in Mexico's regions compared with other OECD countries. However, in Queretaro, the state government has created an aeronautical university, offering courses ranging from 2-year technical degrees to Masters Programmes with the goal of creating an ecosystem of highly sophisticated SMEs acting as suppliers to Bombardier and other lead firms. It has also supported collaboration between the local College for Professional and Technical Education and the federal Council for Science and Technology (CONACYT), which is making possible the training of mid- and high-level technicians for the budding local aeronautics sector. These workforce development efforts illustrate a way forward for the development of more innovative SMEs in other states.

Morelos has placed less emphasis than Queretaro on supplier development. Instead it has focused on its own opportunities to promote SME growth. The state government and its local partners have assessed the requirements for innovative entrepreneurship development as being centred on the need to strengthen business creation and knowledge transfer through its technology parks. One general technology park has been developed at the Technological Institute of Monterrey (ITESM). Another elsewhere in the state is focusing on digital services. The funding for this infrastructure accounts for nearly three-quarters of total SME Fund spending in Morelos.

The approach in Morelos has been flexible enough to exploit the presence of the internationally-recognised Monterrey Technology Institute as a focus for SME innovation and the development of high-tech clusters. As well as the technology park, the state has used SME Fund support to locate business incubators and accelerators at the Institute. It is also promoting education programmes tailored to the entrepreneurial sector and fostering student involvement in business. This is an area where there is an opportunity for further development in universities in other states. In addition, the Technological University Emiliano Zapata (UTEZ) and its Cisco Networking Academy have enabled local information and communications technology firms to widen their customer horizons and obtain the certifications necessary to win contracts with big players in the industry (e.g. Cisco itself and IBM).

These cases show how Mexican SME and entrepreneurship policy arrangements have facilitated adaptation to the reality of local industrial strengths and emergent opportunities. At the same time, however, it is clear that there are some gaps to fill in local policies for innovative entrepreneurship. Some of the interventions that have been promoted in particular states could be usefully adopted in others while retaining local adaptation. This is the case of the workforce skills development approach of Queretaro and the university entrepreneurship teaching of Morelos that could be adapted elsewhere. Furthermore, there are under-exploited opportunities for cluster building. Although policymakers have identified industrial clusters across the country, there has been relatively little emphasis on fostering interactions among clustered SMEs themselves, as opposed to with larger international hub firms. State-level interventions could play an important role by brokering new inter-firm linkages within clusters.

5.2.2. Local initiatives for micro-enterprises

State governments are also very active in promoting micro-enterprises in ways that benefit from local proximity and complement national policy. In Morelos, for example, the state economic development office has introduced a programme for local artisans working on pottery and jewellery. The programme operates through a local business association called *Manos de Morelos* and offers business training and consultancy and subsidies for the purchase of equipment.

5.2.3. Local initiatives for access to finance

State governments are also active in supporting access to finance for SMEs and entrepreneurs. Two examples are IMOFI (*Instituto Morelense para el Financiemiento del Sector Productivo*) in Morelos and SOFEQ (*Programa de Soluciones Financieras*) in Queretaro. IMOFI delivers a business credit programme with features akin to those of the federal SME Productive Project. It helps SMEs to obtain medium-sized credit (i.e. from MXN 70 000 to MXN 1 million, USD 5 500 to USD 79 000) at an annual interest rate of 7.5%. In Queretaro, SOFEQ disburses credit of an average value of MXN 700 000 (USD 55 400) largely for firms

---

Box 5.1. **Local good practice policy initiative: Manos de Morelos**

Tourism employs a significant share of the workforce in the state of Morelos, largely as a result of domestic tourism, especially from close-by Mexico City. In addition to using hotels, restaurants and other services, visitors commonly seek out traditional crafts produced by skilled artisans. *Manos de Morelos* is a crafts association formed and supported through a combination of state and federal funds, bringing together artisans from around the state.

Craft products are typically produced and sold by individuals in outdoor markets. *Manos de Morelos* began in 2008 as a craft exhibition, supported by the local state economic development organisation as a means to promote these artisans. From there, however, the artisans organised themselves into a group. The state has continued to support the organisation in several ways. First, it has provided basic business training to association members, as well as training on workplace safety. It has also offered consulting assistance to increase productivity, and to provide advice on exporting goods. With funding from the state, the artisans have finally purchased new equipment and will also open a permanent gallery for their work in a large mall in central Cuernavaca, the capital city of the state.

The benefits of institutionalising what is typically a fragmented group of unrelated producers go beyond better production and sales techniques, however. One important outgrowth of the organisation has been the development of a recognisable brand that distinguishes local work from those of others, and to which notions of quality and tradition can be attached. Equally, co-operation creates learning opportunities. The artisans collaborate and share new ways of producing and finishing products, as well as new designs, and these innovations can command higher prices.

---

operating in manufacturing. The interest rate is 6%. These programmes help expand the reach of public support into needy areas. They attract strong interest from local SMEs, which in part reflects relatively favourable credit conditions in terms of interest rates and repayment terms compared with the national loan guarantee system.

States also frequently develop industry-specific SME credit interventions that target local sector strengths, sometimes in collaboration with the local offices of NAFINSA, the national development bank. In Morelos, for example, specific credit programmes have been put in place for taxi drivers and micro-enterprises related to tourism.

These interventions help to fill local gaps in provision of SME credit and target them onto the most important sector priorities. Banks of course also deliver credit with the support of the national loan guarantee programme, which permits further targeting to local needs, for example in terms of the volume of loans, the promotion of the programme and the interest rates charged.

There are nonetheless further opportunities to use local interventions to help fill SME finance gaps. These opportunities fall in three main areas. First, there are few mutual guarantee system programmes operating at local level in Mexico promoting lending to local groups of enterprises. The mutual guarantee approach has a number of advantages over individual lending. Transaction costs are reduced because public authorities and banks only deal with the management board of one entity, rather than with a multitude of small borrowers, information asymmetries are lowered because local group members will tend to know each other, and collateral may not be necessary insofar as it is replaced by compulsory savings, group liability, and peer pressure. *Second*, state governments and local partners can play an important potential role in favouring the development of local business angel investor clubs in collaboration with national initiatives. *Third*, state governments can also promote the establishment of local co-operative banks. These can help fill a gap in lending of mid-sized loans to SMEs using a relationship lending approach with local SMEs. While the national government should be tasked with setting the legal framework, the local client base of co-operative banks suggests that state governments should also be involved in their promotion.

5.2.4. *Simplifying local regulations*

The commitment of state governments to regulatory improvement has varied across Mexico, with some states setting up a dedicated commission (CEMER) equivalent to the Federal Commission for Regulatory Improvement (COFOMER), whereas others have delegated the same functions to a unit integrated in the economic development office. Fifteen of the 31 Mexican states have so far decided to establish their own CEMER, including Morelos, whereas Queretaro has kept the responsibility for the simplification of business regulations within the Secretary for Sustainable Development (SEDESU). These new institutional arrangements provide a platform for simplifying local regulations and procedures.

Box 5.2. Local good practice policy initiative: Local Commission for Regulatory Improvement, Morelos

The State of Morelos has set up a Local Commission for Regulatory Improvement (CEMER), focused on simplifying regulations at state and local level. The CEMER has been very proactive by introducing the Rapid System for Business Registration (SARE) in 8 municipalities within the State. This has allowed businesses that do not present social or environmental risks to set up operations in less than 72 hours. In addition, the public registry of business property in Morelos has been made electronic and accessible online, enabling public authorities and private citizens to obtain up-to-date information through the Internet instantly. This advance has been the outcome of collaboration between the CEMER and the local university at no cost to the State authorities, as the system has been digitalised by students as part of their work towards completion of the degree. The CEMER of Morelos estimates that the digitalisation of the registry has resulted in savings for local firms in the range of MXN 14 million (USD 1.1 million) through, for example, lowered notary fees.

The reforms have also involved construction permits, with a new rule that enables some types of micro-enterprises to expand their business up to 200 square metres without requiring special permission, up from the previous limit of 50 square metres. This change in state legislation has especially favoured micro businesses owned by disadvantaged social groups.

Regulatory impact assessment (RIA) is carried out by the CEMER of Morelos for every new law promulgated by the state government. This has permitted the streamlining of business licenses and business permits. However, with a staff of only 17 people, this effort should probably focus only on the acts and rules with the greatest potential impact on business, as is the case of the work of the Federal Commission on Regulatory Improvement.

Finally, Morelos' authorities are also trying to make progress in the area of labour conciliation, where trials opposing business owners and workers can take up to one-and-a-half years to be judged. Morelos has been one of the first states to introduce oral hearings for criminal trials, which replace Mexico's traditional trials based on written communication. It is planning to do the same in the near future for trade-related and labour trials.

5.3. Policy co-ordination

The decentralisation of policy arrangements in Mexico offers the critical advantage of permitting the adaptation of SME and entrepreneurship policies to local needs and preferences. However, this comes with the potential that state and local policies will not always be aligned with national priorities and will not always work in harmony with national interventions. National-local co-ordination of policies is important in the domain of SMEs and entrepreneurship because they must address multiple problems and the success of one intervention often depends on the presence of another, which may be delivered by another level of government or may be absent.

In Mexico, the risks of missing or negative synergies and conflicting policy priorities are minimised by the close involvement of state governments in the operation of the SME Fund and by other co-ordination arrangements across ministries. One of the mechanisms helping to secure co-ordination is the matching funding of the SME Fund by states through the 1:1 rule, which enables state governments to co-fund entrepreneurship and SME policies in their areas if they wish to, on an equal basis with the federal government. This is formalised through a process of discussion and signing of annual co-ordination agreements that identify the respective federal and state contributions to SME Fund initiatives and help to align their efforts. This is an important asset for aligning policies. However, although 1:1 funding is permitted, the state contributions are normally much lower and limited to certain actions.

A second key element supporting federal-state co-ordination of SME Fund-supported actions is the use of intermediary organisations for policy delivery. State governments and local organisations such as chambers of commerce and universities can apply to act as intermediaries to deliver policies on behalf of federal government. For state and municipal governments, as well as local private sector businesses, business associations, public and private universities and so on, working with the SME Fund is an important opportunity to develop and deliver projects that they would not otherwise be able to promote. The initiatives must however fit with national priorities and meet national standards to obtain funding. This is reinforced, by the fact that state governments and federal government jointly accredit SME Fund intermediaries in their states, thus enabling both to have their say on what sort of initiatives and delivery methods should go ahead. Local committees have also often been set up to propose projects to the SME Fund. Through these committees a range of local stakeholders, including the private sector, review and analyse projects and give a view on those that should be accepted.

There are also a number of co-ordination arrangements between national ministries and state governments on other policies and programmes that affect SME and entrepreneurship policy. For example, the federal Councils of Science and Technology often work at the state level to develop stronger communication between research institutions, industry and government, to increase private and state investment in science and technology and to provide more attention to local industrial and social problems. There may be scope nevertheless to reinforce co-ordination at the stage of policy design by exploiting the capacity of the federal delegate offices in the states to act as liaison points between ministries and state level stakeholders.

Finally, policy co-ordination should occur horizontally as well as vertically, i.e. co-ordination is also needed among states. States are all involved in policy design and implementation and have many interesting experiences to share, yet there are few mechanisms to permit best practice exchange among them. It would be useful to build contact networks, share good practices, and provide co-ordination among states in this field, for example under the auspices of the Association of Mexican State Development Secretaries.

5.4. Conclusions

The decentralised economic development arrangements in Mexico and the participation of state governments and local intermediaries in the operation of the SME Fund have allowed for significant tailoring of SME and entrepreneurship policies to state level development needs and for proper co-ordination of policy between federal and state levels. Project applications for many programmes are pre-selected by state governments, permitting the screening-out of projects that are not in line with state priorities. The largest national investments have also always been preceded by a close dialogue between federal and state authorities. The co-funding mechanism, which provides for co-participation by the states in financing local projects, has further enhanced local policy adaptation and national-local co-ordination.

The involvement of state and local governments and partner organisations in the delivery of SME Fund programmes has enabled the formulation and implementation of many projects with strong adaptation to local needs, based on the knowledge and resource contributions of local stakeholders. For example, the state of Queretaro has targeted polices on supplier chain development in the key potential growth sectors of aeronautics and automobiles, while Morelos has focused on technology park and associated technology infrastructure, exploiting the presence of the Monterrey Institute of Technology among other catalysts. States have also developed tailored interventions for micro-enterprise development and micro finance, often around particular local sectors and in complement to federal programmes.

Nonetheless, there are opportunities to strengthen local policy tailoring. In particular, there is further scope for cluster building and for local workforce development, as well as scope for new initiatives to fill gaps in SME financing through the promotion of local mutual guarantee schemes and local co-operative banks.

In terms of policy co-ordination, a more active role could be envisaged for the National Ministry of Economy's state delegations, which are currently "out of the loop" of the policy dialogue between the national and local level and thus unable to perform the role of liaison with which they had originally been charged. In addition, simplification of the SME Fund operating procedures, as discussed earlier in the report, would facilitate the increased participation of state and local organisations in the design, delivery and funding of SME Fund projects, and hence increase the level of co-operation between the federal and state levels.

As with securing the positive evolution of federal programmes, the effective use of evaluation will be critical at local level in directing support to the initiatives that make the most difference to local barriers to entrepreneurship and that best exploit local institutional resources. Strengthening evaluation should therefore be important at local level and the information should be shared with national partners and other states.

Box 5.3. **Specific recommendations on local policy tailoring and co-ordination**

Promote local clusters

- Stimulate the growth of local business clusters by fostering collaboration among SMEs as well as linkages with large firms and universities.

- Provide locally-tailored vocational training and continuing professional development adapted to the needs of local industry clusters, including schemes for placement of students in local SMEs.

Address local gaps in SME access to financing

- Establish local mutual guarantee societies through co-operation between state governments, the national guarantee fund and local intermediaries. Offer state counter-guarantees in addition to those offered by the mutual societies and the national guarantee fund.

- Broker the development of local co-operative banking institutions in collaboration with wealthy individuals and business associations.

- Set up small public venture capital schemes and business angel networks at local level to cater for the needs of growth-oriented SMEs.

Undertake local administrative simplification

- Set up a commission for regulatory improvement in each Mexican state focused on those regulations with the most impact on SMEs and entrepreneurs.

Increase co-ordination in SME and entrepreneurship policy design

- Reinforce the capacity of the federal delegate offices in the states to act as liaison offices between the Under Secretariat for SMEs and the state economic development secretaries and other state-level stakeholders for the purposes of sharing information on policy design.

- Streamline SME Fund operation in order to encourage greater participation of states and local organisations as intermediaries.

- Establish a standing committee on SME and entrepreneurship policy within the office of state economic development secretaries to build contact networks, share good practices, and provide co-ordination among states in this field.

- Undertake local project evaluations in order to provide evidence on which actions and intermediaries are the most effective and efficient in the local context. Share this evaluation information with national partners and other states and use it to set out strategic priorities for the evolution of local programme interventions.

Chapter 6

Framework for the evaluation of public SME and entrepreneurship programmes in Mexico

This chapter examines the framework for the evaluation of public SME and entrepreneurship programmes in Mexico. It sets out the case for evaluation and compares arrangements in Mexico with international good practice. Recommendations are offered on how evaluations might be undertaken for specific SME and entrepreneurship programmes in Mexico. Recommendations are also offered on how arrangements for evaluation could be strengthened at a systemic level, across the entire Mexican SME and entrepreneurship policy portfolio.

6.1. The case for evaluation

The case for evaluation has been consistently put forward by the OECD Working Party for SMEs and Entrepreneurship. It is a critical tool for determining the impact of policies, providing accountability for expenditure, informing choices on the allocation of funds and providing evidence on how policy can continuously be improved.

The main principles of evaluation are discussed in OECD (2007). In short, evaluation can be referred to as (Papaconstantinou and Polt, 1997):

"A process that seeks to determine as systematically and objectively as possible the relevance, efficiency and effect of an activity in terms of its objectives, including the analysis of the implementation and administrative management of such activity."

Evaluation is not undertaken at a single point in time, as a one-off event, but is an on-going process in which information is continuously collected, assessed and fed back into policy making. To be conducted effectively it requires objectives and targets to be set initially, although evaluation can often lead to these being modified or adjusted as evaluation evidence emerges.

Evaluation should also use a careful and rigorous methodology, as a result of which the policy maker can be as confident as possible of being able to assess policy impact. Of course there are always some uncertainties, but the ultimate concern is that policy-makers have to be confident that any observed impact would not have happened in the absence of the policy. Core to this assessment is the use of control groups.

Evaluation can be undertaken at the level of projects, programmes and policy as a whole. Accurate evaluation of the impact of individual SME and entrepreneurship projects and programmes is required. However, this must also be set within the implementation of a system of evaluation which enables a "big picture" assessment of the policy area as a whole and the relative impacts of different measures. This implies the use of consistent methods and the comprehensive application of evaluation across all programmes.

Evaluation has to be linked to clearly specified objectives. For example, the object of policy might be to enhance the survival of new firms, or increase the sales of an SME overseas, or raise rates of patenting or raise rates of new firm formation. These are referred to as "output-based" objectives and their clear specification is critical for any evaluation. Much less desirable are "input-based" objectives, such as the delivery of X hours training to SMEs, the provision of funding for micro-enterprises or the provision of incubation premises. Whilst these are important indicators that can provide information on where activities are operating effectively, they are not an end in themselves and they are not the impact that policy is seeking to achieve. It is the additional economic activity generated from the policy that has to be measured and is the main focus of an evaluation.

In this respect, 2007 OECD Framework for the Evaluation of SME and Entrepreneurship Policies and Programmes makes a distinction between monitoring and evaluation. Monitoring involves only the reporting of the views or observed impact of policies on recipient firms or individuals. What distinguishes evaluation is that it involves a comparison between the firms or individuals in receipt of the assistance and some "control" or "non-treated" group that enables the impact of the policy to be established as the difference in key performance metrics between these two groups.

One of the key challenges in impact evaluation is therefore to identify the control group. However, this is often far from obvious. The most primitive forms of evaluations merely compare the treated firms with a non-treated group that does not differ significantly in terms of observable factors such as age, sector, ownership or geography. Unfortunately this fails to take account of unobservable differences between the treated and the non-treated firms. Techniques have now been developed to better take account of unobservable differences and the "selection bias" problem (see Box 6.1).

Box 6.1. Examples of good practice in SME and entrepreneurship policy evaluation

OECD (2007) made it clear that it is now technically possible to provide accurate measures of programme impact. It showed a set of examples of programme evaluations, assessed in terms of their quality. Since that publication, the examples of good practice have multiplied in both developed and developing countries. Four recent good practice programme evaluation examples are:

- New Zealand Growth Services Range: Business Support Programme providing assistance and advice. Impact on sales; no impact on value-added or productivity (Morris and Stevens, 2010).

- *Impact Evaluation of SME Programs in Latin America and Caribbean* (Lopez Acevedo and Tan, 2010).

- *Evaluating the Effect of Soft Business Support to Entrepreneurs in North Jutland* (Rotger and Gørtz, 2009).

- *Behind the GATE Experiment: Evidence on Effects of and Rationales for Subsidised Entrepreneurship Training* (Fairlie, Karlan and Zinman, 2012).

6.2. The evaluation system

The Mexican government is able to document with great clarity the aggregate scale of expenditure of the SME Fund, the spending on individual programmes and the spending on each ultimate target group – new entrepreneurs, micro-enterprises, etc. The availability of such information is a reflection of the good quality data collected by the Ministry on what are referred to as "inputs" to public funding of SME and entrepreneurship policy.

Monitoring data are also collected on jobs maintained and jobs created by SME Fund and other programmes. This enables estimates of "value for money" to be derived using the internationally recognised concept of "cost per job". The estimates for the SME Fund were set out earlier in Table 3.5. The estimation of costs per job has the advantage that a single metric can be used to compare one programme with another to inform political judgments about impact and about the case for switching of funds from one programme to another. However, the interpretation of such figures requires considerable care.

The major issue is that while the cost information is exemplary, there is considerably less clarity on the outcomes of policy. Estimates are reported of jobs maintained and/or created for SME Fund programmes, but these estimates are not based upon the most robust of methods. The key issue is that programme impact, in terms of job creation or any other metric, has to be assessed on the basis of the "additionality" made by the funding to the outcome achieved. In other words it is vital to be confident that, without the funding, the jobs would either not have been created or would have been lost or not maintained. Obtaining this information directly from the beneficiary enterprises or intermediaries, without any control-group studies, is not a robust approach. Only one example of a robust estimation procedure appears to be in use. The following section describes how individual programmes could be evaluated more robustly.

Second, the horizontal measure of impact for which the most data are available, namely jobs, is not the only objective of policy and therefore not the only the impact to be taken into consideration. Additional objectives include the creation of new enterprises, increasing SME competitiveness, innovation, new firm survival, the creation of gazelles, a reduction in scale of the informal sector, the creation of firms by females and so on. The monitoring and evaluation data are much more limited on these measures, making a full assessment of policy and comparison of programme outcomes difficult.

Even where job impacts are the right measure, it should be clear whether jobs maintained or jobs created are the target, particularly given that jobs created are more likely to be associated with a dynamic economy. Finally it is unclear over what period of time job creation is expected to take place. This is a major issue since job creation in science-based projects may take a decade whereas the impact of business advice programmes may be clear within months.

In respect of indicators, greater clarity is required at the outset on the primary, and then the secondary, objectives of each programme in terms of what outputs they are expected to achieve. Only when clear output-based objectives are documented can a valid assessment be made of the extent to which the existing programmes either meet, or fail to meet, the specified objectives. By "output-based" we mean that objectives have to be of the form of: "improving firm survival" or "increasing new firm creation" or "increasing the share of world patents by Mexican SMEs" or "to reduce the share of informality in the economy". This contrasts with "input-based" targets, examples of which might be the provision of advice to X thousand firms or the provision of Y hours of advice. Once established, such output-based metrics could then be used at the programme level to assess the impact of the five groups of policies and five groups of target enterprise segments, as well as the impact of the individual measures within the groups.

This discussion underlines the need for an over-arching official policy statement on SME and entrepreneurship policy in Mexico able to set realistic objectives and targets for what are viewed as the key elements of SME and entrepreneurship policy.

6.3. Methods for programme evaluation

This section illustrates for five selected federal programmes an evaluation approach that would provide more reliable estimates of impact than those that are currently available. In each case at least one example of an evaluation of a similar programme from another OECD country is provided, emphasising the methodologies used, leading to an outline of what would be required to undertake such an evaluation for the Mexican counterpart programme. Generally only the most robust of evaluations are described.

6.3.1. Evaluating Modernisation and Integration Programmes for micro-enterprises

As described in Chapter 4, the Modernisation and Integration Programmes aim to increase the productivity of micro-enterprises and encourage their participation in the formal economy by the provision of group training and individual consultancy, accompanied by subsidies for the purchase of equipment. There have been a large number of evaluations internationally on the impact of the provision of publicly funded government training and consultancy programmes. The outcome is heavily dependent upon the methodology used.

Two approaches are common. The first is to ask participants for their views of what they received. This self-reported data generally provides very positive views of the service. Typical satisfaction rates are around 85% (Rogoff and Lee, 1996). The second approach uses control groups of otherwise similar businesses which did not make use of these services. Examples include the evaluations of the GATE programme in the US (Fairlie et al., 2012), business and self-employment assistance programmes in the US (Gu et al., 2010) and the Business Link programme in the United Kingdom (Mole et al., 2009). This approach provides more robust impact results, although findings tend to be less positive than evaluations based on beneficiary surveys.

In evaluating the Mexican Modernisation and Integration Programmes in the future it is recommended to track all programme participants for at least two years after they complete the programme rather than rely on surveys of beneficiaries. This tracking could be undertaken at low cost since recipients have to provide information on their business in any case at the time at which they register. They can then be tracked using official data to determine whether they survive and, if they do, whether their employment changes following participation. This does not need to be done for the whole population but for a representative sample. This is preferable to undertaking a survey of programme beneficiaries, which is likely to provide unreliable estimates.

An even better approach would be to construct a control group comprising those enterprises that applied to participate but ultimately chose not to. Clearly this is more problematic since the chances are that they never registered and so cannot be tracked using official data. In this case, these enterprises would have to be contacted via other means and participation rates might be low and information not wholly reliable. Nevertheless it is vital that some form of control group is developed in order to obtain truly robust assessments of impact.

6.3.2. Evaluating the Mexico Emprende Centres

The Mexico Emprende Centres programme has created a national network of one-stop-shop business development centres that provide information and consultancy services to local entrepreneurs and linkages to other public and private programmes. There have been numerous evaluations internationally of the impact of business advisory services to SMEs, and there are good models to follow in seeking to evaluate the effect of the services themselves. For example, in Denmark, an evaluation compared firms that received only basic help with those obtaining more tailored assistance (GØrtz et al., 2012).

However, it is considerably more difficult to assess the impact of bringing together these services into a single organisation, as has been the case in Mexico, since there is no obvious "control group", other than comparing SMEs performance before and after the policy change. For example, the UK Business Links study (Mole et al., 2009) sought to estimate the impact of bringing the delivery of services together via a one-stop-shop as opposed to these offering these services in a more dispersed manner, but it proved impossible to evaluate in practice.

In evaluating the Mexican programme, the first key step will be the identification of key performance criteria. There is an implication in the data compiled by the Ministry of Economy that the support provided by Mexico Emprende Centres is expected to lead to more jobs. The distinction is made between jobs created and jobs maintained and this information is collected for all programme recipients. However other criteria are less clear. For instance, it is not clear whether the jobs specified are to be created only in the recipient firms or whether they can occur more widely in the economy through productivity improvements. Likewise, it is not clear over what period of time the job creation is expected to occur. It might even be an implicit objective for the programme to lower the death/closure rate of enterprises, as reflected in the Mi-Tortilla programme.

Clearly, the impact of the Mexico Emprende Centres will not be accurately measured by quantifying the total number of employees at an assisted enterprise when it receives assistance and inferring that this constitutes jobs maintained, as is currently the case. The conservation of jobs is of course a valid objective of policy and the increased enterprise competitiveness that the programme seeks to create can be expected to increase the probability of firm survival and its ability to conserve jobs in the long run. However, it cannot be argued that all jobs in assisted enterprises are the result of policy support, since many will survive without the assistance. It is equally incorrect to assume that any increases in employment in the firm, following the assistance, is a valid measure of the number of jobs created by the assistance. The impact of the policy is rather the difference between what actually happened and what would have happened to the firm if the policy were not in place, all else held equal. It is therefore not correct to attribute all employment change in the enterprise to the policy when it might have occurred anyway – perhaps because of actions that would have been taken by the owner, or external events in the local or macro-economy.

To address this issue, the central requirement for providing an accurate assessment of the impact of Mexico Emprende Centres is the development of control groups, specifically a group of enterprises that are similar or identical to those benefitting from Mexico Emprende assistance but which did not receive assistance from the programme or received different forms of assistance. The performance of these firms can then be tracked alongside those of the Mexico Emprende firms so as to assess the programme impact. In simple terms, the performance of the control group firms in employment, survival rates etc, would then be compared with that of the assisted or "treated" firms that used the Mexico Emprende Centre's services. It is then the difference between the outcomes of the two groups that constitutes the impact of the service.

6.3.3. Evaluating technology parks

Mexican technology parks provide a range of services and incubation facilities to selected technology enterprises. Such initiatives have been widely evaluated in OECD countries for more than 20 years. An early UK evaluation was carried out by Monck et al. (1988). That study examined the impact of science parks on tenant companies by comparing their performance with that of otherwise comparable off-park firms. The performance measures included not only employment growth but also links with universities and other higher education institutions, R&D intensity, patent activity and the launch of new products and services.

Other more recent examples of technology park evaluations include two studies in Sweden (Löfsten and Lindelöf, 2003; Ferguson and Olofsson, 2004) and one in Italy (Colombo and Delmastro, 2002). These studies also examined differences in performance of between on-park and off-park firms. There was a particular focus on differences in the collaboration with universities of technology based firms located on and off the technology parks.

In order to more robustly establish programme impacts in Mexico, it would be useful to undertake a comparable analysis. This would require a comparison over time of the performance of science park firms with otherwise similar firms not located in a science park, focusing among other issues on their innovation linkages.

6.3.4. Evaluating the Technological Innovation Fund

This Fund is operated through CONACYT and NAFIN and provides subsidies for innovation activities in Mexican SMEs. The selection process for supported projects is important because it suggests how treatment and control groups can be established for the purposes of evaluation. The selection involves the following steps:

- all companies have to demonstrate they are innovative;

- they have to satisfy the size and sector eligibility criteria specified by the Fund;

- they complete an online proposal;

- the proposals are then outsourced to two experts in the subject who provide their scientific judgement on the proposal;

- a Committee makes the final judgement on whether or not the funding is provided.

Approximately 10% of the proposals have been successful. The evaluation opportunity presented by this selection process is to compare enterprises making successful applications with unsuccessful applicants. The latter can be expected to have much more similar characteristics to the successful projects than the population in general. Good data are also available on both groups at the outset. Scorings are also provided by experts that can be used to refine the comparison, for example by assessing the impact of different company characteristics on the score and including that information as a factor influencing the outcome.

The Swedish Innovation Centres (SICs) Programme offers similar services to the Technological Innovation Fund and suggests an evaluation approach that could be used in Mexico. SICs provided seed capital to innovative new and small Swedish enterprises between 1994 and 2003. Firms were required to be less than three years old, able to commercialise their technology and be technically or intellectually advanced. The total public cost of the programme was approximately EUR 170 million. Two main types of financial support were supplied. The first was a financial grant of approximately EUR 4 000 from which the more promising ideas were directed to a second stage, which provided a loan of up to EUR 43 500 which had to be repaid if the project generated revenues.

Norrman and Bager-Sjögren (2010) undertook an official evaluation of the programme. They analysed all limited company applicants and then compared their performance over time with those that were rejected. They nonetheless commented that the selection procedure (similar to that used in the Mexico Fund) perhaps led to "average" firms being selected and high risk/high return firms being rejected, implying a need for some allowance in the evaluation. Furthermore, they observed that, even after seven years, it may still be difficult to assess the impact of this type of programme.

A second example is the National Research Council's Industrial Research Assistance Program (IRAP) in Canada. This is a federal government funded programme designed to assist SMEs improve their innovation capacity. It provides both advisory services and grants to Canadian firms. The programme has a long history and has been evaluated every five years – with the latest being National Research Council (2012). This evaluation also compared the performance of assisted projects with non-assisted applications in terms of growth and innovation rates.

In general, innovation programmes are particularly problematic to assess because of their lengthy gestation periods and non-normal distribution of returns. In the case of the Mexican Technological Innovation Fund, a long term assessment will be required because any effect on innovation in new and small firms is likely to be observed only in the medium to longer term. Taking only a short period risks missing, or under-estimating, developments that can take even up to half a century to become fully commercialised, while conversely, some innovations which have short term impacts fail to continue into even the medium term. The second issue, as identified in the Sweden case above, is that the majority of the impact is delivered by a tiny minority of firms so evaluation has to pick up all these firms and the robustness of small samples is compromised.

A satisfactory evaluation, reaching the same standards as the Sweden evaluation, will require the careful tracking of both successful and unsuccessful applicants over a number of years (at least five) after the funding decision has been made. To undertake such an evaluation, data collection will be vital. Rigorous evaluation requires all applicants, successful and unsuccessful, to provide information on themselves, their prior performance and their business plans. Both groups of applicants then have to be tracked over time.

The simple approach is to use this information to compare changes in the successful and the unsuccessful groups over following five years. However what has consistently emerged is the critical role played by the experts assessing the scientific merit of the projects and the Committee in making the awards. Although such groups consistently assert the vital positive role they play, the evidence, such as that by Wallsten (2000) on the US SBIR programme and Norrman and Bager-Sjögren (2010) in Sweden, implies that they are risk-averse and fail to recognise the truly exceptional projects. This introduces selection bias into comparisons between the assisted and non-assisted groups.

The ideal approach would therefore be to conduct a "randomised trial" of the kind recommended for this programme by Storey (2008). This would place all the rejected proposals in a lottery and a small proportion would be drawn "from the hat". These lucky firms would be allocated funding and support in an identical way to those selected by the experts and the Committee. The information that they were "lottery winners" would not be made known to anyone.

The performance of those selected by the experts and the Committee would then be compared with the lottery firms to assess whether the programme had a positive, negative or no effect. The information on performance would also be linked to the scores given by the experts at the time the applications were assessed in order to provide valuable learning to experts and the Committee on whether their scoring reflected the firms' potential.

6.3.5. Evaluating the National Credit Guarantee Scheme

This scheme offers banks guarantees on SME lending that helps to replace the collateral that SMEs lack. The objectives of the programme are such that it needs to be judged on three grounds. The first is the extent to which SME Fund levers loans from the commercial banks. The second is evidence that access to credit has improved in Mexico over time. The third is whether the SMEs that benefit from the guarantee subsequently improve their performance.

An evaluation of the Mexico programme can be based on experience from evaluations in other OECD countries (see for example Zecchini and Ventura, 2009; Graham, 2004). These studies indicate that in order to evaluation the guarantee fund more accurately, a large sample should be established of some 3 000 SMEs that have expressed interest in the programme. From this sample, three groups would be identified: those that receive the guarantee, those rejected for the guarantee and those randomly excluded. If the guarantee is effective then the recipients of the guarantee should perform significantly better than those in either of the other two groups.

Since the guarantee programme represents a large share of government expenditure on SMEs, it also important to assess whether alternative approaches to stimulating the SME credit market could work more effectively than the provision of guarantees at least in certain areas.

6.4. Developing systemic evaluation expertise

6.4.1. *The systemic approach to evaluation*

All of the major programmes included within the SME and entrepreneurship portfolio of the federal government can be rigorously evaluated individually given the collection of appropriate data and the use of appropriate techniques. However for evaluation to perform its key function of informing and shaping policy it needs to be not only robust in its assessment of key programmes but also to be embedded within the political and institutional system.

Systemic evaluation requires that programmes are compared with each other so that, for example, the impact on SME development of spending on the Mexico Emprende can be compared with the Guarantee Fund. In the event of one programme having considerably greater impact than another there would be a case for resource transfer between the programmes. To make this comparison therefore requires careful evaluation of the individual programmes on a broadly comparable basis (see Box 6.2).

One of the requirements for an evaluation approach that is able to compare the success of different programmes in achieving government objectives is clarity about those objectives. At the heart of a system of evaluation has to be an overarching single high-level statement about SME and entrepreneurship policy that clarifies the objectives of policy and the inevitable trade-offs that need to be made. This currently does not exist in Mexico. For example, the issues that the statement should clarify include:

- The extent to which policy focuses on creating new enterprises (entrepreneurship policy) and enhancing the performance of existing (small) enterprises (SME policy)?
- The extent to which encouraging the transition of existing informal enterprises into the formal sector is a key objective of policy, and the indicators to be used to assess the extent to which policy achieves this.
- Whether higher priority should be given to technology-based enterprises, capable of selling overseas and growing rapidly, compared with smaller scale enterprises.
- The extent to which job creation or productivity growth are the prime "success criteria" for policy.
- Whether there are specific groups in Mexico that merit particular attention such that policy-makers are prepared to accept that, even though the cost of job creation amongst

Box 6.2. **A portfolio approach to SME and entrepreneurship policy evaluation**

One of the major challenges in managing policies across government departments and agencies is to ensure that the set of projects and programmes pursued is the most appropriate for meeting strategic objectives and that the available budget is directed towards the activities that give the greatest returns to public investment.

In the 2011 OECD study on SMEs and entrepreneurship, *Thailand: Key Issues and Policies*, an approach to address this challenge was proposed: a portfolio approach to SME and entrepreneurship policy (OECD, 2011; Hall, 2003). The approach is based on the notion that SME and entrepreneurship policy can be seen as a "portfolio" of different programmes; each with a given a strategic aim or objective in line with the government's current policy priorities.

The approach involves two key components:

1. Each individual programme's: *budget, target enterprise segment* (by stage of development), and *service* to be provided must be determined and clear *key performance indicators* (or objectives) established. These metrics allow for all programmes to be allocated within the portfolio in terms of their **cost** and their intended impact.

2. Systematic evaluation of projects and programmes must be carried out so as to determine the relevant **benefits** of the programme. Once programmes have been evaluated, preferably through cost-benefit analysis, the relative success or usefulness of the programme can be assessed, gaps in programme activity can be identified, and areas where reallocation of resources could improve the performance of the whole portfolio of budget investments can be determined.

Table 6.1 provides an example of such a framework that can be adapted to the policy context of each country, although international comparisons will be facilitated by keeping as closely as possible to these suggested headings. For systemic evaluation, information on costs and benefits needs to be collected for each policy category (1-6) and each enterprise segment (A-G), enabling comparisons of cost effectiveness across the portfolio. This comparison has to recognise that there are different objectives of different interventions and that it is not possible to compare all interventions on a single measure. It also has to recognise that certain objectives may be worth greater spending than others, according to the priorities of government. However, it is only by setting out expenditures and impacts clearly that informed decisions can be made about the balance of effort across the portfolio.

Table 6.1. **A model SME and entrepreneurship policy portfolio**

Enterprise segments (A-G)		Policy and programme categories					
		1	2	3	4	5	6
		Education training, HR	Information knowledge	Finance	Market access and development	Technology innovation	Compliance and assistance
A	Pre-nascent	1A	2A	3A	4A	5A	6A
B	Nascent	1B	2B	3B	4B	5B	6B
C	Start-up	1C	2C	3C	4C	5C	6C
D	Operation	1D	2D	3D	4D	5D	6D
E	Growth	1E	2E	3E	4E	5E	6E
F	International	1F	2F	3F	4F	5F	6F
G	Adjust exit	1G	2G	3G	4G	5G	6G

Source: OECD, 2011.

Box 6.2. **A portfolio approach to SME and entrepreneurship policy evaluation** *(cont.)*

Mexico is in a strong position to implement a portfolio approach to SME and entrepreneurship policy design and evaluation because of the clear design of its SME Fund, which already corresponds to the basic portfolio approach. Since 2007, all programmes are calibrated towards one of five target firms segment and one of five service offerings. This enables the portfolio to be constructed along the two axes: target enterprise segment and category of policy intervention.

The Ministry of Economy is already able to track spending on the various programmes of the SME Fund in a way that matches the requirements outlined above. This allows the "cost" component of cost-benefit analysis to be determined for each programme.

However, two key elements are missing. The first is a White Paper that sets out clearly the key performance indicators (or objectives). Only once the objectives of each programme have been defined can the relevant impacts be reliably measured. Second, more needs to be done in terms of proper impact evaluation, as opposed to monitoring of jobs "created" or "maintained". A rigorous and accurate evaluation of policy impact should be based on a robust and consistent methodology across all programmes.

---

this group is considerably higher than for the remainder of the population, such programmes remain justifiable. Such groups might include women, certain ethnic groups or areas of extreme deprivation or disadvantage.

Clarification of such issues will help to assess the relative weight to put on policy interventions achieving the different objectives, as well as the relative expenditure that is merited to achieve different desired outcomes. If job creation is to be the common metric by which all programmes are judged this makes it easier to compare the impact of programmes. If, instead, individual programmes have very different objectives this also has to be specified so that, although cross-programme impact assessment is made more difficult, the performance of different programmes can be transparent.

In addition to comparing cost effectiveness across programmes, a further role of systemic evaluation in Mexico is to provide information that compares the impact of the various intermediary delivery organisations. Such information would be a mechanism for collective learning about good practice from high-performing intermediaries which can validly be transferred to poorer performing intermediaries. In parallel it may be necessary to transfer resources from poorer performing to better performing intermediaries. A complication is that the various intermediaries are involved in delivering various different programmes. In order to make valid comparisons, it is therefore necessary to compare intermediaries operating *within* specific programmes.

6.4.2. *Implementing a systemic approach to evaluation*

An evaluation system is one in which impact is continually reviewed and assessed as it moves through the cycle of formulation, introduction, implementation, review and re-formulation of policy. This process and the guidance on it that has been produced by OECD governments are set out in OECD (2007). A number of more recent operational manuals that capture the OECD good practice guidance have been produced, an example being the Australian Department of Innovation, Industry, Science and Research's Best Practice Evaluation Handbook outlined in Box 6.3. Preparation and promotion of a similar guidance manual would be useful for promoting best practice evaluation in Mexico.

Box 6.3. **An example of evaluation guidance: The *Best Practice Evaluation Handbook* of the department of Innovation, Science and Research, Australia**

Many governments prepare and disseminate good practice information on evaluation. This is important both to guide specialised evaluation teams in cases where governments set up central evaluation units, and so that programme managers are aware of the practices and principles of evaluation and can assist with the collection of comparable and consistent data and are able to understand and use evaluation results.

The Australian Government promotes a systematic approach to evaluation of SME and entrepreneurship programmes through the use of a *Best Practice Evaluation Handbook*. This provides a common framework for the evaluations of programmes promoted by the Department and ensures that policy-makers consider evaluation, and the key issues related to evaluation, when designing and implementing programmes.

Description

The handbook is designed to be distributed amongst programme managers and to be used throughout the project cycle, from policy formulation to implementation and results and feedback of results into policy re-formulation. The Department has its own Evaluation and Strategy Planning Team (who prepared the handbook) but the purpose of the guidance is to ensure that evaluation is part of everyone's work and not seen as a separate activity undertaken by another team.

The handbook includes guidance in the following areas:

- How to use evaluation: an explanation of what evaluation is and why the Department considers evaluation to be important. Key types and timings of evaluations are also defined.

- How to prepare an evaluation strategy and how this fits in with Departmental Strategy and the Evaluation Team. It is important that each programme has its own evaluation strategy and that this becomes part of programme management.

- Production of an evaluation framework, including comprehensive checklists for different aspects of the framework. The checklists are not a set of boxes to tick, but rather give a list of questions to be answered and issues to be considered.

- Planning and conducting an evaluation including determining what exactly is to be evaluated, and the way in which this will be done (for example whether external consultants should be used).

- Definition of key aspects to be evaluated and the questions which have to be answered in each section. These are defined under the headings: appropriateness, effectiveness, efficiency, integration, performance assessment, and strategic policy alignment. Defining these headings ensures a consistency of approach and use of definitions, and comparability among different evaluations.

- Guidance on methodology, implementation and reporting to ensure common standards.

The handbook has a limited number of annexes which further explain key items (typical terms of reference, table of contents, use of programme logic), but is designed to be read in conjunction with other documents and frameworks related to the design and implementation of programmes.

Box 6.3. **An example of evaluation guidance:**
**The *Best Practice Evaluation Handbook* of the department of Innovation,
Science and Research, Australia** *(cont.)*

Key points

This is a relatively short document (50 pages in total) and is designed to explain key concepts rather than to give comprehensive and detailed guidance on individual evaluations. Its purpose is to ensure that programme managers integrate evaluation into their work. It therefore starts with sections explaining why evaluation is important and how it fits into the other activities of the Department.

The handbook makes considerable use of checklists. However, these are not structured bureaucratically (actions which need to be taken, documents which need to be collected) but rather show a set of issues and questions to be considered. This is important because evaluations can be quite varied in approach and different aspects will be important for different evaluations.

In a short document there is only a limited overview of evaluation methodologies and issues involved in collecting data (for example, difficulties of finding a control group, sample bias, confidence intervals, estimating deadweight). Rather the handbook seeks to raise the issue so that managers can seek detailed technical guidance elsewhere.

Finally, the handbook ensures that there are set of key overall measures which have clear definitions and which will be considered in all evaluations. This ensures some consistency of approach and also that evaluations are comparable (both of several evaluations of the same programme and of contemporaneous evaluations of different programmes).

It is important that evaluation is integrated into each stage of the policy cycle. At the stage of policy formulation it is of paramount importance that the objectives of the policy are clearly specified, perhaps even as part of the legislation. It is also critical that steps are taken from the outset to collect the data that will be needed to evaluate impact at a later stage, since it is often impossible to collect the required information later, when it is time for an evaluation to take place. The policy formulation process clearly should not only look forward to future evaluation arrangements, but should also base choices on policy preferences and design issues with reference to existing evaluation evidence from past programmes.

At the stage of implementation, the key task is to collect data on take-up and use of programmes. It is clear that this is generally available for most current programmes. This data should be consulted as the programme is implemented in order to assess whether there appear to be problems in implementation that need to be corrected.

An evaluation is then undertaken during a review stage. The purpose of the review is to assess, for all individual programmes, their impact in terms of the specified criteria and using the most robust methods. An additional role is to use that information to both compare programmes and also to compare the performance of individual intermediaries within the programme.

At the policy reformulation stage, the evaluation information is used to make judgements about the effectiveness of different programmes and the intermediaries that deliver the programmes. It has to be emphasised that the evaluation data is only one element of any restructuring decision. For example, it is to be expected that the circumstances facing some programmes or some intermediaries may be more challenging than those facing other programmes so their impacts may be smaller. These different circumstances have to be taken into account.

The implementation of an effective evaluation system therefore requires the following:

- Statistical analysis skills of the highest level. This may be inside government if the evaluations are internal or amongst external organisations such as consultants or universities, which has the benefit of greater independence. If external evaluations are used, then government officials must have sufficient evaluation capability to manage these technical contracts.

- Political skills to persuade those delivering programmes to share their detailed knowledge of how programmes operate with the evaluators.

- Close involvement with the key policy makers to ensure that evaluation issues are incorporated at all stages in the policy cycle, i.e. when the policy is being developed, as it evolves and once it is in operation. Failure to engage in any of those stages can mean that the objectives of the policy are never adequately specified or that information is not collected on all applicants to the programme.

- Communication skills in being able to "translate" what can be quite complex inferences from evaluation results into simple concepts that can be widely understood and which lead to policy changes that can be easily implemented and lead to clear improvements.

- A forum within government at which the evaluation findings can be discussed. This forum has to be where key decisions on resource transfers between programmes take place.

Different OECD countries have different approaches to policy evaluation. In some the role is undertaken by a central audit office. This often involves sub-contracting individual evaluations to specialist outsiders. Other countries have specialist evaluation teams within the relevant ministries. The arguments for and against both approaches are set out clearly in OECD (2007), but there are merits in either approach. Examples of different approaches to addressing this issue are presented in Box 6.4.

Box 6.4. Approaches to SME and entrepreneurship policy evaluation within government

Ministry of Economic Development, New Zealand

The Ministry of Economic Development (MED) has established an Evaluation Team within its Organisational Development and Support branch to undertake evaluations of the ministry's programmes and initiatives. A number of the recent evaluations undertaken by the team relate to SMEs. An example is the PLATO evaluation. PLATO is a business advice and mentoring programme that was piloted in Auckland from 2008 to 2010. An evaluation of the pilot was carried out to assess its impact on the participating SME owners and the viability of continuing the programme in Auckland as well as extending it to other regions. It concluded that it was unclear whether there had been a marked improvement in the management capabilities and business performance of the group members. However, attributing performance improvements conclusively to PLATO (and indeed ultimate outcomes) may perhaps be unrealistic especially after a short time period. It was found that the programme had established learning networks that developed a positive sharing of information and better knowledge. This should ultimately result in improved management capabilities and thereby performance.

Box 6.4. **Approaches to SME and entrepreneurship policy evaluation within government** (*cont.*)

Department of Business, Innovation and Skills, United Kingdom

The Enterprise Directorate within the Department of Business, Innovation and Skills works across national and sub-national government in England to develop and influence policies to boost enterprise, start ups and small business growth. It is supported by a strong Analytical Unit, responsible for research, evaluation and statistics for policy design. The Unit has an influential role in promoting and developing evidence-based policy on small business issues. It contributes to the policy development cycle by:

- using research to determine the need (or rationale) for a policy or programme;
- defining a policy/programme's objectives;
- appraising the options for achieving these objectives;
- monitoring progress;
- evaluating effectiveness and cost effectiveness;
- feeding the results back into the further refinement and development of policy.

During 2011-12, the team has undertaken or managed work on issues such as job creation in SMEs, policies to improve access to external equity, the transition from unemployment to self-employment and the role of social enterprises.

6.4.3. Data for an evaluation system

In Mexico a vast amount of data is collected according to the audit requirements of all federal programmes. The participating SMEs are extensively audited and, the data appear to be of high quality. Some programmes for example have, or expect to have shortly, a Client Relationship Management (CRM) system, which implies reliable information.

Despite collecting this data, the Mexican government do not make this data "work" for the benefit of policy design, as is the case with governments in almost all countries throughout the world and in contrast to many large commercial organisations such as banks or retail chains. The current situation is that data are collected and stored, often by individual departments, but are frequently never used or shared with other departments. However, there is much useful information here for evaluation purposes, which could be used if it is shared, subject to reasonable confidentiality requirements, between departments of government. Essentially, every individual enterprise interaction with government should be documented and used in a central database.

In Mexico, every enterprise that is formally registered for tax purposes has one serial number, which is its tax registration number. It is this number that distinguishes the formal from the informal enterprise. Accessing that number for each enterprise, together with recording each interaction with government of the enterprise, would mean that eligible government bodies will be able to identify which government programmes the enterprise has used and for which programmes they have applied. Government should also be able to track their employment, sales and taxes paid over time, before and after receipt of services. This will be tremendously valuable for the implementation of the programme evaluation approaches recommended above.

The availability and use of this information would support government in its policy decisions, providing information about how well programmes work and how well intermediaries work. It will also support government in the process of referral of enterprises to the most relevant services to them. Thus, information on the take-up of programmes by an enterprise would enable government to inform them about other public programmes that might be of interest to them. For example it could be used to inform companies that have received marketing or productivity improvement support about relevant calls for tendering for public procurement contracts. Furthermore, the same information would not have to be provided by the enterprise many times over, so easing the application process for programmes.

There is an information technology challenge to integrate this information into a single enterprise database, but this is comparatively easy once a single enterprise serial number has been allocated. Several developed countries either have that unique serial number (such as Denmark) or are working towards that end (such as New Zealand).

The other challenge is the fear on the part of the SME that sharing tax and possibly employment data would lead to them paying more tax. There is then a risk that this, in turn, could lead to a reduced participation in public programmes and a slowing of the progress made towards a higher proportion of economic output being produced in the formal sector. However, many SMEs are recognising that, whilst there are costs to formality, the gains are potentially considerable, in terms of information and access to funding that enable their business to survive and prosper. Better use of data, enabling better evaluations to be undertaken, benefit the SME and taxpayers more widely and so should be encouraged.

6.5. Conclusions

In Mexico, data on policy "inputs" in terms of public expenditures and their distribution across different programme types and different target groups of entrepreneur and enterprise are of very good quality. This enables an overview of the priorities set for policy and provides the cost side of the information required for cost-benefit analysis and provides a good basis for strengthening the role of evaluation.

The key challenges for the future consist of improving information on the benefit side of cost-benefit assessments of programmes, and putting together programme evaluation information across the whole policy portfolio in a more systemic evaluation approach.

Monitoring data is already collected for certain objectives of government policy, including jobs created and jobs maintained. However, this information is not always collected using the most robust evaluation techniques. Reliable job impact information must be based on an assessment of the "additionality" of the support provided in terms of how it has improved performance over what otherwise would have taken place. This requires the greater development of control group evaluation studies. In addition, other objectives of intervention have to be stated clearly for each programme so that evaluation can then follow the impact against these objectives.

In order to make decisions about where to put resources across different programmes and intermediary organisations, it is important to have comprehensive evaluation results across the entire portfolio of policy that are collected and organised in a consistent manner. The basic framework for portfolio assessment is already in place in Mexico in the form of the SME Fund's "five-by-five" approach, which distinguishes policy expenditures and activities by five policy categories and five enterprise segments. What is required now is further comparable information on outputs based on reliable evaluation methods. This will be supported by a strategic document that sets out clearly the primary and secondary objectives for each programme, together with a unit responsible for undertaking and promoting evaluation within government and able to issue appropriate evaluation guidance.

The availability of good tracking data will be important to simplifying the evaluation process. This can be collected through surveys of firms participating in government programmes and matching them to surveyed non-participants. However, in parallel there is great potential to make better use of existing information on company performance and company interactions with government through sharing information across departments and programmes tied to the single tax registration code of every formal enterprise. This would be facilitated by the creation of a single enterprise database.

Box 6.5. Specific recommendations on the evaluation system

- Information on the impact of public programmes should be improved by the use of control group studies that compare the performance of time of beneficiary firms with matched non-beneficiaries against key performance indicators. Randomised control trials may also be piloted for selected programme evaluations.

- A concise statement or government paper should be produced that sets out clearly the objectives of SME and entrepreneurship policy and the associated targets for policy. These should be specified in terms of output-based targets and not input-based targets.

- A specific unit should be created within government with responsibility for undertaking, promoting and utilising SME and entrepreneurship policy evaluation.

- A single shared database covering all enterprise interactions with government should be developed, which attributes a single serial number, or code, to all enterprises to enable tracking of their use of government programmes and their performance over time.

References

Colombo, M. and M. Delmastro (2002), "How Effective are Technology Incubators? Evidence from Italy", *Research Policy*, 31(7), 1103-1122.

Fairlie, R.W., D. Karlan and J. Zinman (2012), "Behind the GATE Experiment: Evidence on Effects of and Rationales for Subsidized Entrepreneurship Training", *NBER Working Paper*, No. 17804.

Ferguson, R. and C. Oloffson (2004), "Science Parks and the Development of NTBFs: Location, Survival and Growth", *Journal of Technology Transfer*, 29(1), 5-17.

Gørtz, M., G.P. Rotger and D.J. Storey (2012), "Assessing the Effectiveness of Guided Preparation for New Venture Creation and Performance: Theory and Practice", *Journal of Business Venturing*, 27 (4), 506-521.

Graham, T. (2004), *Review of the Small Firms Loan Guarantee*, H.M. Treasury, London

Gu, Q., L.A. Karoly and J. Zissimopoulos (2010), "Small Business Assistance Programs in the United States: An Analysis of What they Are, How Well they Perform, and How we Can Learn More about Them", *International Review of Entrepreneurship*, 8(3), 199-230.

Hall, C. (2003), "The SME Policy Framework in ASEAN and APEC: Benchmark Comparisons and Analysis", Paper to SEAANZ Ballarat conference, 2003.

Löfsten, H. and P. Lindelöf (2003), "Science Parks and the Growth of New Technology-Based Firms: Academic-Industry Links", *Innovation and Markets, Research Policy*, 31(6), 859-876.

Lopez-Acevedo, G. and H.W. Tang (2010), *Evaluation of SME Programs in Latin America and Caribbean*, World Bank/IBRD, Washington, DC.

Mole, K.F., M. Hart, S. Roper and D.S. Saal (2009), "Assessing the Effectiveness of Business Support Services in England: Evidence from a Theory-Based Evaluation", *International Small Business Journal*, 27(5), 557-582.

Monck, C.S.P., P. Quintas, R.B. Porter, D.J. Storey and P. Wynarczyk (1988), *Science Parks and the Growth of High-Technology Firms*, Croom Helm, London.

Morris, M. and Stevens (2010), "Evaluation of a New Zealand Business Support Programme Using Firm Performance Micro-Data", *Small Enterprise Research*, 17, 30-42.

National Research Council (2012), *Evaluation of the NRC Industrial Research Assistance Program* (NRC-IRAP), Final Report, National Research Council Canada, Ottawa.

Norrman, C. and L. Bager-Sjögren (2010), "Entrepreneurship Policy to Support New Innovative Ventures: Is it Effective?", *International Small Business Journal*, 28(6) 602-619.

OECD (2007), *OECD Framework for the Evaluation of SME and Entrepreneurship Policies and Programmes*, OECD Publishing, *http://dx.doi.org/10.1787/9789264040090-en*.

OECD (2011), *OECD Studies on SMEs and Entrepreneurship: Thailand – Key Issues and Policies*, OECD Publishing, *http://dx.doi.org/10.1787/9789264121775-en*.

Papaconstantinou, G. and W. Polt (1997), "Policy Evaluation in Innovation and Technology: An Overview", *OECD Proceedings Policy Evaluation in Innovation and Technology – Towards Best Practices*, OECD, Paris.

Rogoff, E.G. and M.S. Lee (1996), "Putting Governments Role in Perspective: The Impact of Government Programmes on Entrepreneurs and Small Business Owners", *Journal of Developmental Entrepreneurship*, 1(1), 57-73.

Rotger, G.P. and M. Gørtz (2009), "Evaluating the Effect of Soft Business Support to Entrepreneurs in North Jutland", *Working Paper*, No. 18, Danish Institute of Governmental Research, Copenhagen.

Storey, D. (2008), *Entrepreneurship and SME Policy in Mexico*, prepared for the Inter-American Development Bank.

Wallsten, S.J. (2000), "The Effects of Government-Industry R&D Programs on Private R&D: The Case of the Small Business Innovation Research Program, *RAND Journal of Economics*, 31(1): 82-100.

Zecchini, S. and M. Venturo (2009), "The Impact of Public Guarantees on Credit to SMEs", *Small Business Economics*, 32, 191-206.

Chapter 7

Future directions
for SME and entrepreneurship policy
in Mexico

This chapter draws the key conclusions and policy messages from the OECD review of SME and entrepreneurship issues and policies in Mexico. It argues that the significant policy improvements that have been achieved during the last 12 years should be maintained and that further efforts should prioritise strengthening micro-enterprises and reducing informality, supporting innovative SMEs and start-ups, simplifying the operation of the SME Fund, and strengthening the framework for evaluation of SME and entrepreneurship policies and programmes.

SMEs and entrepreneurship make a fundamental contribution to economic and social development in Mexico, and play a critical role in increasing productivity and employment and reducing poverty. This role has been recognised by the Mexican government, which has strengthened the SME and entrepreneurship policy framework and budget over the last 12 years, resulting in substantial improvements in the business environment for SMEs and entrepreneurship, and increased capabilities for domestic enterprises to start-up, be competitive and grow. Indeed, Mexico has one of the highest business start-up rates in OECD countries, and an expanding SME sector.

This review takes stock of the state of SME and entrepreneurship performance and policies at the end of 2012 and highlights directions for policy development in the future that will maintain the momentum in this important area. It highlights the following principal messages:

1. Substantial policy improvements have taken place since the OECD's last review of SME policies in Mexico, published in 2007.

2. Further efforts are needed to strengthen micro-enterprises and reduce informality.

3. Innovative SMEs and start-ups offer great potential for further high impact interventions.

4. Policy delivery may be improved by simplifying the operation of the SME Fund, and by introducing a more robust evaluation framework capable of identifying the programmes and intermediaries with the greatest impact on achieving government objectives with a view to directing funding towards them.

This concluding chapter sets out these key messages in more detail.

7.1. Embedding the SME and entrepreneurship policy framework

Great strides have been made over the periods 2001-06 and 2007-12 in putting SME and entrepreneurship policy in its proper place in the Mexican economy, given the primordial importance of SMEs and entrepreneurship to economic growth and job creation. During this time, the Mexican government has created a policy framework that offers best practice lessons to other countries in several areas, such as the co-ordination of policy by a single body and the clarity and integration of programme measures.

The improvements started in 2001, when the government made "more and better jobs, more and better enterprises, and more and better entrepreneurs" the cornerstone of its entrepreneurship and SME policy agenda. It formulated the Entrepreneurial Development Plan (EDP) 2001-06, which took a major step forward from the sector-based subsidies of the past to a policy that improved business framework conditions and identified specific market failures for SME policy to address. At this time, the Under Ministry for SMEs was created to design and co-ordinate policy and the SME Fund implemented to support programme actions.

During the last 6 years, further important developments have taken place. The SME Fund has provided a growing budget for SMEs, reflecting their importance to the economy and the growing tax take of the country. A system of intermediary organisations has been developed for the delivery of major programmes, which allows government to reach out to enterprises across the country. New business development service networks have been created, including the Mexico Emprende Centres, which act as a one-stop-shop for SMEs and entrepreneurship, and a major expansion of the national business incubator system has been undertaken that has doubled the number of incubators.

One of the key strengths of the current policy arrangements is the "five-by-five" strategic framework developed for the SME Fund, which enables a clear view of policy priorities and offers a "moving walkway" of support for entrepreneurs and enterprises as they develop. It is comprehensive and integrated, covering initiatives for the five segments of nascent entrepreneurs, micro-enterprises, SMEs, gazelles and tractor firms and the five services of financing, training and consultancy, marketing, management, and innovation. The co-funding and co-design arrangements of the SME Fund have further helped to mobilise state and local actors and secure coherent and tailored policy at local level.

The addition of an entrepreneurship policy to work alongside and in full integration with the previous SME policy is also critical in helping to create a pipeline of entrepreneurial people ready to come forward with good quality entrepreneurial ventures and supporting them through their nascent and feasibility stages to business start-up.

New attention has been given to supporting the development of new and micro-enterprises, together with their entry into the formal sector and their up-scaling to small and medium sized enterprises using training, consulting and finance support.

Furthermore, several programmes offering international good practice lessons exist in Mexico, providing models for policy development elsewhere. They include the Business Accelerators Programme, the Supplier Development Programme, the Modernisation and Integration Programmes and the Federal Commission for Regulatory Improvement.

The last 12 years have therefore been a very productive time for policy. The first priority of policy today should be to secure the gains achieved over the past 12 years, and maintain the degree of policy support to the SME and entrepreneurship sector that has been achieved and the good practice structures and programmes that are now in place.

7.2. Strengthening micro-enterprises

One of the main priorities for the future is the further strengthening of micro-enterprises. Mexico has one of the highest proportions of micro-enterprises in the OECD area but these enterprises have relatively low productivity. They are also associated with high levels of informality. This is a barrier both to their own growth and to the ability of government to collect taxes and support improved public infrastructure and services.

The Modernisation and Integration Programmes and the National Credit Guarantee Programme are making a real difference in this area and should need to be maintained given current conditions, although with potential refinements based on the results of impact evaluations that will need to be undertaken. Their activities are appropriate to the needs. However, the number of beneficiaries of both programmes is small relative to the massive scale of the micro firm sector in Mexico, both formal and informal. For example, the government's target for 2011 was to reach 10 000 micro-enterprises with training and consultancy support, but this represents a tiny proportion of the more than 4.9 million enterprises in the business population. Furthermore, the loan guarantee scheme is currently only reaching around 70 000 micro-enterprises per year, despite its high leverage of private finance, although access to bank credit among micro firms is very low in Mexico. An expansion of support to this sector is justified by its scale and by the barriers faced in the operation of markets, and also seems merited from the evidence provided by monitoring data on job creation impacts, although these numbers are not based on rigorous evaluation.

The particular problem of informality, which affects many Mexican micro-enterprises, also requires other actions. The availability of government-backed finance and advice is an incentive to business registration, but the real challenge is further easing of the regulatory burdens on business, continuing the improvements made in recent years and spreading them across all regions of the country. Reduction of barriers in taxation and social security will also play a role.

The pipeline of new entrepreneurs also needs to be stimulated to reinforce the micro-enterprise sector and hopefully to grow larger enterprises as well. Mexico has a high business start-up rate in general. However, more policy effort here is needed on creating the entrepreneurial attitudes and competences that will encourage new entrepreneurs to identify and exploit growth opportunities and raise productivity. Entrepreneurship training and support for young people in universities and vocational and educational training colleges have an important role to play, as well as the continuation of the more general entrepreneurial awareness programmes that are already well embedded.

Finally, improving access to financing will clearly be critical to increasing the productivity and growth of Mexican micro-enterprises. Major improvements have been made in recent years, backed by the national loan guarantee programme and other government measures such as the Unified Registry of Movable Property Collateral, the support of microcredit institutions, and the creation of a network of private sector credit/financing advisors, as well as by fiscal and monetary prudence. Interest rates have fallen, bank credit requirements have softened and the volume of credit to enterprises has increased.

At the same time, domestic credit to the private sector remains low as a percentage of GDP in Mexico compared to the OECD area as a whole. To help fill this gap, the outreach of guarantee instruments can be expanded by developing additional decentralised guarantee mechanisms in co-operation with local intermediaries. In parallel, the quality and coverage of credit bureau data can be improved to reduce information asymmetries in the credit market, financial education can be introduced for SME managers. For the longer term, competition and business entry should be promoted in the banking sector in order to tackle finance market failures at their root, favouring in particular the development of community-based banks such as co-operative banks and savings banks that use decentralised and relationship lending approaches. An exit strategy for the national guarantee scheme should also be stated, based on progressive reduction in support as private investment in SMEs grows. Mechanisms might also be created to channel immigrant remittances into investment in productive entrepreneurial activities, rather than investment in real estate.

7.3. Stimulating innovative SMEs and start-ups

Another priority challenge is to increase the number of innovative SMEs and start-ups in Mexico. This group of firms is associated with relatively rapid productivity and employment growth and internationalisation activity and contributes disproportionately to achieving key government objectives. The government has introduced some important new programmes to promote innovative SMEs and start-ups during the last 6 years, but there is scope to extend and enlarge them.

For example, since 2007, 31 technology parks have been established in key innovation hubs including universities and research institutions. They are often linked to business incubators, accelerators, research laboratories and other facilities that promote innovation and spin-offs. The Business Acceleration Programme is further supporting young, fast-growing gazelle enterprises in innovation and internationalisation in key high-potential sector niches. The Supplier Development Programme is another example of assistance for innovative SMEs, working through the creation of linkages between SMEs and larger firms operating in global value chains.

However, there are also signs of constraints in the system. For example, only 4% of business incubators are targeting high technology start-ups, and the Technological Innovation Fund is oversubscribed, implying that there are many relevant and viable projects that have to be refused funding support. The share of the SME Fund's budget allocated to innovation and technological development projects represented only 6.6% of the total for SME productive projects in the period 2009-11, mostly flowing into the gazelle programme, although programme monitoring data suggest that the benefits compared with the costs are relatively high for this group of programmes. These observations suggest that there is scope to achieve significant economic development benefits by reaching more innovative and potentially innovative SMEs and start-ups through expanded programmes in this field.

It is also important to take complementary actions to strengthen the absorptive capacity of SMEs. The aim of these measures is to enable them to collaborate with research institutes and universities and larger knowledge-intensive companies. Skills development and innovation-purchasing initiatives can fit this purpose, as can staff exchanges and secondments.

Finally, formal and informal equity markets are just starting to develop. This form of financing is particularly relevant to innovative start-ups and SMEs with innovative projects given the high upside risk of these projects (i.e. potential returns that are not captured by providers of debt but are captured by equity holders). Equity finance should be boosted, for example with new fiscal mechanisms aimed at channelling investment by private savers into equity funds investing in innovative SMEs. Expanded support can also be provided to angel investor clubs across the country, and to the creation of public venture capital funds.

7.4. Adjusting the management of the SME Fund and the intermediary system

The SME Fund is a crucial instrument for ensuring that SMEs and entrepreneurs get the support they need. The budget it provides is fundamental. Its use of intermediary organisations to deliver programmes, such as state governments, universities and chambers of commerce, also secures the large-scale outreach and access into distant locations and target populations that is required. There are nonetheless opportunities to increase impact by acting in the following areas.

7.4.1. Simplifying the operation of the SME Fund

The effectiveness of the SME Fund is hindered by the limits of its annual budgeting, its heavy requirements for provision of information on expenditures and activities, and delays for intermediary organisations in receiving approval and payment. This adversely affects the level of interest of some potential co-funders and potential intermediary organisations which could otherwise be ready to help deliver relevant projects.

Simplifying the reporting and compliance procedures of the SME Fund and introducing a multi-year funding formula would make it easier for partners and intermediary organisations to participate and develop longer term projects corresponding to the needs of the enterprise population. Similarly, the disbursement of project money should be processed more quickly than is the case now.

7.4.2. Selection procedures for intermediaries

Even though the current pool of intermediary organisations delivering policy on behalf of government focuses on those organisations that are considered to have the greatest capacities, there are important differences in their quality levels and their abilities to serve the client group at sufficient scale. This implies an opportunity to level-up quality and capacity.

One of the ways of achieving this is to concentrate funding on the better performing organisations, i.e. those intermediaries able to reach the greatest numbers of clients, reach out to under-served groups, refer firms to complementary services and have the most impact on business creation, growth and competitiveness. At the same time, it is important to renew the intermediary pool over time by bringing in new players in order to create competition and encourage innovation in delivery.

Many other countries have also made the choice of delivering public programme support to SMEs and entrepreneurs through intermediary organisations. Australia's Small Business Advisory Service, is an example. The effectiveness of the approaches depends to a significant degree on the systems that are put in place for the selection and management of intermediaries.

Efforts are already being made by the Mexican government to strengthen the intermediary selection processes. Since 2011, stricter requirements for the validation of new intermediary organisations have been put into place, including a requirement of a minimum experience of two years as an organisation and reinforced filtering systems. Furthermore, there has been a rationalisation in the number of intermediary organisations, which has fallen from near one thousand five years ago to approximately three hundred today, enabling concentration on the most capable. However, there are still problems of lack of awareness among potential intermediary organisations of the considerations that will affect whether or not a proposal is accepted.

The efforts to improve selection processes should therefore be continued. In doing so, a particular emphasis should be placed on:

● the use of clear merit criteria for selection and a competitive and transparent selection process;

● marketing, promotion and outreach to involve more potential intermediaries across different sectors, activity areas and regions and encourage them to develop approaches that will succeed in the selection process;

● provision of clear guidelines to potential applicants on the objectives of the programme they are applying to deliver, the criteria that will be applied for selecting intermediaries, the eligible and preferred types of proposals and the arrangements for payment and evaluation of the services delivered;

● the use of impact evaluation to identify the intermediaries with the greatest impacts on achieving objectives within given programmes.

7.4.3. Capacity building for business development service providers

An alternative, or rather complementary, way of levelling up quality and capacity is to identify problems in intermediary organisations and see how government can help overcome them through capacity building efforts. Part of the story is investment in physical infrastructure. However, a further part of the story, which is more likely to be overlooked, is the provision of opportunities for training and knowledge sharing to management and staff on best practice processes and services. This is particularly relevant for the management, staff and consultants of business development services, including the business incubators and Mexico Emprende Centres. The skills of staff play a critical function in the ability of intermediaries and business development services organisations to bring clients into the support system and to provide services that will make a difference to business creation and growth rates.

Despite some existing efforts to provide training, further upgrading of the skills of business development service staff should be envisaged. Better staff will be more able to diagnose the services that can make a difference to supported enterprises, to communicate the policy options to firms and entrepreneurs and to deliver these services in a best practice fashion. Certification of learning is a further important element of the skills upgrading measures for intermediary organisation management and staff.

Sharing of good practices among business development service providers and intermediary organisations is also important and can be co-ordinated through networks of organisations involved in SME and entrepreneurship promotion.

In parallel, national branding of SME Fund-supported services should also be introduced in order to provide greater visibility to services among the population of SMEs and entrepreneurship and to provide potential users with a gauge of their quality, hence increasing their confidence in accessing services.

7.4.4. Introducing and using more robust impact evaluation evidence

One of the main tools available for the continuous improvement of SME and entrepreneurship policies is an evaluation framework that can robustly assess the relevance, effectiveness and efficiency of its various projects and programmes and of its various intermediary organisations. There are key strengths in the existing evaluation approach in Mexico in this respect, notably in the quality of data on programme expenditures and activities and the organisation of the policy within a model portfolio design.

On the other hand, there are two key weaknesses. The first is that programme impact information is generally not based on the most robust methods, meaning that it is difficult to know with confidence which programmes are performing the best against their objectives. The second is that evaluation is not undertaken systematically across all programmes and across all intermediaries operating a programme. The consequence of this is that it is therefore difficult to undertake a "helicopter assessment" of the entire policy portfolio or to make informed choices about where to prioritise spending.

There is a need for a more systemic evaluation approach focused on more comprehensive and robust impact evaluation. The development of such an approach would be favoured by the improvement of methods tracking of beneficiaries and setting up control groups, by the creation of a database shared across ministries recording for each enterprise all its interactions with government as well as available information on its growth and survival performance, and the creation of an effective organisation within government for research and evaluation on SME and entrepreneurship policies and programmes.

Similarly, relevant output objectives should be built into programme documents and the project funding contracts of intermediary organisations to enable the evaluation of impact. This should be supported by the creation of a visible, self-standing, cross-government policy statement on the objectives of government SME and entrepreneurship policy and how it intends to achieve these objectives.

Annexes:
International learning models

A.1. Australia's enterprise connect

This international experience relates to the recommendation regarding the management, co-ordination and capacity building of intermediary organisations in Mexico.

Description of the approach

Enterprise Connect is a national network created by the Federal Government in Australia in 2008. Twelve Enterprise Connect Centres have been established across the country employing 100 business advisors and facilitators. Some of the centres are in manufacturing areas while others are in innovation hubs focused on certain specialisations such as creative industries, defence, and clean energy. They are particularly focused on supporting innovative SMEs.

The Centres aim to connect eligible SMEs to business and management advisory services with a particular focus upon innovation, technology and research. The core service is provided by Business Advisors working out of the Centres through what is called the Business Review, or company diagnosis. This offers a comprehensive, holistic analysis of the firm. It assesses the operational and strategic position of the firm, including relative strengths and weaknesses, strategic business issues, critical areas for business improvement, and potential pathways for growth. The Review results in a report which includes a series of recommendations for improvement, potential pathways forward and provides key linkages. From the review, matched grant funding of up to AUD 20 000 is available to implement recommendations.

Since 2008, Enterprise Connect has assisted 12 000 SMEs – several of which have achieved awards (Department of Innovation, Industry, Science and Research and IP, Australia, 2011). Evaluation results from its responsible body the Department for Innovation, Industry, Science and Research and Tertiary Education show that 96% of Enterprise Connect clients SMEs are implementing at least one recommendation arising from the Business Reviews provided. Substantial improvements have been achieved in the areas of innovation capability, strategic capability, productivity and efficiency. These results highlight the programme's success as an agent of change. Impartial one-to-one advice, coupled with additional services and knowledge linkages have resulted in longer term change in client SMEs.

Factors for success

Several elements of the governance of the programme have contributed to its achievements.

First, Enterprise Connect is a flagship federal government programme enjoying strong support from the national ministry. It provides a focus as a major vehicle for federal government support for SMEs and attempts to complement state government initiatives.

Second, horizontal co-ordination at the local level has been delivered by collaboration between staff from the Department for Innovation, Industry, Science and Research and Tertiary Education and staff based in the regions and other regional partners such as the

Aus-Industry Regional Managers Network. Such collaborations have made possible the provision of complementary services, rather than their overlap. Enterprise Connect staff have co-operated in effective joint working arrangements including cross-referring businesses and delivering shared events such as seminars and workshops.

Third, oversight of the network's development and evolution has been supported by an advisory board, involving experienced members from the private and public sectors, trade unions and research organisations.

Obstacles and responses

Enterprise Connect directly addresses the problems experienced by SMEs in finding the time and knowledge to develop and deliver innovation in their businesses. It engages these challenges by connecting businesses to new ideas and technologies to boost productivity and increase international competitiveness. The changing context has raised further issues for SMEs to which Enterprise Connect has tried to respond through a suite of additional services. Increasing international competition and climate change have been addressed with new elements, including the Clean 21 Technology Innovation Network, the Food and Beverage Industry Network, the Printing and Publishing Industry Network, and "Buy Australian at Home and Abroad" initiatives. Enterprise Connect has gone even further to develop new initiatives for the provision of tailored services, for example addressing the needs of SMEs in the tourism sector affected by floods in 2011. These tourism services have since been extended to tourism based SMEs nationally along with the establishment of the National Tourism Industry Network.

Relevance for Mexico

Enterprise Connect's experience may provide some inspiration for Mexico in terms of the way that the government has developed a national programme for SMEs and entrepreneurs across its extensive national territory using a network of service centres. The institutional frameworks for this are similar in that an Under Ministry in Mexico and a Departmental Division in Australia are used to lead and development the policy framework. Similar too is the use of an indirect network model of intermediate organisations for policy delivery. Enterprise Connect is delivered in partnership with a range of different kinds of intermediate delivery bodies, including business associations (e.g. Australian Industry Group), Chambers of Commerce (e.g. Queensland, Western Australia), sector organisations (e.g. Geelong Manufacturing Council), innovation institutions (e.g. Industry Capability Network, Queensland) and local government (e.g. Gold Coast City Council).

The challenges faced by both countries in managing, co-ordinating and building capacity amongst its network of intermediaries are therefore similar. Both countries have grown delivery networks in relatively short periods of time and each now has comprehensive programmes of support. They are both entering a phase where they need assessment and reflection upon system-wide issues of effectiveness and efficiency, the trade-offs between national coverage and specialisation, and the potential need for further competition amongst providers.

Further information

Ms Judith Zielke, Head of Division
Enterprise Connect Division
Industry House – 10 Binara Street – Canberra ACT 2601
Tel. : (02) 6213 7330
Fax: (02) 6290 8693
E-mail: judith.zielke@innovation.gov.au
www.enterpriseconnect.gov.au

A.2. The National Business Incubators Association: Improving the knowledge and skills of incubator managers, United States

In Mexico, there is a need to support the development of common skills and competencies among managers and staff of the national business incubator programme in order to ensure the consistency and quality of the services offered across the country and to help improve standards. The US-based National Business Incubators Association provides some interesting lessons on this subject. Mexican incubators could participate in the association, seek to arrange to have some of the NBIA training delivered in Mexico or seek to set up a similar national association or branch in Mexico.

Description of the approach

The US National Business Incubators Association (NBIA) is a membership organisation representing incubator managers and economic development professionals with a mission to advance business incubation and entrepreneurship. It has 1 900 members in over 60 countries, three-quarters of which are in the United States. To accomplish its mission, the NBIA serves as a clearinghouse of information on incubator management and development issues and engages in many activities that support members' professional development. Each year, it provides thousands of professionals with information, education, advocacy and networking resources to bring excellence to the process of assisting early-stage companies. It does this by organising conferences and specialised training, conducting research and compiling statistics on the incubation industry, producing publications that describe practical approaches to business incubation, and consulting with governments and corporations on incubator development.

One of the important activities of the NBIA is its training programme for incubator managers leading to a NBIA Certificate in Incubator Management. This training consists of a comprehensive and practical overview of the tasks and responsibilities of incubator management, including incubator and client funding, mission and strategic planning, facilities management, selecting and serving clients, as well as sharing best management practices in each of these areas. The programme requires three full-day workshops, plus five 75-minute conference sessions that are normally offered in conjunction with the NBIA's annual International Conference on Business Incubation.

The training in business incubator management is the main strength of the programme and has resulted not only in the improvement but also in the standardisation of the knowledge and skills of incubator managers and staff members. It is based on three comprehensive workshops that are accessible to incubator managers and staff:

● *The Fundamentals of Incubator Management:* This workshop tackles the challenges faced by incubator managers and deals with defining a mission and governance structure, achieving financial self-sustainability, establishing policies, recruiting clients, developing graduation criteria, generating revenue, handling leases and other agreements, etc.

- *Serving Client Companies:* This deals with the programmes and services an incubator offers as well as best practices for coaching clients. Specific topics include teaching business basics, creating service provider networks, setting up financing programmes, sharing services and space, etc.

- *Facilities Management:* This addresses aspects of overseeing the operation of the building that houses an incubation programme, including managing lease agreements, collecting rents and service fees, cutting costs in innovative ways, etc.

The NBIA website also includes a simple (10-minute) benchmarking survey that allows an incubator to compare its incubation programme management with NBIA-accepted best practices. It evaluates an incubation programme's performance in 10 best practice areas, such as: governance and staffing, selecting and serving clients, financing, marketing, support for post-incubation enterprises, facilities management, and measuring impact. Comparing results with best practices enables the incubator staff to identify their areas of comparative excellence and areas for improvement. The site can be accessed at *www.nbia.org/resource_library/peer/benchmark/survey.php.*

Factors for success

The development of international best practices in incubator management responded to a global need. Organising a membership network of incubator managers from a number of countries has also expanded the sharing of experience and practice, which provides much value to members.

Obstacles and responses

The training is offered in conjunction with the NBIA's annual conference. This poses travel expenses for incubator managers and thus may act as a barrier to their participation in some cases. However, all of the other material is accessible on line.

Relevance for Mexico

One of the weaknesses in the management of incubators in Mexico's national system of incubation concerns the quality of incubator managers and staff and the possible inconsistency in the delivery of comprehensive incubator services to support incubating enterprises. While the national association of incubators in Mexico is seeking to upgrade the professionalism of incubator management in the country and has already developed some linkages with the NBIA for technical support, the Ministry of Economy should invest additional resources, in the short-term, to enable the incubator managers and staff to pursue the NBIA Certificate in Incubator Management. In the medium-term, there would be advantages to developing a Mexican programme to prepare professionals for the occupation of incubator manager following or participating in some of the practices developed by the NBIA.

Further information

National Business Incubators Association (NBIA)
20 East Circle Drive – #37198 Athens – OH 45701-3751
Phone: (740) 593-4331
Website: *www.nbia.org*

"NBIA Incubator Management Certificate Program":
www.nbia.org/member_services/certificate/index.php

A.3. Small Business Investment Company (SBIC) Programme, United States

The Small Business Investment Company Programme (SBIC) represents an interesting model to strengthen the availability of growth capital to SMEs, this being one of the main constraints in enterprise financing identified in this report.

Description of the approach

The Small Business Investment Company (SBIC) programme was created by the US Congress in 1958 to help small US businesses raise the capital they need to fuel business growth, particularly patient long-term capital not available through banks or other private capital sources.

The mission of the programme is "to improve and stimulate the national economy and small businesses by stimulating and supplementing the flow of private equity capital and long term loan funds for the sound financing, growth, expansion and modernisation of small business operations while insuring the maximum participation of private financing sources" (*www.sba.gov/about-offices-content/1/2890*) (*www.sba.gov/about-offices-content/1/2890*).

SBICs are privately owned and managed investment funds, licensed and regulated by the Small Business Administration (SBA) to make equity and debt investments in qualifying small businesses (with maturities of at least five years) using their own capital, plus additional funds they can raise through the SBA by sale of SBA-guaranteed securities, on an "as needed" basis to support fund investments and expenses. Funds secured through the SBA can potentially increase the total capital available for investment up to three times the private capital.

SBICs fill the gap for SME financing in the USD 250 000 to USD 5 million range, either in the form of subordinated loans, not made by banks, or equity investments that are too small to be of interest to other private equity firms. They also provide management assistance to their client companies. A maximum of 10% of an SBIC's total capital may be invested in a single small company unless the SBA approves a larger investment.

To be able to operate as an SBIC, the qualifications and business plans of the private sector management teams are approved in advance in a rigorous SBA licensing process. Before it receives its license, an SBIC must prove that its management and directors are experienced individuals with a broad range of business and professional talents. In addition, it must raise between USD 5 million and USD 10 million in private capital, most of which comes from private investors, such as high net-worth individuals, state development funds, pension funds, investment companies, or even commercial banks.

The two primary criteria for licensure as an SBIC are qualified management and sufficient private capital. Applying for an SBIC license is a two-part process, beginning with the completion of the Management Assessment Questionnaire (which requires about 40 hours of time to complete and is used to assess whether the investment company has the professional capabilities to manage an SBIC (see *www.sba.gov/content/application-forms*), *www.sba.gov/content/application-forms*), followed by the formal licensing phase. Once licensed, each SBIC is subject to annual financial reporting and biennial onsite compliance examinations by the SBA, and is required to meet certain statutory and regulatory restrictions regarding approved investments and operating rules.

Costs are associated with becoming a licensed SBIC. The private investment company pays a USD 10 000 fee when filing a licensing application, and an additional USD 5 000 for licensees structured as limited partnerships. When approved, the SBIC also pays a commitment fee of 1% up front, a 2% draw down fee at issuance of its debentures and a variable annual charge of around 1%, paid semi-annually.

In terms of procedures, the SME owner submits a detailed business plan, its funding requirements, and how the financing will be used to the benefit of the company. The SBIC then performs its due diligence and structures the financing appropriately in negotiation with the SME owner. SBICs can make only long-term loans or equity investments, and are prohibited from taking control of the companies in which they invest; therefore, the interests of the SBIC and their clients are compatible, both want to grow and prosper. Because SBICs are often interested in generating capital gains, they may prefer to purchase stock in the company or advance funds through a loan with conversion privileges or rights to buy stock at a predetermined later date.

If the SBIC money is provided to the SME in a subordinated position, it will often allow leveraging of other financing. For example, industry averages show that for every SBIC dollar placed with a small business, two additional senior dollars become available from commercial banks or other sources.

To provide incentives for SBICs to focus their investments towards new businesses with higher risk, the SBA also makes provisions for Specialized Small Business Investment Company (SSBICs), which operate similar to SBICs, except that they can access additional government financial assistance for these activities. Furthermore, the programme can be adjusted to meet emerging needs. A recent example is the SBAs proposal for a new SBIC programme to promote American innovation and job creation by encouraging private sector investment in job-creating early-stage small businesses as part of President Obama's 2011 "Start-Up America Initiative". This initiative is proposing to commit up to USD 1 billion in SBA guaranteed leverage over a five year period to selected early-stage venture funds using its current debenture programme authorization. This Early Stage SBIC Initiative will target the gap that early-stage growth companies face accessing financing rounds between USD 1 million and USD 4 million, particularly those without the necessary assets or cash flow for traditional bank funding. Since January 2006, less than 10% all US venture capital dollars have gone to seed funds investing at those levels.

Factors for success

The US SBIC programme has a number of strengths. It increases the overall supply of equity finance capital in two ways. Firstly, it provides an incentive for more people to set up venture capital funds by leveraging their own investment. For example, the investor with USD 5 million might receive another USD 15 million through the SBA. In addition, many SBICs do not have to make interest payments to the SBA during the first few years of operations. In lieu, the SBA will take up to 10% of the profits as they are realised, taking away the burden of paying interest on the SBA guaranteed loans while the SBIC invests in long-term opportunities. Second, investors purchasing shares of an SBIC are eligible for tax breaks and rollovers which make it attractive for them to invest in the SBIC funds.

SBICs have a range of flexibility in determining how to operate. They can establish the investment value ranges they will serve, and the preferred size of the loan or investment they choose to make. They can also decide whether to focus on certain industries or types of businesses in which their officers and directors have specialised knowledge or experience or to invest more generally. Generally, SBICs prefer to invest in companies located *within a reasonable distance* of the SBIC office. In some cases, more than one SBIC will work together in making loans or investments, if the amount required exceeds the investment capacity of one SBIC.

Smaller companies are not excluded from the programme. The SBIC Programme defines a company as "small" when its net worth is USD 18 million or less and its average after tax net income for the prior two years does not exceed USD 6 million. However, SBICs must commit to making 25% of their investments in "smaller businesses" defined as those with tangible net worth of less than USD 6 million and an average of USD 2 million in net income over the previous two years.

The SBICs are networked through the Small Business Investor Alliance, which is their national association. The Alliance promotes the growth and vitality of the industry. It represents the SBIC members, identifies new investors for the SBIC funds, advocates for reduced regulatory burdens and better programme management, sponsors and co-ordinates industry meetings and educational programmes, including an annual Venture Capital Institute on venture investing.

In terms of results, since 1958 SBICs have invested almost USD 60 billion in 107 000 "small enterprises". The businesses financed by SBICs have far outperformed national averages in terms of increases in sales, profits, assets, and new job creation and benefited from the money and management counselling made available to them by the SBICs. For example, companies such as Intel, Apple, Callaway Golf, Whole Foods Market, Staples, Quiznos, Federal Express, Outback Steakhouse, and Costco all received early-stage financing from SBICs.

The number of SBICs continues to grow; in 2010, the SBA licensed 23 new SBICs with USD 654 million in initial private capital. At the end of fiscal year 2010, SBICs held USD 16.5 billion in capital resources; USD 8.6 billion of which was private capital and USD 7.9 billion was SBA-guaranteed capital or commitments.

At the fiscal year-end 2011, there were 299 SBICs of all types operating in 43 states, the District of Columbia, and Puerto Rico. In 2011, these SBICs invested USD 2.83 billion in financing dollars in 1 339 small businesses, 34% of which were in low-to-moderate income areas or were minority- or women-owned businesses, creating an estimated 56 211 jobs. The SBA issued USD 1.82 billion in new commitments to SBICs.

Obstacles and responses

The SBIC programme offers its licensees access to debt capital with a 10-year maturity and semi-annual interest payments. The structure of this financing means that most SBICs focus primarily on providing small businesses with debt or debt with equity features. SBICs will typically focus on companies that are mature enough to make current interest payments on the investment so that, in turn, the SBIC can meet its interest obligations to the SBA.

This implies the existence of barriers to the financing of new enterprises, which have been partly addressed through new branches of the programme targeting the early stage of business development in companies that lack necessary assets or cash flow for traditional bank funding.

Relevance for Mexico

The private equity market is underdeveloped in Mexico. The number of Angel Investment Clubs is small and they have been not been multiplying at a very rapid rate, leaving SMEs in many parts of the country without the benefit of such a programme. A model similar to the SBIC approach might bring a more systematic approach to escalating the amount of risk capital available to early-stage and growth-oriented SMEs, as well as being a complement to the business acceleration programmes and the high-technology incubators.

The Ministry of Economy would probably need to adjust the definition of a qualifying "small" business to be more compatible with the Mexican context. Since the incentive structure for the SBICs is based on leveraging the investment fund through government-guaranteed loans to the SBIC and tax breaks for investors in the SBIC, these policy issues would have to be examined by the Ministry of Economy.

Further information

Office of Investment
The Small Business Administration
409 Third Street S.W. – Suite 6300 – Washington, DC, 20416
Website: *www.sba.gov/content/sbic-program-overview-2*

Small Business Investors Alliance (SBIA)
1100 H Street NW – Suite 610 – Washington, DC, 20005
Phone: (202) 628-5055
Website: *www.SBIA.org*

A.4. Women's Enterprise Centre initiative, Canada

This policy model can be a source of inspiration to reach out to more women-owned enterprises, women's participation being one of the principles against which the Mexican government measures the effectiveness of SME policies

Description of the approach

The Women's Enterprise Initiative (WEI) was established by Western Economic Diversification Canada (WD) in 1994 to encourage the establishment and growth of women-owned and controlled businesses, encourage self-employment and business development, and promote economic equality between men and women in Western Canada. The network of Women's Enterprise Centres (WECs) was part of this effort to better address the challenges faced by women entrepreneurs.

WECs are present in each of the four provinces of Western Canada, are operated by not-for-profit organisations, and are awarded five-year renewal contracts to offer advice, business planning assistance, mentoring/matchmaking, networking opportunities, information, and referrals to accountants and lawyers specifically to women. They also deliver loan funds (pools of up to CAD 5 million) targeted to new or existing businesses owned by women with loan values of up to CAD 150 000. The loans, particularly when combined with business advice and assistance in the development of a business plan, are considered the most significant service received by clients.

Factors for success[1]

The WECs have provided a one-stop shop for women thinking about starting a business or already managing one and women entrepreneurs with existing businesses. The strong capabilities of the staff, the support provided by the Board of Directors and other volunteers, and strong linkages developed with other programmes and services, have been key to the success of the initiative.

From 2003-08, the network of WECs provided 28 000 advisory services and trained 21 000 women. This assistance led to new start-ups and jobs, job retention in existing client firms, increased revenues, and higher survival rates than for the average Canadian SME (Ference and Weicker, 2008). WECs issued 572 loans totalling approximately CAD 22.9 million. Businesses that received the loans had average revenues of CAD 475 000 and 5.8 employees; assisted-businesses which did not access the loan component had revenues averaging CAD 272 000 and 2.8 workers.

---

1. The source of this results data is from the evaluation report prepared by Ference Weicker & Co. (2008), "Impact Assessment of the Women Enterprise Initiative (WEI)," prepared for Western Economic Diversification Canada, Vancouver, BC.

The most significant impacts on client firms have been the following, based on the results of the evaluation of the programme:

● helped them to further develop their business, management and/or personal skills (39% reported a significant impact);

● increased their access to other programs and services through referrals from staff as well as the information and resources available through the offices (38%);

● enabled them to network with other entrepreneurs to exchange information and build business relations with each other (37%);

● increased their access to information for decision making (35%);

● encouraged them to start and/or further develop their own business by assisting with business planning (34%);

● increased access to financing or capital from sources other than the WECs (e.g. local, provincial and federal sources of assistance and commercial banks) (14%).

Particularly relevant because of its impact has been the loan programme. The main results are reported below:

● The revenues of the average business receiving loans increased from about CAD 57 000 in the year prior to receiving the loan (most of the businesses were not yet in operation) to CAD 163 000 in the first year to over CAD 550 000 in the fifth year after receiving the loan. Over a five-year period, the average WEC client business which remained in business would generate about CAD 1.9 million in additional revenues.

● Based on the evaluation results, 75% of businesses are still operating after five years. After adjusting for survival rates, the average WEC-assisted enterprise (including those still operating and those that had ceased to operate) generated revenues of approximately CAD 1.5 million over the five-year period.

● The majority of impacts are incremental in that they would not have occurred in the absence of the support provided by the programme. On average, these clients estimated that there is only a 34% chance that they would have been able to develop their business to the extent they have without the assistance of the WEC. Overall, the clients attribute 55% of their current business revenues to the services provided by the WEC.

● Over time, the loan clients invested about CAD 2.35 in their businesses for every dollar in loan funding received. The loan clients estimated that 36% of their investment is incremental in that it would not have been made in the absence of the services received from the WECs.

● The evaluation team estimated that over the five-year period from when assistance was initially provided, the CAD 22.9 million in loan funding generated about CAD 660 million in incremental revenues and 8 000 incremental person years of employment. Of this amount, CAD 363 million in revenues and 4 430 person years of employment is attributed by clients to the services provided.

● In terms of return on the government's investment, the WECs received CAD 18.8 million in operating funding over the five years from 2003 to 2008. The evaluation of their performance revealed that, taking only into consideration their loan clients, the WECs contributed to a person year of employment for every CAD 4 246 in operating funding that they received from the government. Per dollar of operating funding, loan clients attributed CAD 19.30 in revenues, CAD 0.96 in export revenues, CAD 4.43 in wages, and CAD 1.46 in new investment to the services received from the WECs.

Obstacles and responses

The main problems concerned the lack of follow-up or follow-on services; concerns about staff turnover and/or the capabilities of the staff; and a poor fit between their needs and the focus of the training sessions or seminars (i.e. mainly because training sessions were not sufficiently tailored to the characteristics of their business or of their stage of development). This indicates the importance of providing follow-up services to centre clients, and ensuring that staff is fully trained and capable of meeting clients' needs, including by adjusting training material to the different stages of growth of an enterprise.

Relevance for Mexico

Although support for women-owned SMEs is a criterion for gauging the efficiency of Mexico's SME programmes, as per the rules of operation of the SME Fund, there is little evidence of specific measures to reach out to the women's market. The experience from Canada, as described above, as well as in other countries, suggests that targeting women with directed measures can lead to increased growth, both in terms of the number of women-owned enterprises and the growth of these enterprises with a positive impact on job creation and economic spin-offs.

The Canadian model is a simple one to replicate because many of the components of a WEC are already delivered in Mexico through other entities, although not targeted specifically to women and not as such a cohesive package. The model could be easily adapted in Mexico by including a call for proposals from intermediary organisations to operate a Women's Enterprise Centre, coupled with appropriate training and skills development of staff working in the centres.

Further information

Alberta Women Entrepreneurs
308, 10310 Jasper Avenue – Edmonton, AB T5J 2W4
Toll Free: 1-800-713-3558
Website: *www.awebusiness.com*

British Columbia Women's Enterprise Centre
Suite 201, 1726 Dolphin Avenue – Kelowna, BC V1Y 9R9
Toll Free: 1-800-643-7014
Website: *www.womensenterprise.ca*

Manitoba Women's Enterprise Centre
100-207 Donald Street – Winnipeg, MB R3C 1M5
Toll Free: 1-800-203-2343
Website: *www.wecm.ca*

Women Entrepreneurs of Saskatchewan Inc.
Suite #108, 502 Cope Way – Saskatoon, SK S7T 0G3
Toll Free: 1-800-879-6331
Website: *www.womenentrepreneurs.sk.ca*

A.5. Quick Deregulation Strategy, Ukraine

Ukraine's Quick Deregulation Strategy provides an example of successful simplification of business regulations, which is key to Mexico's objectives of promoting the creation of more firms and the regularisation of existing ones.

Description of the approach

In 2005, the State Committee on Regulatory Policy and Entrepreneurship began implementation of the Quick Deregulation Strategy as a response to pressures to improve the business environment and reduce the informal economy. To push the reform at the national level, a regional Quick Deregulation effort was undertaken through assistance to municipalities in seven cities.

Support was given to local municipalities in the following forms:

1. Creation of an agenda for the Working Groups. The most critical areas of regulation were agreed centrally, but local municipalities and Working Groups could then concentrate on different individual regulations.

2. Analytical capability. Consultants were made available to analyse the impact of individual regulations and proposed changes so that discussions in the Working Groups could be relatively objective.

3. Organisation of monitoring and evaluation. This included commissioning base line and follow up surveys of the local SME sector.

Out of 785 regional regulations in the seven cities, 340 were abolished and 172 amended to become more market-friendly.

The Quick Deregulation effort in Donetsk is a good example of how the process worked in the regions. The mayor of Donetsk launched a quick review of regulations enacted by the city council and mayor by signing a resolution in April 2005. He also created a public-private sector working group that reviewed 92 regulatory acts against three criteria: 1) is it needed?; 2) was it enacted legally?; 3) is it efficient and market-friendly? The working group recommended that the government abolish 17 regulations and amend 13 to be market-friendly.

The speed, popularity, and impact of the Quick Deregulation initiative in the seven cities did not go unnoticed by the national government. In May and June 2005, President Yushchenko signed Decree No. 779 "On Liberalisation of Entrepreneurial Activity and State Support for Entrepreneurship" and Decree No. 901 "On Measures to Ensure Implementation of State Regulatory Policy," which officially launched the quick deregulation initiative at the national level. All of Ukraine's cities were encouraged to follow the example set by the seven pioneer cities.

By September 2005, 9 866 regulations issued by executive power authorities were reviewed and 5 599 (56.8 per cent) were found to be inconsistent with the law "On Regulatory Policy in the Sphere of Economic Activity" and were subject to repeal or amendment, including: 249 acts of the Cabinet of Ministers (4.4 per cent); 737 regulations of national executive power authorities (13.2 per cent); 4 613 regulations of local executive power authorities (82.4 per cent);

and 66 presidential acts. In the regions, 5 100 local self-government regulations were examined and almost 35 per cent were scheduled for repeal or amendment.

At all levels of the Ukrainian government, the first phase of the Quick Deregulation initiative in 2005 resulted in the review of about 15 000 of regulations, the identification of 7 000 of those as not business-friendly and burdensome for entrepreneurs, and the repeal of more than 4 900 of them.

Factors for success

This model shows the degree to which regulations can be changed quickly when there is political direction and a clear strategy. Central political support and party political support in the selected municipalities had a significant bearing on the process.

It equally shows the importance of collaboration and co-ordination between national and local level in this specific area of reform. Businesses are affected both by national and local legislation, which implies a twofold action on both levels to reduce administrative burdens on start-ups and extant firms.

Since corruption was a significant issue, holding the hearings in public and maintaining adequate publicity were significant factors in success, particularly in making clear to the public the commitment to reform by regional and national policy-makers.

Target areas for the initial programme were chosen on a number of factors, but particularly through the commitment of the local authorities. This was important since the visible success of the first pilots was important both in engaging other areas, and in bringing issues to national attention.

Resourcing of the working groups was important, in particular in ensuring good quality independent background material for discussions. This allowed a degree of objectivity in decision-making and mitigated against defence of unnecessary regulation by vested interests.

Obstacles and responses

Commitment of high-ranking officials was important, but many such people had very high workloads and needed incentives to attend. In the first stages, therefore, working group members were paid an honorarium to attend.

Public cynicism and corruption were seen as significant barriers to reform. This was countered by a variety of publicity measures, making sure that WG meetings were held openly and publicising results.

In some cases, regulations are necessary but the implementation of the regulations and co-ordination between regulatory bodies is a greater issue. In Ukraine, this particularly applied to issuance of permits, where the system was confusing and not transparent, again giving chances for corruption. A parallel project introduced one stop shops and streamlined and made clear the regulatory framework.

Relevance for Mexico

The number and complexities of business regulations are a barrier to setting up businesses and an additional spur to remaining in the informal economy. Mexico has made recent important progress in this area, but OECD data show that product markets are still restrictive of competition and nascent entrepreneurs are still faced with obstacles when trying to set out an activity. Further reform is therefore needed in this area, and political endorsement at the highest level can jump-start the process and introduce changes faster.

A.6. Innovation Vouchers in the Netherlands

With a view to strengthening support to innovation in Mexico and improving the productivity of SMEs, innovation vouchers represent a simple solution to help firms establish linkages with research organisations and benefit from knowledge networks.

Description of the approach

The main objective of the Innovation Voucher scheme is to introduce SMEs to public research institutions. The issuing of the voucher has two main impacts, both of which overcome major incentive barriers to the usual engagement between SMEs and public knowledge providers. First, the voucher empowers the SME to approach knowledge providers with their problems, something that they might not have done in the absence of such an incentive. Second, the voucher provides an incentive for the public knowledge provider to work with SMEs when their tendency might either have been to work with larger firms or to have no industry engagement.

Cornet, Vroomen, and van der Steeg (2006) summarise the objectives of the Dutch programme as follows:

● to introduce SMEs to knowledge providers (lowering the cost threshold);

● to make research institutions operate in a more demand-oriented way (managing demand);

● to enable SMEs to purchase research capacity from research institutions in order to answer application-oriented research questions;

● to ensure that SMEs use more of the available knowledge among knowledge providers (bridging the knowledge gap).

In other words, the Innovation Voucher provides a means of enabling demand-led knowledge transfer rather than the more traditional supply-led model.

The Dutch Innovation Voucher scheme worked broadly as follows. First, the availability of vouchers was advertised widely in the print media. SMEs then submitted an application using a simple application form which contains simple eligibility criteria (including a State Aids *de minimus* statement) as well as a brief description of the problem they would like to solve. The typical problem should be "application-oriented", in the sense that the SME should be able to use the knowledge to improve its products or operational processes. Examples include solving a minor technological problem or setting out the possible solutions for a more complex technological problem. Vouchers are then awarded to all firms meeting the eligibility criteria by the operating agency, which in the case of the Netherlands was an organisation supported by the Dutch Ministry of Economic Affairs.

Factors for success

The Innovation Voucher scheme is an innovative approach to stimulating demand-led technology transfer. It has proved effective in encouraging SMEs to articulate barriers to innovative development and seek assistance from knowledge providers. In some cases, the

Innovation Voucher programme has also stimulated new innovation network or partnership development as SMEs collaborate to pool vouchers. It has also proved effective in encouraging knowledge providers to engage – very often for the first time – with SMEs. The programme has also stimulated institutional developments within some knowledge providers as specific offices have been set up to facilitate Innovation Vouchers.

From a firm's point of view, the Innovation Voucher scheme has been attractive because:

● it has helped the company to harness university expertise to overcome a barrier to developing innovation activity at low cost;

● the application procedure and "red tape" involved in the scheme is minimal;

● the decision time before the firm knows it has been granted an Innovation Voucher is minimal;

● there are no reporting requirements other than an acknowledgement that the agreed package of work has been completed by the knowledge provider;

● there is the potential to pool vouchers to create larger packages of funding;

● receipt of an Innovation Voucher – and the partnership with the university – has some value as a signal of R&D and product quality.

Similar factors, along with the obvious revenue stream, have also made the scheme attractive to knowledge providers.

Obstacles and responses

Before the initial Pilot phase of the scheme it was not clear whether the scheme would fail due to weaknesses on either the demand (firm) or supply (knowledge provider) side. In fact both demand and supply have worked effectively, with the light-touch brokerage working relatively well. In this sense there have been few obstacles to the development of the scheme.

Some administrative procedures have had to be changed as the scheme has matured including a move from a paper based processing system to an electronic application and processing system. In addition, as the scheme has grown there has been a move from an application date based system to an open application system which has helped with managing work flow. These changes seem to have been dealt with effectively by the operating agency and caused little operational difficulty.

Relevance for Mexico

Mexico needs to strengthen the absorptive capacity of SMEs and enable them to collaborate with research institutes and universities, as well as with larger knowledge-intensive companies. Innovation-purchasing initiatives such as the vouchers would help go in this direction.

Further information

Cornet, M., B. Vroomen and M. van der Steeg (2006), "Do Innovation Vouchers Help SMEs to Cross the Bridge Towards Science?", *CPB Discussion Paper*, 58, Den Haag, The Netherlands.

A.7. Brazil's Sector Funds: Stimulating links between industry and academia

This example illustrates an approach to incentivising productive linkages between industry and academy for the purpose of developing innovative SMEs.

Description of the approach

Measures to reform the higher education system often overlook the dissemination of new knowledge to industry. The reference response has continued to be the formation of offices of technology transfer and licensing, with little attention given to increasing the establishment of collaborative partnerships between academics and companies. The latter is an important step that is far from automatic, requiring careful calibration of incentives, complex negotiations regarding intellectual property rights, and in many cases considerable shifts in institutional cultures in both business and the academy.

In 1999, Brazil therefore created the Science and Technology Sector Funds to finance domestic research, development and innovation. The programmes provide non-reimbursable subsidies for scientific and technological research, with the specific aim of stimulating partnerships between universities and enterprises as a means to build a stronger innovation system. The funds are administered by Brazil's Research and Projects Financing Agency (FINEP), and are allocated as part of the National Fund for Scientific and Technological Development (FNDCT), the Brazilian equivalent of Mexico's CONACYT. Funding is not delivered directly to private firms, but is instead contingent on participation with universities and research centres in co-operative projects.

The Sector Funds are made possible by a special tax on corporate earnings from licensing on government-owned natural resources, with participating firms contributing matching contributions. There are 16 funds in total, targeting such sectors as biotechnology, petroleum, information technology and energy. Two of the 16 funds cut across sectors. One of these "horizontal" funds is an infrastructure fund aimed at supporting the improvement of academic research infrastructure. The second is the Green-Yellow Fund (*Fundo Verde Amarelo*), whose aim is to support meaningful interaction between universities and private firms.

Budgets for the Sector Funds have grown considerably since they became operational. The entire programme had approximately BRLD 300 million at its disposal in 2002. In 2011, the Green-Yellow Fund alone was able to disburse over BRLD 330 million, while the size of the entire Sectorial Funds grew to BRLD 3.2 billion. This expansion has made it possible for new ways of encouraging business innovation to be adopted, such as the granting of a subsidy to any company carrying out Technological and Industrial Development Programs (PDTI). The Fund will also incentivise the formation of venture capital funds. The decree authorises the use of resources from the fund for a direct participating stake in the company's capital, particularly in those firms that have been recently created.

Factors for success

In an evaluation of the programme performed by de Negri et al. (2006) involving a sample of 80 000 participant and non-participant firms, the Sector Funds have shown initial signs of success. They have incentivised considerable spending on technological upgrading, and created a wealth of new links between firms and academia. At the same time, in 2006, there was little unambiguous evidence of improved economic performance among participant firms, though these effects are likely to take some time to appear.

One important source of success of the Funds is their stable funding, tied to corporate taxes. The FNDCT considered this to be an explicit rationale for the creation of the Funds, without which support was at the mercy of annual budgets. Another factor in success is that, by opting for a direct subsidy, rather than tax exemptions, the Funds are likely to be better suited to the needs of small firms, which might otherwise have insufficient funds to undertake collaborative projects.

The major strength, however, is simply the emphasis on collaboration. By making linkages between firms and universities and research centres entirely central in the Sector Funds, the FNDCT has clearly identified the need to go beyond technology licensing offices. Instead, the Sector Funds are directive in their aim of fostering meaningful and deep collaboration between the private sector and higher education institutions.

Obstacles and responses

While the Brazilian emphasis on university-industry co-operation makes strategic sense, there is less available information with regard to the manner by which academic agents are motivated to participate. As in Mexico, this could be a problem that results in less-than-optimal take-up of the programme among knowledge-producers in academia. There are scant details on this point in existing reviews of the Funds, and no mention of responses to this potential problem. A second potential issue is the absence of observed productivity gains. Ultimately, the aim of such co-operative ventures between industry and the academy ought to be substantive improvements in processes and the introduction of new goods and services. These innovations ought to enhance firm productivity. One plausible explanation is that it simply may take more time for technological investments to bear fruit.

Relevance for Mexico

The Brazilian reforms address two bottlenecks in Mexico with respect to inadequate of financing of innovation and disparities in the level of scientific development among different states. It illustrates a national policy response that has potential for Mexico. Studies have consistently found positive benefits when researchers engage in linkages with private firms. The Brazilian experience suggests a way of incentivising Mexican academics to participate in these collaborations, since they may also serve as source for new research that could result in publications. Some innovation systems have a more pronounced division of labour, with universities focused primarily on basic research. But the evidence suggests that greater interaction between Mexican academic and industry would be mutually beneficial.

Further information

www.mct.gov.br/index.php/content/view/1419.html.

De Negri, J., M. Lemos and F. De Negri (2006), "Impact of R&D Incentive Program on the Performance and Technological Efforts of Brazilian Industrial Firms", *OVE Working Papers*, 1406, Inter-American Development Bank, Office of Evaluation.

A.8. Chile's PROFO: Creating greater horizontal collaboration

This example relates to the recommendation of strengthening collaboration among geographically co-located firms in related sectors, or local clusters.

Description of the approach

The government of Chile created the Programmes of Managerial Development (PROFO) in order to stimulate greater collective efficiency among SMEs in the same industry by encouraging the formation of horizontal networks. It is hoped that this will enable SMEs to overcome scale-based barriers related to the ability to license technology, access markets and hire skilled managers by overcoming co-ordination problems and creating trust.

Legally, a PROFO is a partnership in which SMEs participate for a maximum of three to four years. There must be at least 5 firms to form a PROFO. Operating costs are shared between the public and private sectors, with public support starting at 70% in the first year, falling to 60% in the second year and 50% for the third year. Correspondingly, participating businesses finance at least 30% of the costs the first year, 40% the second and 50% the third. The agreement usually is made for three years, but an extension for a fourth year may be obtained if positive results can be demonstrated and if the group of companies decides to extend its partnership by undertaking joint investments or forming further consortia.

The amount of the government subsidy can be as much as USD 100 000 per year per group, with a contribution limit of USD 12 000 per participating company. The activities and types of expenditure that these funds can finance are: the remuneration of the PROFO manager (appointed by the member companies) and other support staff, technology transfer seminars, exhibitions, shows and consultancy work, travel, training and purchases of specialist books and reviews.

Corporacion de Fomento de la Production (CORFO), the state agency responsible for the promotion of national productive activity, is responsible for approving PROFO projects and allocating funds. PROFOs have been initiated by diverse entities such as public-sector bodies and private-sector trade associations such as the Chilean Textile Institute. The program is very grassroots and adaptive. CORFO has no direct operation oversight of individual PROFOs.

Factors for success

CORFO's model has generated cost savings over a centralised government programme and has led to experimentation and locally calibrated innovative approaches, but also has important limitations. Despite the increased outreach and low administrative costs, locally hired managers tend to limit their work to more standardised functions, and are noted not to contribute to the strategic side of CORFO operations. Moreover, there does not appear to be consistency in the service intermediation model, and clients have complained that agents offer what they know rather than what local business requires to become more efficient, competitive or profitable.

Benavente and Crespi's (2003) evaluation of Chile's PROFO programme found significant net improvements in total factor productivity growth (TFP) ranging from 11.7 to 22.9 per cent. Qualitative analysis of the survey of PROFO beneficiaries attributed many of these gains to reorganisation of the production process, implementation of joint marketing strategies, introduction of quality control techniques, and managerial training.

Obstacles and responses

The evaluation performed by Benavente and Crespi (2003) revealed a variety of benefits enjoyed by SME participant firms in PROFO. However, one area where the intervention proved less successful is in the generation of process and product innovation. This might reflect an unmet challenge of the policy. If so, it is one that has not yet been adequately responded to by CORFO.

Relevance for Mexico

In field studies, Mexican SMEs appear to put insufficient value on inter-firm collaboration with other small firms in their sector, preferring instead to seek out linkages with large MNCs and anchor firms in global supply chains. However, the two are not mutually exclusive, and in fact achieving collective efficiency may promote supply chain activity, as a result of raised productivity and other benefits. Chile's PROFO program may be the kind of incentive required to get small and medium-sized Mexican firms working together to maximise collective benefits.

Further information

www.investchile.com.

Benavante, J.M. and G. Crespi (2003), "The Impact of an Associative Strategy (the PROFO Program) on Small and Medium Enterprises in Chile", *SPRU Electronic Working Paper, Series Paper*, No. 88, University of Sussex.

ORGANISATION FOR ECONOMIC CO-OPERATION AND DEVELOPMENT

The OECD is a unique forum where governments work together to address the economic, social and environmental challenges of globalisation. The OECD is also at the forefront of efforts to understand and to help governments respond to new developments and concerns, such as corporate governance, the information economy and the challenges of an ageing population. The Organisation provides a setting where governments can compare policy experiences, seek answers to common problems, identify good practice and work to co-ordinate domestic and international policies.

The OECD member countries are: Australia, Austria, Belgium, Canada, Chile, the Czech Republic, Denmark, Estonia, Finland, France, Germany, Greece, Hungary, Iceland, Ireland, Israel, Italy, Japan, Korea, Luxembourg, Mexico, the Netherlands, New Zealand, Norway, Poland, Portugal, the Slovak Republic, Slovenia, Spain, Sweden, Switzerland, Turkey, the United Kingdom and the United States. The European Union takes part in the work of the OECD.

OECD Publishing disseminates widely the results of the Organisation's statistics gathering and research on economic, social and environmental issues, as well as the conventions, guidelines and standards agreed by its members.

OECD PUBLISHING, 2, rue André-Pascal, 75775 PARIS CEDEX 16
(85 2013 01 1 P) ISBN 978-92-64-18692-7 – No. 60439 2013-01